"Gentry and Wellum offer a third way ̶ ̶ ̶ ̶ ̶ ̶ ̶ ̶ ̶ ̶ ̶ ̶ dispensationalism, arguing that both of these theological systems are not informed sufficiently by biblical theology. Certainly we cannot understand the Scriptures without comprehending 'the whole counsel of God,' and here we find incisive exegesis and biblical theology at its best. This book is a must-read and will be part of the conversation for many years to come."

Thomas R. Schreiner, James Buchanan Harrison Professor of New Testament Interpretation, The Southern Baptist Theological Seminary

"*God's Kingdom through God's Covenants* is hermeneutically sensitive, exegetically rigorous, and theologically rich—a first-rate biblical theology that addresses both the message and the structure of the whole Bible from the ground up. Gentry and Wellum have produced what will become one of the standard texts in the field. For anyone who wishes to tread the path of biblical revelation, this text is a faithful guide."

Miles V. Van Pelt, Alan Belcher Professor of Old Testament and Biblical Languages and Director, Summer Institute for Biblical Languages, Reformed Theological Seminary, Jackson, Mississippi

"This is not the first volume that has attempted to mediate the dispensational/covenant theology divide, but it may be the culminating presentation of that discussion—just as Bach was not the first Baroque composer but its highest moment. *God's Kingdom through God's Covenants* should be read by all parties, but I won't be surprised to learn in twenty years that this volume provided the foundation for how a generation of anyone who advocates regenerate church membership puts their Bible together."

Jonathan Leeman, Editorial Director, 9Marks; author, *Church and the Surprising Offense of God's Love*

"Gentry and Wellum have provided a welcome addition to the current number of books on biblical theology. What makes their contribution unique is the marriage of historical exegesis, biblical theology, and systematic theology. *God's Kingdom through God's Covenants* brims with exegetical insights, biblical theological drama, and sound systematic theological conclusions. Particularly important is the viable alternative they offer to the covenantal and dispensational hermeneutical frameworks. I enthusiastically recommend this book!"

Stephen G. Dempster, Professor of Religious Studies, Crandall University

"The relationship between the covenants of Scripture is rightly considered to be central to the interpretation of the Bible. That there is some degree of continuity is obvious, for it is the same God—the God of Abraham, Isaac, and Jacob as well as the Father of our Lord Jesus Christ—who has revealed himself and his will in the covenants. That there is, however, also significant discontinuity also seems patent since Scripture itself talks about a new covenant, with the old one passing away. What has changed and what has not? Utterly vital questions to which this new book by Gentry and Wellum give satisfying and sound answers. Because of the importance of this subject and the exegetical and theological skill of the authors, their answers deserve a wide hearing. Highly recommended!"

Michael A. G. Haykin, Professor of Church History and Biblical Spirituality, The Southern Baptist Theological Seminary

"*God's Kingdom through God's Covenants* is directly applicable to a pastor faithfully seeking understanding of God's Word as it reveals the structure that supports the narrative of God's message. The study of the covenants provides a framework for understanding and applying the message of the Bible to life in the new covenant community. I have found this study enriching for pastoral ministry."

Joseph Lumbrix, Pastor, Mount Olivet Baptist Church, Willisburg, Kentucky

GOD'S KINGDOM

through

GOD'S COVENANTS

GOD'S KINGDOM

through

GOD'S COVENANTS

A CONCISE BIBLICAL THEOLOGY

PETER J. GENTRY AND
STEPHEN J. WELLUM

WHEATON, ILLINOIS

CONTENTS

ILLUSTRATIONS

PREFACE

One of the dangers of writing a long and detailed book on the biblical covenants is that it becomes potentially inaccessible to those who are looking for a more succinct treatment of the subject. When we coauthored *Kingdom through Covenant* (Crossway, 2012), it was our intent to write an in-depth treatment of the interrelationship of the biblical covenants. Given our conviction that the progressive unfolding of the biblical covenants is the backbone to the metanarrative of Scripture and, more importantly, that one cannot properly understand God's glorious redemptive plan apart from thinking through the biblical covenants, it was necessary to discuss the biblical covenants in detail.

In addition, it was our goal to demonstrate that our understanding of kingdom through covenant was slightly different from other ways of thinking through the Bible's storyline current in evangelical theology. In evangelicalism, the dominant biblical-theological systems of covenant theology and dispensationalism (and their varieties) are the way that most Christians conceive of the Bible's larger story. It was our conviction that both of these views—as much as we agree with them on most matters related to the gospel—were not quite right in their specific way of rendering the Bible's plotline. Hence, it was necessary for our book to interact with technical details in exegesis, biblical theology, and systematic theology.

We offer this shortened version of the earlier book for readers who are more interested in a succinct treatment of the subject, who want to be able to see our proposal of "kingdom through covenant" without all of the technical discussion and theological debate. In fact, it was the prodding of many seminary students, pastors, and lay leaders who desired a shorter, more accessible version of our larger work that was the genesis of this book. In this work, we have done our best to summarize our basic proposal, to avoid a lot of the technical discussion and debate, and to simply outline how we understand the unfolding of the biblical covenants and thus, how our triune God's plan has been brought to its wonderful consummation in Christ.

As in the first book, we begin by discussing why the covenants are foundational to the biblical storyline, along with some interpretative observations on how to read Scripture correctly. We then unpack each covenant in its own context before we show the progressive development of how each covenant builds on the previous one and then how all the covenants find their *telos*, terminus, and fulfillment in our Lord Jesus Christ. The last chapter summarizes our findings by succinctly describing exactly what we mean by the expression "kingdom through covenant." To make this work more accessible, we have kept the footnotes to a minimum, have mostly eliminated the discussions of how our view differs from that of dispensational and covenant theology, and have not given a detailed defense of our view. For the most part, the view argued in the previous book is assumed, yet now written in such a way that the reader is able more easily to discern what that overall view is and how the biblical covenants serve as the Bible's own way of unfolding, revealing, and disclosing God's one, eternal plan of redemption. If the reader desires the warrant and bibliographic discussion for the overall argument of this work, all he needs to do is turn to the previous work and find it there.

We have read with great care and interest every review of *Kingdom through Covenant* known to us. Frequently, the reviews have told us more about the metanarrative of our reviewers than the evidence presented in the book. Only rarely have reviewers actually engaged the extensive exegesis. We would like to thank Doug Moo for pointing out problems in my (Peter's) treatment of Ezekiel 16 and the relation of Deuteronomy to the Sinai Covenant. We believe we are developing in our own understanding of the Scriptures and appreciate correction. Further research has resulted in new proposals, which are incorporated into this abridgement.

A number of people have asked about the artwork used for the covers of both the larger work and this abridgement. Pieter Bruegel the Elder, a Flemish Renaissance painter, produced three versions of *The Tower of Babel*; only two of them survive. The painting chosen for the larger work, *Kingdom through Covenant*, was done in 1565 and is in the Museum Boijmans Van Beuningen, in Rotterdam. The painting chosen for this abridgement was done in 1563 and resides in the Kunsthistorisches Museum in Vienna. *The Tower of Babel* is not only an interpretation of the biblical text but a commentary on the construction going on in Antwerp at the time. These pictures portray an attempt to establish the human kingdom through unified effort.

The result is laughable. The Devil offered Jesus all the broken, tattered kingdoms of this world, but the only kingdom that will stand is the one now laughed at by men: the kingdom of God.

There are many people to thank in seeing this book come to fruition. We especially want to thank Crossway for their ongoing support of our work, and especially Justin Taylor for his encouragement and confidence in us. We also want to thank the administration and our colleagues at The Southern Baptist Theological Seminary, where we both teach and serve. It is a privilege to serve alongside colleagues who love the gospel of our Lord Jesus Christ and an administration who encourages us to teach, write, and minister as servants of the King of kings. In addition, Peter wants to dedicate this work to his dearest wife, Barb, who for more than thirty-five years has not only been a lover and sweetheart but has served as a close teammate in ministry and has epitomized *hesed* and *'ĕmet* in covenant relationship. Stephen gladly dedicates this work to his dearest wife, Karen, who for almost thirty years has served alongside him as a wonderful and faithful wife, mother, and partner in gospel ministry. Without the loving care and devotion of our wives, we would not have been able to write this work or do anything we have done in our marriage, in our family, and in the Christian ministry.

It is our prayer that this shortened work, *God's Kingdom through God's Covenants*, will be an encouragement to the church by helping Christians know a bit better the "whole counsel of God" as given through the unfolding and progression of the biblical covenants. It is our prayer that this work will help us think through how our great and glorious triune God has acted to redeem us in Christ, and thus has led us to a greater adoration and knowledge of, love for, and obedience to our covenant Lord. To God be all the glory in his church and in the world, until we sit at Jesus' feet, lost in wonder, love, and praise.

Written, this time, above the clouds.
Peter J. Gentry
Stephen J. Wellum
November 2014

PART ONE

INTRODUCTION

Chapter 1

THE IMPORTANCE OF COVENANTS IN GRASPING THE BIBLE'S STORY

> The idea of covenant is fundamental to the Bible's story. At its most basic, covenant presents God's desire to enter into relationship with men and women created in his image. This is reflected in the repeated covenant refrain, "I will be your God and you will be my people" (Exodus 6:6–8; Leviticus 26:12 etc.). Covenant is all about relationship between the Creator and his creation. The idea may seem simple; however, the implications of covenant and covenant relationship between God and humankind are vast . . .[1]

The purpose of this book is to demonstrate how central and foundational "covenants" are to the entire narrative plot structure of the Bible. One cannot fully understand Scripture *and* correctly draw theological conclusions from it without grasping how *all* of the biblical covenants unfold across time and find their *telos*, terminus, and fulfillment in Christ. We do *not* assert that the covenants are *the* central theme of Scripture. Instead, we assert that the covenants form the backbone of the Bible's metanarrative and thus it is essential to "put them together" correctly in order to discern accurately the "whole counsel of God" (Acts 20:27). Michael Horton nicely captures this point when he writes that the biblical covenants are "the architectural structure that we believe the Scriptures themselves to yield. . . . It is not simply the concept of the covenant, but the concrete existence of God's covenantal dealings in our history that provides the context within which we recognize the unity of Scripture amid its remarkable variety."[2] If this is so, which we contend it is, then apart from properly understanding the nature of the biblical covenants and how they relate to each other, we will not correctly discern the message of the Bible and hence God's self-disclosure which centers on and culminates in Christ.

---

[1] Alistair I. Wilson and Jamie A. Grant, "Introduction," in *The God of Covenant: Biblical, Theological, and Contemporary Perspectives*, ed. Jamie A. Grant and Alistair I. Wilson (Leicester, UK: Apollos, 2005), 12.
[2] Michael S. Horton, *God of Promise: Introducing Covenant Theology* (Grand Rapids, MI: Baker, 2006), 13.

This is not a new insight, especially for those in the Reformed tradition who have written extensively about the importance of covenants and have structured their entire theology around the concept of covenant. Yet it is not only Reformed theology that acknowledges this point; almost every variety of Christian theology admits that the biblical covenants establish a central framework that holds the Bible's story together. Since the coming of Christ, Christians have wrestled with the relationships between the covenants, especially the old and new covenants. In fact, it is almost impossible to understand many of the early church's struggles apart from covenantal debates. For example, think of the many issues concerning the Jew-Gentile relationship in the New Testament (Matt. 22:1–14, par.; Acts 10–11; Romans 9–11; Eph. 2:11–22; 3:1–13); the claim of the Judaizers, which centers on covenantal debates (Galatians 2–3); the reason that the Jerusalem Council assembled (Acts 15); the divisions between strong and weak in the church (Romans 14–15); and the question of how to live in relation to the old covenant now that Christ has come (Matthew 5–7; 15:1–20, par.; Acts 7; Romans 4; Hebrews 7–10). All of these issues are simply the church wrestling with covenantal shifts—from old covenant to new—and the nature of covenant fulfillment in Christ.

Christians have differed in their understanding of the relationship between the covenants. This is one of the primary reasons that we have different theological systems, which is best exemplified today by the theologies of dispensationalism and by covenant theology. Even though these two views agree on the main issues central to the gospel, at the heart of these two systems there is disagreement on what the biblical covenants are and how they relate one to another. Thus, beyond our basic agreement that the story of Scripture moves from Adam to Abraham to Sinai, ultimately issuing in a promise of a new covenant whose advent is tied with Jesus' cross work (Luke 22:20; 1 Cor. 11:23–26), there is disagreement on how the covenants are related. This disagreement inevitably spills over to other issues, especially the question of what applies to us today as new covenant believers. It is at this point, on such matters as the Sabbath, the application of the Old Testament law to our lives, the relationship between Israel and the church, and many more issues, that we discover significant differences among Christians.

For this reason, correctly "putting together" the biblical covenants is central to grasping the Bible's story, drawing correct theological conclusions, and rightly applying Scripture to our daily lives. If we are going to make progress in resolving disagreements within the church, then how we put together the biblical covenants must be faced head-on and not simply assumed. We are convinced that the current ways of putting together the covenants, especially as represented by covenant or dispensational theology, are not quite right, even though it is important *not* to overplay the differences among us. All Christians seek to do justice to the overall unity of God's plan, and to acknowledge some kind of "progressive revelation," redemptive epochs (or "dispensations"), fulfillment in Christ, change in God's plan across time, and so on. Yet there is disagreement in regard to the specifics of God's plan, the kind of changes that result, and the relationship between Israel and the church, which still requires resolution. What follows is an alternative reading of the covenants, which seeks to build on the insights of both of these theological systems while offering a slightly different way of understanding the unfolding of the covenants and their fulfillment in Christ.

"Kingdom through covenant" or "progressive covenantalism" is our proposal for what is central to the Bible's storyline. *Progressive* underscores the unfolding of God's plan from old to new, while *covenantalism* stresses that God's unified plan unfolds *through* the covenants, ultimately terminating and culminating in Jesus and the new covenant. Our triune God has only *one* plan of redemption, yet we discover what that plan is as we trace his salvation work *through* the biblical covenants. Each and every biblical covenant contributes to that one plan, but in order to grasp the full depth and breadth of that plan, we must understand each covenant in its own redemptive-historical context by locating that covenant in relation to what precedes it and what follows it. When we do this, not only do we unpack God's glorious plan; we also discover how that plan is fulfilled in our majestic Redeemer (see Heb. 1:1–3; 7:1–10:18; cf. Eph. 1:9–10). In addition, given that Christians live in light of the achievement of Christ's glorious work, we can apply Scripture rightly to our lives only if we think through how all of the previous covenants find their fulfillment in Christ and the new covenant he inaugurates.

Before we unpack "kingdom through covenant," in the remainder of this chapter and in preparation for chapters 2–10 we will focus on two issues. First, we will briefly discuss how we conceive of the nature of biblical theology and its relation to systematic theology, since this book is an exercise in both disciplines and, sadly, there is no unanimous agreement in regard to these disciplines. Second, we will outline our hermeneutical approach in this study and thus describe something of our theological method. Let us now briefly turn to each of these areas.

BIBLICAL THEOLOGY AND ITS RELATION TO SYSTEMATIC THEOLOGY

Any attempt to understand the progressive nature of the biblical covenants is an exercise in "biblical theology." It is also the first step in drawing legitimate theological conclusions from Scripture and thus applying the "whole counsel of God" to our lives, which is the task of "systematic theology." Since people mean different things by "biblical" and "systematic" theology, let us explain how we are using these terms and how we understand the relationship between them.

At the popular level, for most Christians, when the term "biblical theology" is used it is understood as expressing the desire to be "true to the Bible" in our teaching and theology. Obviously, to be "biblical" in this sense is what all Christians ought to desire and strive for, but this is *not* exactly how we are using the term. In fact, in church history, "biblical theology" has been understood in a number of ways.[3]

Generally speaking, before the past few centuries biblical theology was often identified with systematic theology, even though many in church history practiced what we currently call "biblical theology," that is, an attempt to grasp the redemptive-historical unfolding of Scripture.[4] One can think of many examples, such as Irenaeus (c. 115–c. 202), John Calvin (1509–1564), and Johannes Cocceius (1603–1669). In this sense, biblical theology is not entirely new, since the church has always wrestled with how to "put together" Scripture, especially in light of Christ. Any position, then, that seeks to think through the Canon is doing "biblical theology" in some sense. Granting this point, it is still accurate to note that, in the past, there was a tendency to treat Scripture in more logical and atemporal categories rather than to think carefully through the Bible's developing storyline. Even in the post-Reformation era, where there was a renewed emphasis on doing a "whole-Bible theology," biblical theology was mostly identified with systematic theology, and systematics was identified more with "dogmatic" concerns.

---

[3] For a history of biblical theology, see C. H. H. Scobie, "History of Biblical Theology," in *New Dictionary of Biblical Theology*, ed. T. D. Alexander, Brian S. Rosner, D. A. Carson, and Graeme Goldsworthy (Downers Grove, IL: InterVarsity Press, 2000) [hereafter *NDBT*], 11–20.

[4] For an example of this approach to biblical theology see Graeme Goldsworthy, *According to Plan: The Unfolding Revelation of God in the Bible* (Downers Grove, IL: InterVarsity Press, 2002).

With the rise of the Enlightenment, however, biblical theology began to emerge as a distinct discipline. But it is crucial to distinguish the emergence of biblical theology in the Enlightenment along two different paths—one, an illegitimate path tied to Enlightenment presuppositions, and the other, a legitimate one that developed previous insights in church history but now in a more precise, detailed, and historically conscious manner, dependent upon the Bible's own internal presentation.

In regard to the illegitimate Enlightenment approach to biblical theology, there was a growing tendency to read Scripture *critically* and uncoupled from historic Christian theology. This resulted in approaching Scripture "as any other book," rooted in history but also open to historical-critical methods which viewed the Bible within the confines of *methodological* naturalism.[5] This meant that the Bible was not approached on its own terms, i.e., as God's Word written. Instead, the idea that Scripture is God-breathed through human authors—a text that authoritatively and accurately unfolds God's redemptive plan centered in Christ—was rejected. The end result of this approach was not only a denial of a high view of Scripture but also an increasingly fragmented reading of Scripture, given the fact that the practitioners of this view did not believe Scripture to be a unified, God-given revelation. Biblical theology as a discipline became merely "descriptive," governed by critical methods and non-Christian worldview assumptions. "Diversity" was emphasized more than "unity" in Scripture, and ultimately, as a discipline seeking to grasp God's unified plan, it failed. In the twentieth century, there were some attempts to overcome the Enlightenment straitjacket on Scripture, but none of these attempts produced a "whole Bible theology," given their low view of Scripture.

Contrary to the Enlightenment approach, there is a legitimate way to do biblical theology. In the history of the church, specifically in the post-Reformation and post-Enlightenment era, this path also emphasized a renewed attempt to root the Bible in history by stressing the "literal sense" (*sensus literalis*) tied to the intention(s) of the divine and human author(s). Yet, it was rooted in a larger Christian worldview and, as such, it operated self-consciously within Christian theological presuppositions, as illustrated in such people as Johannes Cocceius and the post-Reformation Reformed

---

[5] "Methodological naturalism" is the view that approaches the study of history (including study of the Bible) and science without considering God's involvement in the world, and divine action as represented by divine revelation and miracles. *Methodological* naturalism does *not* necessarily entail atheism, since it is also consistent with deism and panentheism (both Enlightenment views), which also deny God's action in an effectual sense.

Protestant scholastics who came after him.[6] Probably the best-known twentieth-century pioneer of biblical theology, who sought to follow a path distinct from that of the Enlightenment, was Geerhardus Vos, who developed biblical theology at Princeton Seminary in the early twentieth century.[7] Vos, who was birthed out of Dutch Calvinism, along with such figures as Abraham Kuyper and Herman Bavinck, sought to do biblical theology with a firm commitment to the authority of Scripture. Vos defined biblical theology as "that branch of Exegetical Theology which deals with the process of the self-revelation of God deposited in the Bible."[8] In contrast to the Enlightenment view, Vos argued that biblical theology, as an exegetical discipline, not only begins with the biblical text; it must also embrace Scripture as God's own self-attesting Word, fully authoritative and reliable. Furthermore, Vos argued, in exegeting Scripture, biblical theology seeks to trace out the Bible's unity and diversity and find its consummation in Christ and the inauguration of the new covenant era. Biblical theology must follow a method that reads the Bible *on its own terms*, following the Bible's own internal contours and shape, in order to discover God's unified plan as it is disclosed to us over time. The path that Vos blazed was foundational for much of the resurgence of biblical theology within evangelicalism, in the twentieth and now twenty-first century.

Following this evangelical view, we define "biblical theology" by employing Brian Rosner's helpful definition: "Biblical theology" is "theological interpretation of Scripture in and for the church. It proceeds with historical and literary sensitivity and seeks to analyze and synthesize the Bible's teaching about God and his relations to the world on its own terms, maintaining sight of the Bible's overarching narrative and Christocentric focus."[9] In this definition, Rosner emphasizes some important points crucial to the nature and task of biblical theology. Biblical theology is concerned with the overall message of the whole Bible. It seeks to understand the parts in relation to the whole. As an exegetical method, it is sensitive to the liter-

---

[6] For a detailed treatment of the post-Reformation Protestant scholastics, see Richard Muller, *Post-Reformation Reformed Dogmatics: The Rise and Development of Reformed Orthodoxy, ca. 1520 to ca. 1725*, 4 vols. (Grand Rapids, MI: Baker, 2003). See also the application of some of the insights of the Protestant scholastics for biblical and systematic theology in Michael S. Horton, *Covenant and Eschatology: The Divine Drama* (Louisville: Westminster John Knox, 2002); Richard Lints, *The Fabric of Theology: A Prolegomenon to Evangelical Theology* (Grand Rapids, MI: Eerdmans, 1993).

[7] See Geerhardus Vos, *Biblical Theology: Old and New Testaments* (Grand Rapids, MI: Eerdmans, 1948; repr., Carlisle, PA: Banner of Truth, 2004); Richard B. Gaffin, Jr., ed., *Redemptive History and Biblical Interpretation: The Shorter Writings of Geerhardus Vos* (Phillipsburg, NJ: P&R, 2001).

[8] Vos, *Biblical Theology*, 5.

[9] Brian Rosner, "Biblical Theology," in *NDBT*, 10 (italics removed from original).

ary, historical, and theological dimensions of Scripture, as well as to the interrelationships between earlier and later texts in Scripture. Furthermore, biblical theology is interested not merely in words and word studies but also in concepts and themes as it traces out the Bible's own storyline, on the Bible's own terms, as the plotline reaches its culmination in Christ. In a similar way, D. A. Carson speaks of biblical theology as an inductive, exegetical discipline which works from biblical texts, in all of their literary diversity, to the entire Canon—hence the notion of *intertextuality*. In making connections between texts, biblical theology also attempts to let the biblical text set the agenda. This is what we mean by saying that we are to read Scripture *on its own terms*, i.e., *intratextually*. Scripture is to be interpreted in light of its own categories and presentation, since Scripture comes to us as divinely given, coherent, and unified.[10] In fact, it is our contention that if one asks the most basic questions—How has God given Scripture to us? What are the Bible's own internal structures? How ought those structures shape our doing of biblical theology?—working through the biblical covenants is the Bible's own way of presenting its internal structures and learning how to read Scripture as God intended it to be read.

With these ideas in mind, let us now summarize what we believe biblical theology is. Simply stated, it is the *hermeneutical* discipline that seeks to do justice to what Scripture claims to be and what it actually is. In regard to its *claim*, Scripture claims to be *God's* Word written, and as such, it is a *unified* revelation of his gracious plan of redemption. In regard to what Scripture actually *is*, it is a *progressive* unfolding of God's plan, rooted in history and developed along a specific storyline primarily demarcated by the biblical covenants. Biblical theology as a hermeneutical discipline attempts to exegete texts in their own context and then, in light of the entire Canon, to examine the unfolding nature of God's plan and carefully think through the relationship between *before* and *after* in that plan, which culminates in Christ.[11] In so doing, biblical theology provides the basis for understanding

---

[10] On these points see D. A. Carson, "Systematic Theology and Biblical Theology," in *NDBT*, 89–104.

[11] Two words that describe how biblical theology seeks to interpret texts first in their immediate and then in their canonical context are *synchronic* and *diachronic*. Synchronic refers to viewing events occurring at a given time, hence to read texts synchronically means reading them in their immediate context. As we exegete texts, we place them in their redemptive-historical context, we interpret them according to the grammatical-historical method, and we inquire about the theology of a particular prophet, book, or corpus. Biblical exegesis begins at this level as it involves an analytical examination of the "parts." Our interpretation of Scripture, however, does not end here. The unity of Scripture drives us to say more, which introduces the notion of diachronic. *Diachronic* refers to viewing events over time. Texts must be read not only in terms of their immediate context but also in terms of the "whole." Scripture is both unified and progressive. Thus biblical theology is concerned to read the "parts" in terms of the "whole" and to trace out how God's plan develops *throughout* redemptive-history, leading us to Christ.

how texts in one part of the Bible relate to all other texts, according to God's intention, which is discovered through human authors but ultimately at the canonical level. In the end, biblical theology is the attempt to think through the "whole counsel of God," and it provides the basis and underpinning for all theologizing.

If this is what biblical theology is, then what is systematic theology? As with "biblical theology," there are various ideas as to what "systematic theology" is. It is not necessary to delve into all of these diverse views; rather, we will simply state how we conceive of the discipline. For our purposes, we will employ the definition given by John Frame: systematic theology is "the application of God's Word by persons to all areas of life."[12] In our view, this entails at least two key components.

First, in order to *apply* Scripture properly, we must first interpret Scripture correctly, which requires the doing of biblical theology, as just described. This is why we contend that biblical theology is the basis for all theologizing, since we are not doing theology unless we correctly understand how the entire canon of Scripture fits together.

Second, systematic theology goes further than biblical theology, since it involves the *application* of Scripture *to all areas of life*. Systematic theology, then, inevitably involves theological construction and doctrinal formulation, grounded in biblical theology and done in light of historical theology, but it also involves interacting with all areas of life—history, science, psychology, ethics, and so on. In so doing, systematic theology leads to worldview formation as we seek to set the biblical-theological framework of Scripture over against all other worldviews and learn "to think God's thoughts after him," even in areas that the Bible does not directly address. In this important way, systematic theology presents a well-thought-out worldview, over against all of its competitors, as it seeks to apply biblical truth to every domain of life. As a discipline it is also *critical* in seeking to evaluate ideas within and outside the church. *Outside* the church, systematic theology takes on an apologetic function as it first sets forth the faith to be believed and defended, and then critiques and evaluates views that reject the truth of God's Word. In this way, apologetics is properly a subset of systematic theology. *Within* the church, theology is critical by analyzing theological proposals first in terms of their fit with Scripture and secondly in terms of their implications for other doctrines. In all these ways, systematic theology is the discipline that

---

[12] John M. Frame, *The Doctrine of the Knowledge of God* (Phillipsburg, NJ: P&R, 1987), 76.

attempts "to bring our entire thought captive to Christ" (see 2 Cor. 10:1–5), for our good as the church and ultimately for God's glory.

How, then, should we think of the relationship between biblical and systematic theology? In our view, biblical theology is primarily a *hermeneutical* discipline, since it seeks to rightly divide God's Word (2 Tim. 2:14–15). This is why the conclusions of systematic theology must first be grounded in the exegetical conclusions of biblical theology. But then systematic theology goes further: on the basis of biblical theology it attempts to construct what we ought to believe from Scripture for today, to critique other theological proposals within the church, and also the false ideas of non-Christian worldviews, so that we learn anew to live under the Lordship of Christ.

How does this discussion apply to what we are doing in this book? In this book we are setting forth a proposal for understanding the nature and interrelationships of the biblical covenants. In truth, we are *doing* systematic theology by first grounding it in biblical theology. In order to make our case, we will expound the biblical covenants before we turn to systematic reflection. But before we do this, let us outline the basic hermeneutical approach we will follow.

HERMENEUTICAL BASICS: BEING "BIBLICAL" IN OUR READING OF SCRIPTURE AND THEOLOGY

What does it mean to be "biblical"? How do we rightly exegete biblical texts and draw proper theological conclusions from them? At the heart of Christian theology is the attempt to "take every thought captive to obey Christ" (2 Cor. 10:5, ESV). But how does one know that one's theological proposals are biblically warranted? Obviously these questions are not new; they have been with us since Scripture was first given and interpreted. And, it must be admitted, these questions are not as easy and straightforward to answer as many assume. We have all experienced diversity of opinion within the church, even among those of us who affirm Scripture's full authority. This has apparently led some to treat the Bible like a wax nose, i.e., twisting and shaping it at will to fit a variety of viewpoints, with the conclusion that it is not possible to demonstrate one interpretation as more biblical than another.

How, then, do we approach Scripture, interpret it, and draw our theological conclusions? In theological debates, adjudication between viewpoints is often complicated. As most admit, theological positions involve more than merely appealing to one or two texts; entire positions involve a discussion of how texts are understood in their context, how those texts are interrelated to other texts, and ultimately how the entire canon of Scripture is put together. Before we develop our proposal, "kingdom through covenant," we will first outline our basic hermeneutical commitments. Obviously, in this regard, much could be said; we can only scratch the surface. In addition, most of what follows is in agreement with a majority of approaches to evangelical hermeneutics, but regardless, it is important to describe how we approach the task of reading and applying Scripture and thus how we move from text to theological conclusions.

Let us describe our hermeneutical approach by developing the following statement: In order to be *biblical* in our theology, our interpretation and application of Scripture must (1) take seriously what Scripture claims to be; and (2) interpret Scripture in light of what it actually is as God's unfolding revelation across time. Let us develop these two points a bit more.

The Scriptural Claim for Itself: Scripture's Self-Attestation

In order to be *biblical* in our theology we must take seriously what Scripture claims to be. What, then, does Scripture claim for itself? We cannot give a full-blown explication and defense of the doctrine of Scripture; many books have undertaken that task and have done it well.[13] In agreement with historic Christianity, we affirm that Scripture is God's Word written, the product of God's mighty action through the Word and by the Holy Spirit whereby human authors freely wrote exactly what God intended to be written and without error.

Why has the church throughout the ages affirmed this about Scripture? The answer is straightforward: Scripture makes this claim about itself. The church does not confer authority upon this book because she desires it to be God's Word; rather, Scripture itself testifies that it is God's authoritative Word, written through the agency of human authors, and that it is the product of the sovereign-personal "God who is there" and from "the God who is not silent."[14] As such, Scripture both attests to and bears the marks of its divine origin and is thus completely authoritative, sufficient, and reliable. Certainly some biblical scholars and theologians have challenged this claim, but when Scripture is read on its own terms, it can be shown repeatedly to make this

---

[13] See, for example, John M. Frame, *The Doctrine of the Word of God* (Phillipsburg, NJ: P&R, 2010).
[14] The expressions "the God who is there" and "the God who is not silent" are taken from two works of Francis A. Schaeffer: *The God Who Is There* (Downers Grove, IL: InterVarsity Press, 1968) and *He Is There and He Is Not Silent* (Carol Stream, IL: Tyndale, 1972).

claim. In what follows, we assume this view of Scripture in our interpretation of it.

How, then, does this view of Scripture impact our interpretation of it? Two answers may be given. First, given that Scripture is *God's* Word, from the triune, sovereign, and all-knowing God of the universe, we expect *an overall unity and coherenc*e between the Testaments, despite its diversity, that together declares God's unfailing plan and purposes in this fallen world. As we think through the biblical covenants, given our view of Scripture, we will not view the covenants as independent and isolated from each other but as together, in all of their diversity, unfolding the one plan of God centered in our Lord Jesus Christ (Eph. 1:9–10).

Second, given that Scripture is God's Word *through human authors*, we discover God's intent by reading what the biblical authors say; hence the expression, what God says, Scripture says (i.e., the biblical authors), and vice versa. Ultimately, this point leads us to a canonical reading of Scripture in order to discover how to interpret the meaning of specific texts. It is not enough to read Scripture in a "thin" manner, i.e., as isolated texts apart from the whole. Instead we must read texts in a "thick" way, i.e., texts read in light of the entire canon of Scripture.[15] We discover God's intent through the writing(s) of the biblical authors, but given the diversity of authors throughout time, we must interpret biblical authors in light of the entire Canon. It is only by reading Scripture "thickly" that we discover the true meaning of Scripture, i.e., what God's intent is, and how Scripture applies to us today. This observation is simply another way of stating the important Reformation principle that "Scripture must interpret Scripture."

It is also another way of speaking about the "fuller meaning" of Scripture or what has been labeled *sensus plenior*. This expression is understood in diverse ways, so it requires careful definition. We agree with Greg Beale's understanding of the term when he argues that, for example, "the Old Testament authors did not exhaustively understand the meaning, implications, and possible applications of all that they wrote."[16] As authors who wrote under divine inspiration, what they wrote was God-given, true, and authoritative. However, they might not, and probably did not, understand where the entire revelation was going, given the fact that God had

---

[15] See Kevin J. Vanhoozer, "Exegesis and Hermeneutics," in *NDBT*, 61–62.
[16] G. K. Beale, "Did Jesus and His Followers Preach the Right Doctrine from the Wrong Texts?" in *The Right Doctrine from the Wrong Texts: Essays on the Use of the Old Testament in the New*, ed. G. K. Beale (Grand Rapids, MI: Baker, 1994), 393.

not yet disclosed all of the details of his eternal plan. Thus, as more revelation is given through later authors, we discover more of God's plan and where that plan is going. It is for this reason that the New Testament's interpretation of the Old Testament becomes definitive, since later texts bring with them greater clarity and understanding. In other words, we must carefully allow the New Testament to show us how the Old Testament is brought to fulfillment in Christ. In this way, as Beale rightly acknowledges, the New Testament's interpretation of the Old may expand the Old Testament author's meaning in the sense of seeing new implications and applications. However, given that we discover God's intent through the human authors, later texts do *not* contravene the integrity of the earlier texts, "but rather [develop] them in a way which is consistent with the Old Testament author's understanding of the way in which God interacts with his people"[17] in previous eras of redemptive-history.[18] Thus, Scripture as an entire canon must interpret Scripture; the later parts must "draw out and explain more clearly the earlier parts,"[19] and theological conclusions must be exegetically derived from the entire Canon.

On this point, it is also important to stress that, given what Scripture is, a canonical reading is not an optional way to interpret Scripture. In fact, to read the Bible canonically is demanded by the very nature of Scripture and its claim regarding itself. Thus, *not* to read Scripture in this way is to fail to interpret it correctly and is to be less than "biblical." Grammatical-historical exegesis, then, needs to be set in the larger context of a canonical reading; the parts must be read in terms of the whole. Let us now turn to the second point, i.e., in order to be "biblical" we must interpret Scripture in light of what it actually is as God's unfolding revelation across time.

Interpreting Scripture According to What It Is

What *is* Scripture? Here we are not thinking in terms of what Scripture says about itself but more in terms of the actual phenomena of Scripture, or better, how God has chosen to give us his Word and disclose himself to us through human authors. Let us discuss the phenomena of the Bible by focusing on two points: Scripture is a word-act revelation and a progressive revelation.

---

[17] Ibid.
[18] It is customary among biblical scholars and theologians to refer to the history of God's plan of redemption with the hyphenated phrase "redemptive-history."
[19] Ibid.

SCRIPTURE IS A WORD-ACT REVELATION

A helpful way of describing the phenomena of Scripture is by viewing it as a word-act revelation. What does this mean? Simply stated, it means that Scripture is God's own authoritative interpretation of his redemptive acts through the agency of human authors. Let us think about this in three steps.

First, we affirm that all of God's redemptive acts are revelatory of him, his plan, and his purposes. God has disclosed himself in history through his mighty acts, what we often identify as special revelation in contrast to God's revelation in the natural world. For example, in the Old Testament, the greatest revelatory redemptive act of God was his deliverance of Israel from their slavery in Egypt (cf. Ex. 6:6–7). In the New Testament, the proclamation of the gospel involves the recitation of God's acts in history (cf. Acts 2:22ff.; 3:13ff.; 10:36ff.; 13:26ff.; 1 Cor. 15:3f.). In fact, supremely, the focal point of Scripture is what God has done in Christ. The New Testament continually proclaims that what God had promised in ages past, what the Old Testament prophets anticipated, God has now brought to fulfillment in the life, death, and resurrection of our Lord Jesus—the greatest display of God's mighty acts (cf. Mark 1:15; Luke 4:21; Gal. 4:4).

Second, as important as it is to affirm that God acts in order to reveal himself and to redeem his people, God's redemptive acts are never left to speak for themselves, and they never appear separated from God's verbal communications of truth. Word *and* act always accompany each other. Furthermore, just as redemption is historically successive, so also is revelation, for God's revelatory word interprets God's redemptive acts. For example, Exodus 15:1–18 interprets the events of the Red Sea crossing; they are never left as self-interpreting. In fact, word and act often follow a general order in Scripture: first there is a preparatory word, then the divine act, followed by the interpretive word. For example, in the giving of the old covenant we first see a preparatory word (Exodus 19), then the divine act of giving the law (Exodus 20), followed up by an interpretative explanation of the law (Exodus 21ff.). This same order may be observed of the Bible as a whole. The Old Testament reveals the predictive word and anticipates greater realities tied to the coming of our Lord; the Gospels give the account of the redemptive-revelatory fact of the coming of the Son; and the remainder of the New Testament supplies, along with the Gospels, the final interpretation of not only who the Son is but the full implications of what he has achieved in the inauguration of the new covenant era and the fulfillment of the prophetic word.

Third, as a word-act revelation, Scripture is the product of God's own mighty actions. Scripture not only chronicles the activities of God's redemption in history; it not only is a word that interprets God's redeeming acts; it is itself a product of God's own redemptive acts for the purpose of teaching, edification, instruction, and as such is fully authoritative and sufficient for our thinking and lives. Scripture, then, as a written text, is in its final form God's own divine interpretation, through human authors, of his own redemptive acts that carries with it a true and authoritative interpretation of his redemptive plan. Though it is not an exhaustive revelation, nonetheless it is a true, objective, and first-order text that requires us to read it as a complete canonical text on its own terms, according to its own structure and categories, in order to discern correctly God's intent and redemptive plan. Once again, this reminds us that Scripture must be read as an entire revelation in order to discern God's overall plan. This point is further underscored by viewing Scripture as a *progressive* revelation.

SCRIPTURE IS A PROGRESSIVE REVELATION

Scripture as a word-act revelation also involves historical progression, since, just as God's plan of redemption and mighty acts did not happen all at once, so the word-interpretation of those acts unfolds over time.[20] Revelation, alongside redemption, unfolds in a progressive manner by unique twists and turns in separate but related epochs, largely demarcated by the biblical covenants, which ultimately find their terminus in the person and work of Christ.

Hebrews 1:1–3 beautifully describes this point. "Long ago," the author reminds us, "God spoke to our fathers by the prophets," and he did so "at many times and in many ways" (ESV). God's word-act revelation took place over a period of time, and as it was given it pointed beyond itself to something more to come. In fact, this is the precise point that the author makes by his use of "at many times and in many ways," i.e., not only was the Old Testament revelation repetitive, it was also incomplete. In the progress of revelation, more and more of God's plan was disclosed to us, pointing forward to and culminating in the coming of Christ. But now, with the coming of the Son, the last days have dawned; the last days that the Old Testament revelation anticipated have now come to fulfillment literally "in Son" (*en huiō*; v. 2), underscoring that in Christ the final, definitive, complete revela-

---

[20] "Progressive" is used in the sense of the unfolding plan of God, not in the sense that an earlier era was inferior and the later era has progressed or has reached a superior stage.

tion has now come. In this way, the author of Hebrews, along with the entire New Testament, places the Son in a qualitatively different category than the prophets who preceded him. The effect of this is not to downplay the authority of the Old Testament prophetic revelation; rather, the point is that the previous revelation was incomplete and, by its very nature, was intended by God to point beyond itself to God's full self-disclosure in his Son. This is why the Son is more than a mere prophet (though he is the fulfillment of the prophetic institution): he is the one about whom the prophets spoke; he is the one who fulfills the previous incomplete Word. Even more: in the Son, all of God's revelation and redemptive purposes culminate.

All of this is to say that Scripture as a word-act revelation is also a *progressive* revelation. Hermeneutically speaking, this has important implications for how we read and apply Scripture and thus draw conclusions from Scripture and warrant our theological proposals. Our reading of Scripture must trace out how Scripture unfolds God's plan of redemption, which is the task of "biblical theology." Biblical theology attempts to give a theological reading of Scripture, grounded in exegesis, that grasps "the whole counsel of God" in terms of its redemptive-historical progression. Scripture consists of many literary forms which all must be interpreted carefully, but underneath all of these literary forms is a storyline, beginning in creation and moving to the new creation, which unfolds God's redemptive plan. And it is crucial that we read Scripture in such a way that we do justice to the Bible's own presentation and within its own categories, which is precisely why the biblical covenants are so important.

Michael Horton stresses these exact points as he thinks through theological method.[21] Given what Scripture is, Horton contends that the most "biblical" theological method is one that is "redemptive-historical-eschatological." By these terms he is saying what we have just described. Given the authority of Scripture and how it has come to us, we are to interpret Scripture according to its own intrasystematic categories, i.e., on its own terms, which Horton contends are captured by the terms "eschatological" and "redemptive-historical."

By "eschatological" Horton means more than a mere doctrinal topic. Rather, it is a lens by which we read Scripture and do our theology. Scripture itself comes to us as a redemptive revelation, rooted in history, unfolding God's eternal plan worked out in time, and as such the very "form" and

---

[21] See Horton, *Covenant and Eschatology*, 1–19, 147–276.

"shape" of Scripture is eschatological. Scripture is more than a storehouse of facts or propositions; Scripture unfolds for us a *plot*, a divine interpretation of the drama of redemption, that is eschatological at heart and Christological in focus, and as such, our reading of Scripture and our drawing of theological conclusions must reflect this. By "redemptive-historical," Horton is referring to Scripture's own presentation of itself as "the organic unfolding of the divine plan in its execution through word (announcement), act (accomplishment), and word (interpretation)."[22] Given that redemption is progressive and unfolding, so is revelation, as it is God's own interpretation of his action and human response in actual historical contexts.

Given this understanding, for Horton there are a number of important implications for our interpretation of Scripture and for the doing of theology. We will focus on one of them. Our reading of Scripture and our doing of theology must attend to the historical unfolding of redemptive history that is *organically* related and ultimately centered on Jesus Christ. The very "form" and "shape" of Scripture reminds us that God did not disclose himself in one exhaustive act but in an organic, progressive manner, and in fact, it is this organic quality of revelation that serves to explain the diversity of Scripture. Theology, as a result, must be very careful not to proof-text without considering the redemptive-historical structure and progression in Scripture and reading Scripture as a canonical text.[23]

"Putting Together" the Canon: The Three Horizons of Biblical Interpretation

What does this discussion have to do with biblical covenants? The simple answer is, *everything*. As we think through the biblical covenants, since God has not disclosed himself in one exhaustive act but progressively, we must carefully think through every covenant first in its own immediate context, then ask what has preceded that covenant, and then relate that particular covenant to that which comes after it and how it is fulfilled in Christ's new covenant. It is only when we do this that we begin to understand how each covenant relates to previous and later covenants, and how *all* the biblical covenants relate to Christ. We must also be careful as we trace out the historical unfolding of God's plan as demarcated by the biblical covenants and their covenant heads—Adam, Noah, Abraham, Israel, David, and then our

---

[22] Ibid., 5.
[23] Ibid., 1–19, 147–276.

Lord—noting how the entire plan is *organically* related while at the same time preserving its diversity, thus maintaining a proper balance between the continuity and discontinuity of God's plan as it culminates in Jesus.

In this regard, the work of Richard Lints is helpful. Lints, in laying out an evangelical theological method, stresses the same points we have stressed, especially in regard to how we must interpret any text of Scripture. He rightly contends that biblical theology is foundational to the doing of systematic theology. He also proposes, given what Scripture is, that we interpret biblical texts according to three horizons: textual, epochal, and canonical.[24] By emphasizing these three horizons, Lints helps us think about how to interpret Scripture properly—in light of what Scripture is—while also enabling us to avoid "proof-texting." He also reminds us that, in biblical interpretation and theological formulation, "context" is king and, in fact, three contexts are crucial in "putting together" the entire Bible, including the biblical covenants. Let us briefly discuss each of these "contexts" for a proper biblical-theological interpretation of Scripture.

CONTEXT, CONTEXT, CONTEXT

Our interpretation of Scripture begins with a specific text, what Lints calls the *textual horizon* or the immediate context. In terms of this context, biblical hermeneutics has sought to interpret texts according to the grammatical-historical method, seeking to discern God's intent through the human author's intent by putting the text in its historical setting, understanding the rules of language the author is using, analyzing the syntax, textual variants, word meanings, figures of speech, and the literary structure, including the genre of the text. By paying careful attention to the text, a reader discovers what authors are seeking to communicate. Standard books in hermeneutics work through these areas, and we assume all of this in our exegesis of individual passages of Scripture. Yet it is important to note that our interpretation of texts does not terminate here, which leads to the second horizon of biblical interpretation.

The *epochal horizon* is the second context by which we interpret texts. Here we seek to read texts in light of where they are located in God's unfolding plan. Since Scripture is a progressive revelation, texts do not come to us in a vacuum; rather, they are embedded in a larger context of what has come *before* them. As God communicates through biblical authors, these same

---

[24] See Lints, *Fabric of Theology*, 259–311.

authors write in light of what has preceded them. When Lints labels this context the "epochal horizon," he does not intend to convey, nor do we, that the "epochs" embody different plans of God; rather, they simply remind us that God's revelation of redemption occurs over time. There is a unity within this development, given that it is God's plan, but this fundamental unity should not lead us to minimize the differences among epochs, hence the balance between continuity *and* discontinuity in Scripture.

Furthermore, locating texts in redemptive-history also helps illuminate *intertextual* links between earlier and later revelation. As later authors refer to earlier texts, they build upon what is given, but not only in terms of greater understanding of where God's plan is going: they also begin to identify God-given patterns between earlier and later events, persons, and institutions within the unfolding of God's plan—what is rightly labeled "typology." It is by this means, but not limited to it, that God's plan moves forward and ultimately reaches its *telos* in Christ. As later authors draw out these God-given patterns (types), they do not arbitrarily make connections; rather, they develop these patterns in ways that God intends and in ways that do not contravene earlier texts. It is only by reading texts first in their immediate context and then in relation to where these texts are in God's unfolding plan that we begin to grasp God's overall plan and purposes. Individual texts do not become fragmented, and the road from "text" to "reader" is not merely a matter of one's intuition, preference, or prejudice.

Is it necessary to be precise as to what the epochal differences are in Scripture? Probably not; people may disagree on these differences. The important point is to always read texts in light of what has preceded them in reference to God's redemptive actions and plan. Most agree that the most significant epochal division is between the Old Testament era and the fulfillment of God's plan in the coming of Christ. But there are also other divisions that are crucial, and Scripture does divide up redemptive-history in a number of ways. For example, in Romans 5:12–21 Paul divides all of human history under two heads: Adam and Christ. Under these two heads, Paul further subdivides redemptive-history by the following epochs: Adam (vv. 12–13), from Adam to Moses (vv. 14–17), and from Moses and the giving of the law-covenant to Christ (vv. 18–21). Or, in Acts 7:1–53, Stephen identifies three distinct periods: the age of the patriarchs (vv. 2–16), the Mosaic age, which included the time of the exodus and conquest of the Promised Land (vv. 17–45a), and the age of the monarchy (vv. 45b-53). Or, in the genealogy in Matthew 1, Matthew divides up redemptive-history into three distinct periods: Abraham to David (vv. 2–6a); Solomon to the exile (vv. 6b-11); and the exile to Christ (vv. 12–17).

It is Matthew's structuring of redemptive-history that Graeme Goldsworthy follows. However, in addition to the three epochs from Matthew, Goldsworthy adds a prior epoch that includes creation (Genesis 1–2), the impact of the historic fall (Genesis 3), and primeval history (Genesis 4–11), thus speaking of the era of Genesis 1–11, prior to Abraham. Concerning this first epoch—creation, fall, primeval history—Goldsworthy argues that it provides the main theological presuppositions to all of redemptive-history, which are then worked out as God's plan unfolds and ultimately culminates in Christ.[25]

For our purposes, what is most significant to note is that most of these epochal divisions follow the unfolding of the biblical covenants, which we contend is *the Bible's own way of making these epochal divisions*. For many like Goldsworthy, the unfolding of the "kingdom" is the backbone to the storyline of Scripture, yet if we follow the Bible's own "intrasystematic" categories, it is "kingdom through covenant" that captures the Bible's own *internal* structure, and thus better grasps the various epochal divisions in God's plan of redemption.

At this point it is important to ask whether these epochal differences, tied to *before* and *after* categories in Scripture, are really that hermeneutically significant? Or, better, is this how Scripture, on its own terms, "puts itself together"? Does thinking through where various texts are located in God's plan impact the conclusions we draw from Scripture, especially in how we understand the biblical covenants? The answer is *yes*. For example, let us think about Paul's argument in Romans 4. In Romans 4, Paul argues that Abraham serves as the paradigm, for Jews *and* Gentiles, of one who was justified by grace through faith apart from works. Warrant for this assertion is found in Genesis 15:6, where God declares Abraham righteous on the basis of his believing the promises of God. But in order to demonstrate that God's declaration of justification is for both the Jew and the Gentile, Paul then argues that in the life of Abraham this declaration took place *before* he was circumcised (which took place in Genesis 17, which comes *after* Genesis 15), thus demonstrating that Abraham's justification was *not* tied to circumcision but was solely on the basis of his faith in the promises of God. It is for this reason that Abraham can serve as the paradigm of faith for

---

[25] See Goldsworthy, *According to Plan*, 80–234.

Jews *and* Gentiles. This is not to say that circumcision was not significant in the Old Testament; it certainly was. But it is to affirm that one cannot draw the conclusion, which the Judaizers sadly did, that Gentiles had first to be circumcised in order to enter into covenant relationship with Yahweh. In the life of Abraham, not only was this *not* the case, but now that Christ has come, that covenant sign is no longer in force (1 Cor. 7:19), due to the fact that, in the plotline of Scripture, God was teaching us that salvation was always by grace through faith. Paul's argument works, however, only if circumcision is instituted *after* Genesis 15, thus illustrating the point that texts must carefully be interpreted in terms of what comes *before* and *after* them, in order to draw correct "biblical" conclusions.

Galatians 3 is another example of this point and is a very significant text in thinking through covenantal relationships. In Galatians 3, Paul is countering the Judaizers who, like many conservative Jews, "saw in the law given at Sinai not only a body of instruction but a hermeneutical key to the rest of Scripture."[26] In this way these individuals viewed the old covenant as an end in itself and not as a means to a larger end found in Christ and the inauguration of the new covenant. That is why, in order for a Gentile to become a Christian, these Judaizers argued that Gentiles had to come under the Mosaic law-covenant. Conversely, Paul's argument is that, now that Christ has come, Christians are not bound by the Mosaic law-covenant; rather, we come to Christ by faith apart from the law (vv. 1–6). How does Paul warrant his point? He first appeals to Genesis 15 to demonstrate that Abraham was justified by grace through faith (vv. 6–9) and then argues that God's declaration of justification in Abraham's life took place long *before* the giving of the Mosaic law (vv. 15–29). In light of this, Paul wrestles with the obvious question of why the law was given, but his conclusion is the same: since Abraham was declared just *before* the old covenant was given, the old covenant cannot set aside the previous covenant.

Hermeneutically and theologically speaking, then, in order to grasp how God's plan fits together, and, for our purposes, how the biblical covenants fit together, one must locate each covenant in its proper place in redemptive-history and discern how it relates to what preceded it and what follows it. Unless we read Scripture this way, we will misread it and fail to understand how the parts of God's plan fit with the whole.[27] In fact, this was one of the

---

[26] Carson, "Systematic Theology and Biblical Theology," 98.

[27] Other examples could be multiplied, specifically from the book of Hebrews. In chapters 7–8, the author makes the same argument that Paul makes in Romans 4 and Galatians 3, namely that one must read texts in terms of their

key failures of a Jewish reading of Scripture. Old Testament Jews, along with the Judaizers, did not interpret the law-covenant in relation to its place in redemptive-history. If they had done so, they would have drawn the same conclusion that the New Testament draws: in God's overall plan, the Mosaic law-covenant is temporary, leading us to what that old covenant was ultimately pointing forward to, namely, Christ and the new covenant. Yet, we must not end our reading of Scripture here: texts must also be read in terms of what comes *after* them, namely, the canonical horizon.

The third and final context that must be considered in our interpretation of any biblical text is, therefore, the *canonical horizon*. Given the fact that Scripture is *God's* Word and is a *unified* revelation, texts must be understood in relation to the entire Canon. As Kevin Vanhoozer notes, it is only when Scripture is read canonically that we are interpreting it in a truly "biblical" manner—"according to its truest, fullest, *divine* intention."[28] In fact, to read the Bible canonically corresponds to what the Bible actually *is*. That is why, "To read the Bible as unified Scripture is not just one interpretative interest among others, but the interpretative strategy that best corresponds to the nature of the text itself, given its divine inspiration."[29] As texts are placed along the storyline of Scripture and ultimately interpreted in light of the culmination of God's plan in Christ, we begin to read Scripture the way God intended and thus "biblically."

What, then, does it mean to be "biblical?" If we take seriously Scripture's claim for itself and what Scripture actually is, a three-horizon reading of the Canon is the place to start—a *theological* reading, which may be summarized as a grammatical/literary-historical-canonical method of interpretation. In this way, we are letting Scripture interpret Scripture; we are seeking to unfold how the Bible itself is given to us, in its own intrasystematic categories and storyline, so in the end, we read, apply, and draw theological conclusions from Scripture "biblically."

At this point it is legitimate to ask, in what ways does Scripture itself link the Canon together in terms of its own intrasystematic categories? Much could be said here, but Lints is on track when he notes that, in the big

---

placement in the Bible's storyline. For example, in Hebrews 7, the author concludes that the Old Testament did not view the Levitical priesthood as an end in itself but something that was temporary, given God's announcement of another priest, in a different order, in Psalm 110, *which came after the establishment of the Levitical priesthood* (Heb. 7:11, 28). Also in Hebrews 8, building on his argument in chapter 7, the author concludes that since the promise of the new covenant in Jeremiah 31 comes *after* the establishment of the old covenant, this is proof that in God's plan the old covenant was temporary and anticipatory of something greater.

[28] Vanhoozer, "Exegesis and Hermeneutics," 61 (emphasis his).

[29] Ibid.

scheme of things, "essential to the canonical horizon of biblical interpretation is the continuity between the promises of God and his fulfillment of those promises."[30] That is why one of the important ways that God has glued the diverse epochs of redemptive-history together is the *promise-fulfillment* motif. But note: it is almost impossible to think of God's promises apart from unpacking the biblical covenants, since the triune God who makes promises to his creatures, in terms of both creation and redemption, does so by entering into covenant relations with them. In truth, unpacking the "promise-fulfillment" motif is another way of unfolding the biblical covenants across time, and this is why the covenants serve as the backbone to the Bible's metanarrative. By unfolding the covenants, the biblical authors are able to grasp both the continuity of God's plan (tied to his promises) and its discontinuity (how fulfillment in Christ brings with it God-intended changes). Thus, as we trace out the storyline of Scripture, as we move from promise to fulfillment and unfold the biblical covenants across time, we are better able to see how Scripture hangs together and reaches its consummation in Christ. We begin to appreciate even more that the diverse stories of Scripture are not randomly thrown together but are part of a larger tapestry that finds its terminus in Christ.

In addition, Lints suggests that closely associated with the "promise-fulfillment" theme is biblical typology. In fact, one of the crucial means by which God's plan unfolds—indeed, how the "promise-fulfillment" motif is developed—is the use of God-given "typology." Typology, no doubt, is a hotly disputed topic in biblical and theological studies, and it means different things to different people. In this work, we will not fully enter that debate. Instead, we will outline how we understand typology and how it relates to our proposal of "kingdom through covenant."

THE NATURE AND IMPORTANCE OF TYPOLOGY

It is first crucial to distinguish typology from "allegory." The major difference is that typology is grounded in *history*, the *text*, and *intertextual* development, where various "persons, events, and institutions" are intended by God to correspond to each other, while allegory assumes none of these things. In addition, since allegories are not grounded in authorial intent, which is (inter)textually warranted, "allegorical interpretation" depends on some kind of extratextual grid to warrant its explanation. As Vanhoozer

---

[30] Lints, *Fabric of Theology*, 303.

notes, allegorical interpretation is represented by the interpretive strategy for declaring "*This* (word) means *that* (concept),"[31] with *that* being determined by an extratextual framework. This is not what typology is and how typology functions in Scripture. In fact, when one investigates the six explicit New Testament typological texts (Rom. 5:14; 1 Cor. 10:6, 11; Heb. 8:5; 9:24; 1 Pet. 3:21), a consistent picture emerges that distinguishes it from allegory. What exactly is that pattern? Let us describe it by first defining typology and then explaining its key features.[32]

We will employ Richard Davidson's definition of typology. Typology is the study of the Old Testament salvation-historical realities or "types" (persons, events, institutions) which God has specifically designed to correspond to, and predictively prefigure, their intensified antitypical fulfillment aspects (inaugurated and consummated) in New Testament salvation history.[33] There are two explanatory points to note from this definition.

First, typology is symbolism rooted in *historical* and *textual* realities. As such, it involves an *organic* relation between "persons, events, and institutions" in one epoch and their counterparts in later epochs. The early "person, event, and institution" is called the "type," while the later one is the "anti-type." As Lints reminds us, "The typological relation is a central means by which particular epochal and textual horizons are linked to later horizons in redemptive revelation. It links the present to the future, and it retroactively links the present with the past. It is founded on the organic connection of God's promises with his fulfillment of those promises."[34]

Second, typology is *prophetic* and *predictive* and thus divinely given and intended. In other words, God intended for the "type" to point beyond itself to its fulfillment or "antitype" in a later epoch of redemptive-history. Typology ought to be viewed as a subset of predictive prophecy, not in the sense of verbal predictions but in the sense of predictions built on models/patterns that God himself has established, that become known gradually as later texts reinforce those patterns, with the goal of anticipating what comes later in Christ. In this way, typology is a more "indirect" kind of prophecy which corresponds well with the Pauline emphasis on "mystery" (see, e.g.,

---

[31] Kevin J. Vanhoozer, *Is There a Meaning in This Text? The Bible, the Reader, and the Morality of Literary Knowledge* (Grand Rapids, MI: Zondervan, 1998), 119.

[32] Our discussion of typology is indebted to Richard Davidson, *Typology in Scripture: A Study of Hermeneutical TUPOS Structures*, Andrews University Seminary Doctoral Dissertation Series 2 (Berrien Springs, MI: Andrews University, 1981).

[33] This definition is compiled from the summary discussion in Davidson, *Typology in Scripture*, 397–408.

[34] Lints, *Fabric of Theology*, 304.

Eph. 1:9–10; 3:1–10). In a number of places, Paul states that the gospel was hidden in the past, but now, in light of the coming of Christ, is made known and disclosed publicly for all to see. Simultaneously, then, Scripture says that the gospel was *promised* beforehand and was *clearly* revealed through the prophets (e.g., Rom. 3:21), while it was *hidden* in ages past and *not* fully known until the coming of Christ (e.g., Rom. 16:25–27). A crucial way to reconcile this tension is through typology. Given the indirect nature of it, not only does typology require careful discernment; it also requires the passing of time in order to determine how the "type" is fulfilled in the coming of Christ.

It is also important to note that typology depends on a high view of divine providence and knowledge. How so? While the type has significance for its own time, its greater significance is directed toward the future; it testifies to something greater than itself that is still to come. But the future antitype *will* surely come, not only because God completely knows that it will, according to his eternal plan, but also because God sovereignly *guarantees* that the prophetic fulfillment of the original type will occur in Christ. The relationship between type and antitype is not arbitrary—a construction by the reader; it is an organic relationship ordained by God so that specific types do in fact point beyond themselves to their fulfillment in Christ. Apart from this high view of God, our view of typology makes no sense. This is not to say that everyone associated with the Old Testament type understood and knew the pattern to be pointing forward. Rather, it is to say that when the type is *discovered* to be a type (at some point along the trajectory of its repeated pattern), it is then viewed as such and as God-intended.

Given this basic description of typology, how, then, does it work in Scripture? Typology exhibits a twofold character. First, typology involves a *repetition* of the "promise-fulfillment" pattern of redemptive-history so that various types find their fulfillment in later persons, events, or institutions, but ultimately *all types first find their fulfillment in Christ before they have application to us.* So, for example, Scripture presents Adam as a type of Christ (Rom. 5:12–21; 1 Cor. 15:21–49). As redemptive-history unfolds, other "Adams" (the idea of repetition) show up on the stage of human history and take on the role of the first Adam (e.g., Noah, Abraham, Israel, David), but these "other Adams" are not the ultimate fulfillment. Instead, it is only in Christ that we have the "last Adam"—the one whom all these other persons point to and anticipate. In this way, God intends the first Adam to point beyond himself to Christ, and we come to know God's intention as the Adamic pattern *intertextually develops* and finds its ultimate fulfillment in Christ. This is why types are viewed as both predictive and hidden. They are *predictive* since God intends for them to anticipate Christ in a variety of ways. They are *hidden* not only due to their indirectness but also because we come to know them as types only as God's redemptive plan unfolds and later texts pick up the recurring pattern.

Or, for example, think of the nation of Israel. Israel not only is presented in Scripture as "another Adam" who, as the son (Ex. 4:22–23), takes on Adam's role in the world; Israel also anticipates the coming of the true Son, the true Israel, the true servant, the true vine, namely, Christ (see, e.g., Isa. 5:1–7; Hos. 11:1; Matt. 2:15; John 15:1–17). Furthermore, since types find their fulfillment first in Christ and not in us, we as God's people participate in the typological pattern only by virtue of our relationship to Christ. Thus, in the case of Israel, Christ is first its fulfillment and we, as the church, are viewed as the "Israel of God" only because of our relation to Christ. We, as the church, are not the antitypical fulfillment of Israel in the first sense; Christ alone fills that role. Yet in union with Christ, we are the beneficiaries of his work. In relationship to Christ, the true Son/Israel, we become adopted sons (Gal. 3:26–4:7), the "Israel of God" (6:16), Abraham's spiritual offspring (3:29), restored to what God created us to be (Eph. 4:20–24). It is in this way that the new covenant promise given to the "house of Israel/Judah" (Jer. 31:31) is applied to the church. Christ, as the antitypical fulfillment of Israel, takes on the role of Israel, and by our faith union in him, his work becomes ours as his new covenant people.

A second characteristic of typology is its *a fortiori* (lesser to greater) quality, or the fact that it exhibits *escalation* as the type is fulfilled in the antitype. For example, as one moves from Adam or David to the prophets, priests, and kings, and through the covenants to the last Adam, the true Davidic King, the great High Priest, and so on, the antitype is *always* greater than the previous types. Yet it is important to note that escalation across time does not occur incrementally from the original type to each "little" installment and then to Christ, as if there were a straight line of increase. Rather, escalation occurs fully only with the coming of Christ. The previous typological patterns point forward to the greater one to come (Rom. 5:14), but the *greater* aspect is realized only in Christ. So, for example, Adam serves as a type of Christ, and "little Adams" arise across time, yet all of these "other

Adams" (e.g., Noah, Abraham, Israel, David) fail in their obedience and faith; there is *not* an increase in them. Yet, all of them anticipate the coming of a greater Adam—the last Adam—who will *not* fail in his obedience. Or, think of David and his sons. Rooted in the Davidic covenant, they serve as types of Christ. As one moves from David to Solomon there is a minimal escalation, but it does not last long. During his life, Solomon horribly fails. In fact, all of the Davidic kings fail, including David, and as such they are not able to usher in God's saving rule and reign (kingdom) and fulfill their God-appointed purpose. It is only in the coming of David's greater Son, our Lord Jesus Christ, that we have escalation as he brings the Davidic pattern to its antitypical fulfillment.

This observation is important for a number of reasons. Not only does the *a fortiori* quality of typology serve as the crucial means by which Scripture unpacks the unique identity of Christ; it is also how Scripture grounds the uniqueness of the new covenant era. When fulfillment arrives, legitimate *discontinuity* between the old and new in God's unified plan is established. When the antitype arrives in history, or better, when it is inaugurated, not only are the previous types brought to their *telos* but the entire era introduced entails massive changes. This is why the era of fulfillment inaugurated by Christ (the "already"), even though it still awaits the consummation (the "not yet"), has introduced greater realities—realities that are directly linked to the inauguration of the new covenant era and the dawning of the new creation.[35]

One last point is crucial to note before this section is concluded. In Scripture, typology and covenants are intimately related. Try to think of any biblical types and patterns that are *not* tied to the biblical covenants! In fact, to reflect upon typological patterns and their development is simultaneously to walk through the biblical covenants. For example, Adam and the "other Adams" who follow him are all associated with the covenants of creation, Noah, Abraham, Israel, and David. In all these covenant heads, the role of Adam is continued in the world, and each one of them points forward to the coming of the last Adam, who through his obedience accomplishes our redemption.[36] Or, think of the promise to Abraham regarding his "seed." As the seed promise unfolds, it does so in Isaac, later in the nation of Israel, in the Davidic king, and ultimately in Christ, and then by extension to the

---

[35] For a discussion of inaugurated eschatology see Thomas R. Schreiner, *New Testament Theology: Magnifying God in Christ* (Grand Rapids, MI: Baker, 2008), 41–116.
[36] See texts such as Genesis 1–3; 5:1–2; 9:1–17; 12:1–3; Exodus 4:22–23; 2 Samuel 7:5–16; Psalm 8; Romans 5:12–21; Hebrews 2:5–18.

church as Abraham's spiritual offspring.[37] Or, think of how Moses, who is foundational for the entire institution of prophets and who inaugurates the entire priestly role under the old covenant, is developed in terms of an entire institution of prophets and priests that ultimately culminates in Christ.[38] Many more examples could be given in relation to David and his sons, the entire tabernacle-temple structure, the event of the exodus (which anticipates a greater exodus to come), and so on. *All* of these types are organically related to the covenants. One cannot properly think of them apart from wrestling with how the covenants relate to each other and how the covenants as a whole point forward to the coming of Christ and the new covenant age. In this way, all of biblical history is prophetic, not merely in terms of verbal predictions but in types/patterns associated with the covenants, which anticipate and predict the dawning of the end of the ages in the coming of Christ. This is why the entire New Testament is Christological in focus, since Jesus is the one whom the covenants and prophets anticipate (e.g., Matt. 5:17–18; 11:11–15; Rom. 3:21, 31). This is another reason why "putting together" the biblical covenants is the means by which we grasp the "parts" of God's plan in light of the "whole" and thus understand Scripture.

With these points in place, let us now turn to the exposition of the biblical covenants. In doing so, we will follow the hermeneutical method as outlined above. Each biblical covenant will first be placed in its own immediate context, then understood in terms of what comes *before* it, and then finally in terms of what comes *after* it, in God's plan. Ultimately we will seek to understand how *all* of the biblical covenants find their *telos*, terminus, and fulfillment in Christ, as we see the unfolding of God's glorious plan under the rubric of "kingdom through covenant."

---

[37] See texts such as Genesis 12:1–3; 17:1–22; Exodus 1:1–7; 2 Samuel 7:5–16; Galatians 3:16, 29. On the development of this theme, see T. D. Alexander, "Seed," in *NDBT*, 769–773.
[38] See Exodus 19–20, 24, 32–34; Leviticus 8–9; Deuteronomy 18:14–22; 34:10–12; John 1:14–18; Hebrews 1:1–3; 3:1–6.

PART TWO

EXPOSITION OF THE BIBLICAL COVENANTS

Chapter 2

COVENANTS IN THE BIBLE AND THE ANCIENT NEAR EAST

COVENANTS IN THE BIBLE

The meaning of "covenant" as found in the Bible and biblical world, and likely even the term, is foreign to our culture, society, and thought-world today. A brief overview of covenants in the Old Testament and in the ancient Near East along with definitions will begin to adjust our perspective to that of the Bible.

Covenants in the Old Testament

In the Old Testament the Hebrew word for covenant is *běrît*. The same word is used in Scripture for a wide diversity of oath-bound commitments in various relationships. It is used to refer to international treaties (Josh. 9:6; 1 Kings 15:19), clan alliances (Gen. 14:13), personal agreements (Gen. 31:44), national agreements (Jer. 34:8–10), and loyalty agreements (1 Sam. 20:14–17), including marriage (Mal. 2:14).

INTERNATIONAL TREATIES

In Joshua 9, when Joshua led Israel into the land of Canaan and attacked the Canaanites who were living in the land at that time, they were deceived and tricked by the Gibeonites into making a treaty with them. This was a peace treaty between two nations.

In 1 Kings 5:12, Hiram, king of Tyre, a city in ancient Phoenicia, and Solomon, king of Israel, made an international treaty. There were peaceful relations between the two countries and agreements for commerce and trade.

CLAN/TRIBAL ALLIANCES

In Genesis 14:13, powerful nomads of the desert formed an alliance to help each other in case of attack by enemies. This is essentially an alliance between clans or tribes.

PERSONAL AGREEMENTS

After years of attempting to best and outwit each other, Laban and his nephew Jacob finally made an agreement not to harm each other (Gen. 31:44). This was a private agreement between two individuals.

LOYALTY AGREEMENTS

Jonathan, the son of King Saul, developed a deep friendship with David during the years when Saul sought to get rid of David and kill him. This friendship was formally solemnized twice by agreements of loyalty (1 Sam. 18:3; 23:18).

MARRIAGE

The marriage relationship is a loyalty agreement formally solemnized by a vow before God. This is clearly indicated by Proverbs 2:17 and Malachi 2:14.

NATIONAL LEGAL AGREEMENTS

In Jeremiah 34:8–10, King Zedekiah made a covenant with the people to proclaim freedom for all the slaves. Although this may seem somewhat similar to a legal agreement or contract, it was different in character from contracts and legal documents of today. Since the covenant was made between king and people, it operated at a national level.

DEFINITION AND ILLUSTRATION

Defining the term "covenant" (*bĕrît*) can be difficult since it is used for such a wide variety of agreements. Bruce Waltke's definition is minimal: "*covenant* . . . means a solemn commitment of oneself to undertake an obligation."[1] The definition of Gordon Hugenberger is also brief and clear:

> A covenant, in its normal sense, is an elected, as opposed to natural, relationship of obligation under oath.[2]

The following description, adapted from Daniel C. Lane, is similar but fuller:

---

[1] Bruce K. Waltke with Charles Yu, *An Old Testament Theology* (Grand Rapids, MI: Zondervan, 2007), 287.
[2] Gordon Hugenberger, *Marriage as a Covenant: A Study of Biblical Law and Ethics Governing Marriage Developed from the Perspective of Malachi*, Supplements to Vetus Testamentum 52 (Leiden, Netherlands: Brill, 1994), 11.

A covenant is an enduring agreement which defines a relationship between two parties involving a solemn, binding obligation(s) specified on the part of at least one of the parties toward the other, made by oath under threat of divine curse, and ratified by a visual ritual.[3]

Scholars debate whether *běrît* can denote a relationship between parties, or simply the obligation one party takes upon himself. This seems to be based on a false dichotomy. Fulfilling any obligation between human parties involves a relationship formalizing some understanding between them, and no relationship between human parties is without obligations unless it functions only at a merely animal level.

Studies of the origin of the word *běrît* have not been helpful as to its meaning. Analysis of usage provides better help in understanding the term. In the branch of the Semitic family to which Hebrew belongs, *běrît* is attested as a loanword in Egyptian texts as early as 1300 B.C. This indicates that the use of the word was already established well before that time.

Behind each example of covenant is the use of family categories for those who are not bound by ties of natural kinship. Thus, by a ceremony or legal process, people who are not kin are now bound as tightly as any family relationship. Marriage is the best example of this. A man and a woman, who are not previously related, are now bound closer than any other bond of blood or kinship.

COVENANTS IN THE ANCIENT NEAR EAST

We must not think that the kind of agreements or covenants described in the Bible were entirely unique to the nation of Israel. Covenants or treaties either identical or similar to those mentioned in the Old Testament were common all across the ancient Near East, in lands and regions known today as Egypt, Iraq, Syria, and Turkey. Two types of treaties in the ancient Near East are especially noteworthy: (1) the suzerain-vassal treaty and (2) the royal charter or land grant. The first type is a diplomatic treaty between a great king or suzerain and client kings or vassals. The focus of these treaties was to reinforce the interests of the suzerain by arguments from history and

---

[3] Adapted from Daniel C. Lane, "The Meaning and Use of the Old Testament Term for 'Covenant' (*bᵉrît*): with Some Implications for Dispensationalism and Covenant Theology" (PhD diss., Trinity International University, 2000). Lane's actual wording is as follows: "A *berith* is an enduring agreement which establishes a defined relationship between two parties involving a solemn, binding obligation to specified stipulations on the part of at least one of the parties toward the other, which is taken by oath under threat of divine curse, and ratified by a visual ritual" (314).

oath-bound affirmations of loyalty on the part of the vassal states, backed up by divine sanctions. The second type of treaty involves a grant of property or even a privileged position of a priestly or royal office given as a favor by a god or king. The focus of these treaties is on honor and the interpersonal relationship.

Scholars have found it helpful to compare and contrast biblical covenants in form and structure to treaties in the ancient Near East. For example, the book of Deuteronomy is identical in form (but not in content) to the international treaties in the ancient Near East, especially the suzerain-vassal treaties of the Hittites from the late fourteenth century B.C. Discussion of the biblical covenants in this work will benefit from noting both differences and similarities between the major covenants in the Old Testament and those in the nations surrounding Israel. Two important points have frequently eluded scholars as they have attempted to use models or patterns of treaties in the ancient Near East to analyze and characterize those in the Old Testament. First, it may be that the biblical treaty in question is an adaptation of a genre or literary model in the ancient Near East and not necessarily a consciously close imitation of the literary structure in all aspects, so that one need not "discover" every feature of the genre or model in the biblical example. Second, although one may distinguish these two types of treaties, they represent different emphases on a continuum rather than polar opposites. Thus, rather than categorizing a treaty as either suzerain-vassal or royal grant, it may be that a covenant in the Old Testament has features of both types, and it would diminish the communication of Scripture to represent the covenant solely in terms of one model.

MAJOR COVENANTS IN THE BIBLE

While there are a great number and variety of covenants or treaties described in the Old Testament, certain covenants between God and other parties—be they groups or individuals—stand out in the plot structure of the narrative as determined by the canon of the Old Testament. Table 2.1 concisely lists the major covenants:

Table 2.1: The Major Covenants

Covenant	Main Scripture Texts
1. The Covenant with Creation	Genesis 1–3
2. The Covenant with Noah	Genesis 6–9

Covenant	Main Scripture Texts
3. The Covenant with Abraham	Genesis 12/15/17/22
4. The Covenant at Sinai	Exodus 19–24
5. The Covenant with David	2 Samuel 7/Psalm 89
6. The New Covenant	Jeremiah 31–34/Isaiah 54/Ezekiel 33–39

Some debate exists as to what should or should not be included in a list such as this. Not all are persuaded that the features portrayed in Genesis 1–2 can be labeled a covenant. Some would add to this list covenants such as the covenant with Levi (Num. 25:6–13; cf. Mal. 2:1–9). At least the six covenants in this list, however, need to be discussed and studied.

THE MAJOR COVENANTS AS THE FRAMEWORK OF THE BIBLICAL METANARRATIVE

We may well ask, what, in literary terms, is the plot structure of the Old Testament or even of the entire Bible as a single text? The basic idea of this book is that the *covenants* constitute the framework of the larger story. They are the backbone of the biblical narrative.

The biblical story begins with the fact that there is only one God. He has created everything and especially has made humankind to rule under him. In this context, God is the center of the universe and we humans find our purpose in having a right relationship to God and to one another. The first man and woman, however, rejected this way. Now, what happens when God is no longer the center of our universe? Who steps in to take his place? Why, we do! I want to be at the center of the universe. Will this work? No, because you want to be there too. So chaos and evil have reigned since the rebellion of Adam and Eve, because we no longer had a right relationship with God and did not treat each other as genuinely human.

God judged the entire human race and made a new start with Noah. This too ended up in chaos and evil, as is clear from the story of the Tower of Babel.

Finally, he made a fresh start with Abraham. He would restore a creation and humanity ruined by pride and rebellion by using Abraham and his family as a pilot project. The people of Israel would be a light to the world, an example of what it meant to be properly related to God and to treat each other properly according to the dignity of our humanity. They would be blessed for obedience, cursed for disobedience. We may call this the Mosaic covenant, set forth in Exodus and restated in Deuteronomy.

But the people of Israel did not keep the Mosaic covenant. That is why the biblical story begins talking about a new covenant. This time it would be possible to keep this covenant.

This summary of the biblical story illustrates that in less than three hundred words—the amount of space normally permitted for a PhD dissertation abstract—the covenants adequately account for the literary or plot structure of the Bible as a text.

The claim here is that the covenants are the key to the larger story of Scripture, the biblical metanarrative. While this claim is based on the idea that Scripture is a *single* book or text and not just an *anthology* of texts, it is not the same as discovering a plan in the arrangement of the books (although that is in part related). Rather, it is a question of the literary plot structure of the metanarrative as a whole. Even genres that are not narrative have at their base a larger story that provides the framework for understanding them. Thus even the nonnarrative genres are based on the larger story.

Nor is this claim the same as the goal pursued by the biblical theology movement of the twentieth century, where the aim was to find a "center" for, e.g., the Old Testament. The claim here is not that "covenant" is *the* center of a biblical theology of the Old Testament, but rather that the covenants (plural) are at the heart of the metanarrative plot structure.

A COMPARISON OF CONTRACT AND COVENANT

In North American culture, the biblical understanding of a covenant relationship is disappearing and being replaced by the notion of contract. In table 2.2, Elmer Martens provides a comparison and contrast between covenant and contract that clarifies and sharpens our understanding of the biblical idea of a covenant relationship:[4]

Table 2.2 Comparison and Contrast between Covenant and Contract

Category	Contract	Covenant
Form/Literary Structure	1. Date 2. Parties 3. Transaction 4. Investiture 5. Guarantees 6. Scribe 7. List of witnesses	1. Speaker introduced 2. History of relationship 3. General command 4. Detailed stipulations 5. Document statement 6. Witnesses 7. Blessings and curses

---

[4] Elmer A. Martens, *God's Design: A Focus on Old Testament Theology* (Grand Rapids, MI: Baker, 1981), 73. Used by permission.

Category	Contract	Covenant
Occasion	Expected benefit	Desire for relationship
Initiative	Mutual agreement	Stronger party
Orientation	Negotiation Thing-oriented	Gift Person-oriented
Obligation	Performance	Loyalty
Termination	Specified	Indeterminate
Violation	Yes	Yes

Various categories help to highlight the similarities and differences between contract and covenant and so enable us to appreciate the significance of the loyalty aspect in covenant. The most obvious difference between contract and covenant is the form or literary structure. We have many contracts in Egyptian Aramaic from the fifth century B.C. A consistent format gives the date, lists the parties, describes the transaction, and is followed by guarantees and witnesses. This format differs markedly from that of the covenants or treaties, whether of the second or first millennium B.C. Yet beyond the aspect of form there are other fundamental differences. Martens comments helpfully on these as follows:

> The occasion for contract is largely the benefits that each party expects. Thus for a satisfactory sum one party agrees to supply a specified quantity of some desired product for the other party. The contract is characteristically thing-oriented. The covenant is person-oriented and, theologically speaking, arises, not with benefits as the chief barter item, but out of a desire for a measure of intimacy. In a contract negotiation an arrival at a mutually satisfactory agreement is important. In a covenant, negotiation has no place. The greater in grace offers his help; the initiative is his. 'Gift' is descriptive of covenant as 'negotiation' is descriptive of contract. Both covenant and contract have obligations, but with this difference. The conditions set out in a contract require fulfillment of terms; the obligation of a covenant is one of loyalty. A covenant, commonly, is forever; a contract for a specified period. A ticking off of terms in check-list fashion can reveal a broken contract, and the point of brokenness can be clearly identified. A covenant, too, can be broken, but the point at which this transpires is less clear, because here the focus is not on stipulations, one, two, three, but on a quality of intimacy. Of all the differences between covenant and contract, the place in covenant of personal loyalty is the most striking.[5]

---

[5] Ibid., 72–73 (emphasis his). See also George E. Mendenhall, *The Tenth Generation: The Origins of the Biblical Tradition* (Baltimore: Johns Hopkins University Press, 1973), xi-xiii, 16–31, where he discusses the differences

At the heart of covenant, then, is a relationship between parties characterized by faithfulness and loyalty in love. In the Hebrew of the Old Testament there is a word pair which is consistently used to express this: *ḥesed* and *'ĕmet*. Neither word has a convenient and simple equivalent in English. The first, *ḥesed*, has to do with showing kindness in loyal love. The second, *'ĕmet*, can be translated by either "faithfulness" or "truth." As a word pair, one cannot easily reduce the meaning of the whole to the sum of its constituent parts, just as one cannot explain the meaning of "odds and ends" in English by describing "odd" and "end." This word pair operates, then, within covenant relationships and has to do with demonstrating faithful, loyal love within the covenant context.

REFLECTIONS ON COVENANT RELATIONSHIP

An excellent illustration of the word pair *ḥesed* and *'ĕmet* is found in Genesis 47:29–30:

> [29] When the time drew near for Israel to die, he called for his son Joseph and said to him, "If I have found favor in your eyes, put your hand under my thigh and promise that you will show me kindness and faithfulness [*ḥesed* and *'ĕmet*]. Do not bury me in Egypt, [30] but when I rest with my fathers, carry me out of Egypt and bury me where they are buried."
>
> "I will do as you say," he said. (NIV)

Jacob, also called Israel, is asking his son Joseph to bury him in Canaan and not in Egypt. There is a covenant relationship between father and son, since family relationships are covenantal in the Old Testament. There is an obligation on the part of the stronger party, Joseph, to help the weaker party, Jacob. The fulfillment of this obligation is referred to as showing *ḥesed* and *'ĕmet*, i.e., faithful, loyal love:

1. Covenant relationship
2. Obligation to help weaker party
3. Fulfillment of obligation demonstrates faithful, loyal love

When Solomon dedicated the temple, he affirmed in his prayer, "there is no God like you, in heaven above or on earth beneath, keeping covenant and showing steadfast love to your servants who walk before you with all their heart" (1 Kings 8:23, ESV).

---

between covenant societies and contract societies: in the former the emphasis is on obligations, in the latter, on rights; in the former on the common good, in the latter on the private interest group.

Another wonderful illustration is Psalm 117:

[1] Praise the LORD, all you nations;
   extol him, all you peoples.
[2] For great is his love [*ḥesed*] toward us,
   and the faithfulness [*'ĕmet*] of the LORD endures forever.
   Praise the LORD. (NIV)

This is the briefest and shortest hymn in the whole of Israel's Songbook (Psalms). According to the format standard for a hymn, there is a call to praise Yahweh, followed by the reason for praise. In Psalm 117, verse 1 is the Call to Praise and verse 2 is the Reason for Praise. In the section giving the reason for praise, the word pair *ḥesed* and *'ĕmet* is split over parallel lines. Thus the reason for boasting about the Lord is his faithful, loyal love in his covenant with his people Israel. In fact, the celebration of this quality summarizes the entire Psalter.

Chapter 3

THE COVENANT WITH NOAH

Whether or not a covenant is entailed in Genesis 1–3 is debated. The first occurrence in the Bible of the word "covenant" (*bĕrît*) is in Genesis 6:18, where it refers to the covenant with Noah. God says to Noah, "But I will establish my covenant [*bĕrît*] with you" (NIV). Consequently Genesis 6–9 and the covenant with Noah will be discussed first, and only then, the issues raised by Genesis 1–3 will be considered.

First we need to consider the context in which God makes this statement to Noah (in Gen. 6:18) and the meaning of the language used in this text.

In the previous verse, God informs Noah that he is going to destroy all life upon the earth—all human and animal life in the entire world. The means of destruction will be a cataclysmic event—floodwaters covering the entire earth. God instructs Noah, however, to construct a big "box" which will be the means of rescue and deliverance from the destruction of the flood.

The earlier part of chapter 6 explains why God had apparently given up on the human race and decided upon such a severe judgment. In verse 5 we are told, "The LORD saw how great the wickedness of the human race on the earth had become, and that every inclination of the thoughts of their hearts was only evil all the time." A bit further on in verses 11–13 we read,

> Now the earth was corrupt in God's sight and was full of violence. God saw how corrupt the earth had become, for all the people on earth had corrupted their ways. So God said to Noah, "I am going to put an end to all people, for the earth is filled with violence because of them." (NIV)

Verse 5 describes the human situation as "bad," "evil," or "wicked," and traces this to the condition of the human heart, the center of our being where we feel, reason, and make decisions and plans. In verses 11–13, two terms in particular stand out: "corrupt" and "violence." The first word occurs three times and the second word twice, so that the cumulative effect is pronounced. It is difficult for the reader to miss the message! The term "corrupt" shows that a beautiful and good situation is now ruined, spoiled, and twisted.

Frequently, not many hours after opening the presents on Christmas Day, children manage to ruin and spoil beautiful and intricate toys so that they are damaged in appearance and function. The term violence (*ḥāmās*) is a word that refers specifically to social violence and conditions in human society where social justice is lacking.

The evil of the human heart, resulting in corruption and social violence, brings a response from God, according to verses 6 and 7:

> The LORD was grieved that he had made man on the earth, and his heart was filled with pain. So the LORD said, "I will wipe mankind, whom I have created, from the face of the earth—men and animals, and creatures that move along the ground, and birds of the air—for I am grieved that I have made them." (NIV)

The flood, then, is a divine judgment in response to the evil of the human heart and the resultant corruption and violence.

COVENANT MAKING IN THE OLD TESTAMENT AND ANCIENT NEAR EAST

Before further consideration of God's covenant with Noah, it is necessary to acquire a better grasp and understanding of covenant making in the culture of the biblical world. What is normally involved in initiating a covenant or treaty? The events described in Genesis 21:22–34 provide an excellent example of what is entailed in covenant making in the ancient Near East. The narrative concerns the king of Gerar (a city in the south of Canaan, just west of Beersheba), who makes a covenant/treaty with Abraham. The agreement between the parties resolves a dispute over water rights relating to the well of Beersheba. Four features characterize this treaty and, in fact, are normative of covenants in general:

(1) A covenant does not necessarily begin or initiate a relationship. It can formalize in binding and legal terms an agreement between parties who have developed a relationship before the covenant is made. Abimelech and Abraham already have a relationship. When the covenant is made, Abimelech appeals to this already established understanding between them by speaking of the lovingkindness (*ḥesed*) he has shown Abraham in the past (v. 23). It is true that the covenant does specify a new level to this relationship, but the parties have had dealings in the past.

(2) There is conventional language for initiating covenants or treaties

that is standard in the Old Testament. The standard expression for initiating a covenant is "to cut a covenant" (*kārat běrît*; 21:27, 32). How and why this peculiar expression arose will become clear shortly.

(3) A covenant gives binding and legal status to a relationship by means of a formal and solemn ceremony. As a general rule, covenants belong to the public rather than the private sphere. This is why, for example, elopement is inappropriate for marriage: no formal or public ceremony is involved.

(4) Covenant making involves a commitment or oath or promise and, frequently, signs or witnesses. Here the parties of the treaty solemnly swear to the agreement. While an oath is an important part of the covenant, it is not the covenant itself.

In the ceremony, animals are slaughtered and sacrificed. Each animal is cut in two and the halves are laid facing each other. Then the parties of the treaty walk between the halves of the dead animal(s). This action is symbolic. What is being expressed is this: each party is saying, "If I fail to keep my obligation or my promise, may I be cut in two like this dead animal." The oath or promise, then, involves bringing a curse upon oneself for violating the treaty. This is why the expression "to cut a covenant" is the conventional language for initiating a covenant in the Old Testament.

Many other covenants and treaties are recorded in the Bible. As examples, one may mention the covenant between Joshua and the Gibeonites (Joshua 9), between the men of Jabesh Gilead and Nahash the Ammonite (1 Sam. 11:1–3), two covenants between David and Jonathan (1 Sam. 18:3; 23:18), one between David and Abner (2 Sam. 3:12–21), David and Israel (2 Sam. 3:21; 5:1–3), Ahab of Israel and Ben-Hadad of Syria (1 Kings 20:31–34), and between Jehoiada the high priest and King Joash of Judah (2 Kings 11:17). While the components and also the nature and status of the parties differ, and the language varies somewhat, in each case a covenant concluded involves a commitment or promise solemnized by oath in which an agreement and level of relationship between parties is specified.

INITIATE VERSUS AFFIRM COVENANT

The first occurrence(s) of the term "covenant" (*běrît*) in the Old Testament is significant. The word appears first in the flood narrative (Gen. 6:18; 9:9, 11, 12, 13, 15, 16, 17). In four instances God speaks of "confirming" or "establishing" a covenant with Noah (Gen. 6:18; 9:9, 11, 17). The construction in Hebrew is *hēqîm běrît*. The remaining four occurrences have to do with the sign of the covenant and remembering the covenant. Thus, when we consider the covenant God made with Noah ar ' his descendants, we can see right away that the standard expression or la'   ᷉ covenant initiation is lacking. Nowhere do we read of God "cutt᷉   ᷉*ıt běrît*), even though the word "covenant" is frequent/   ᷉nt here, and what does this signify? An exhaustiv   ᷉ᴴe Hebrew Bible reveals a completely consistent usa᷉ a covenant" (*kārat běrît*) refers to covenant initiatiᴸ "to establish a covenant" (*hēqîm běrît*) means to affirm tinued validity of a prior covenant, i.e. to affirm that one is stıᴸ the covenant relationship established in a preexisting covenant. So᷉   ᷉s *hēqîm běrît* can have a more particular or specific use meaning to carry out or fulfill the obligations of a covenant made previously, i.e., to make good on one's commitment, obligation, or promise.

The difference in the expressions can be illustrated in the case of the covenant with Abraham. In Genesis 15, God's promises to Abraham of land and seed, given earlier in chapter 12, are formalized in a covenant. Notice that in 15:18 we have the standard terminology in the Hebrew text: "cut a covenant" (*kārat běrît*). Later, in Genesis 17, God *affirms* his covenant promise. Verses 7, 19, and 21 consistently employ the expression *hēqîm běrît*, while the expression *kārat běrît* is not used. Here God is affirming verbally a commitment in the covenant made previously, in chapter 15. So God affirms his promise and specifies further that Sarah will have a baby within the year.

Therefore the construction *hēqîm běrît* in Genesis 6 and 9 indicates that God is not initiating a covenant with Noah but rather is affirming to Noah and his descendants a commitment initiated previously. This language clearly indicates a covenant established earlier between God and creation, or between God and humans at creation. When God says that he is affirming or upholding his covenant with Noah, he is saying that his commitment to his creation—the care of the Creator to preserve, provide for, and rule over all that he has made, including the blessings and ordinances that he initiated through and with Adam and Eve and their family—are now to be with Noah and his descendants.

The distinction in usage between *kārat běrît* and *hēqîm běrît* has been challenged, but exhaustive study has shown that there is not one single case either in the Hebrew Bible or in the later Hebrew of the Dead Sea Scrolls where this distinction in idiomatic usage does not hold true. Jeremiah 34 is a nice example. The expression *kārat běrît* is employed in Jeremiah 34:8, 13, and 15 as well as a similar expression *bô'bibrît* ("enter a covenant") in 34:10 for initiating or making a covenant between King Zedekiah and all the people of Jerusalem to proclaim freedom for Hebrew slaves. The people then fulfilled the obligation by freeing the slaves, but later reneged on the covenant and re-enslaved the manumitted slaves. Jeremiah was sent to challenge this covenant violation (see the expression *'ābar běrît* in 34:18) and called upon the people in 34:18 to "uphold the covenant" (*hēqîm běrît*), meaning to fulfill the promise given in the covenant made previously to free the slaves. The people must make good on the commitment and promise made in the covenant. A simple, straightforward reading of this text, then, shows that a strong case can be made for the distinction in usage between *kārat běrît* and *hēqîm běrît*.

Note that the expression *kārat běrît* is sometimes used in covenant renewals, because in every case where this happens, people are making a covenant to keep a covenant made previously. This is like a couple renewing wedding vows on their twenty-fifth anniversary. They are actually making *new vows* to keep *previous ones* and are not simply affirming verbally that the original covenant commitment stands.

In summary, based on the expression *hēqîm běrît*, linguistic usage demonstrates that when God says that he is affirming his covenant with Noah, he is saying that his commitment initiated previously at creation to care for and preserve, provide for and rule over all that he has made, including the blessings and ordinances that he gave to Adam and Eve and their family, is now to be with Noah and his descendants. This can be further supported by noting the parallels between Noah and Adam, and between the covenant terms given to Noah and the ordinances given to Adam and his family.

PARALLELS WITH ADAM/THE CREATION NARRATIVES

In terms of literary techniques, we note that key words, dominant ideas, parallel sequences of actions, and similar themes clearly link the Noah narrative of Genesis 6–9 to the creation narratives in Genesis 1 and 2.

The Flood Story as a New Creation

First, the flood story is presented in the narrative as a new creation. Just as God ordered the original heavens and earth out of the chaotic deep or ocean (Gen. 1:2; Heb. *tĕhôm*), so here God orders the present heavens and earth out of the chaotic floodwaters. Genesis 8:1 records that God caused a wind

(Heb. *rûaḥ*) to pass over the waters of the flood covering the entire earth, which reminds one of the creation narrative, where the Spirit (Heb. *rûaḥ*) of God hovers over the waters of the original chaotic deep. In the creation narrative, God gathers the waters together and the dry land emerges; then he commands the earth to bring forth vegetation. After the flood, the dry land emerges as the waters subside, and the earth brings forth vegetation, as we see when the dove returns with an olive leaf in her beak. These parallels indicate that, after the flood, we have a new beginning like the first beginning.

Noah as a New Adam

Second, Noah is presented in the narrative as a new Adam. The blessing and commission given to Noah is the same as the one given to Adam (Gen. 9:1 = 1:28a). In this way the narrator portrays Noah as a new Adam. When we look at the terms of the covenant, we will see that Noah is recommissioned with all of the ordinances given at creation to Adam and Eve and their family.

In the flood narrative in Genesis 6–9, then, both the language used and the literary techniques indicate a covenant affirmed which had been initiated previously. This covenant entails a divine-human relationship initiated and specified at creation. Such a covenant could not, by definition, involve a ceremony between both parties, since what was involved was the creation of one of the parties in the relationship. That is a possible reason why the standard language "to cut a covenant" is absent in Genesis 1–5.

THE TERMS OF THE COVENANT

In Genesis 9:1–7 God blesses Noah and commissions him as a new Adam, giving him Adam's mandate, modified somewhat to suit the circumstances of a fallen world. Genesis 9:8–17 describes the covenant, its parties, and its sign. This passage, then, is an expansion on the statement made to Noah in Genesis 6:18. Let us briefly note the blessing and terms set before Noah in verses 1–7 of chapter 9.

(1) First, Noah is told to "be fruitful," to "increase in number," and to "fill the earth." As already noted, this is the blessing originally given to Adam at creation. This command is repeated in verse 7, with stylistic variation, and so provides brackets or bookends, i.e., a framework for the covenant stipulations and terms.

(2) Second, we read in 9:2 that "the fear of you and the dread of you will be upon all the wild animals of the earth and upon all the birds of the

sky, upon all the creatures that crawl on the ground, and upon the fish of the sea" (ESV). In Genesis 1, mankind was commanded to rule over the earth and subdue it. God now assists humans in this task in a fallen world by placing the fear of them upon the animals, birds, fish, and all creatures that move. The animals' fear of humans may also assist humans in catching creatures for consumption and nourishment, which may then relate to the next instruction or stipulation.

(3) Third, the animals are given to the human race for food, just as the plants were given at creation for food (Gen. 1:29–30). There are two important restrictions to this provision. First, humans are not to eat flesh or meat with its blood in it. Later, instructions given in the Mosaic law clarify this stipulation. Several passages discuss properly draining the blood from meat when animals are slaughtered, before the meat can be eaten (Lev. 3:17; 7:26–27; 19:26; Deut. 12:16–24; 1 Sam. 14:32–34). So, while God gave the flesh of birds, fish, wild animals, and all creatures that move to sustain human life, he makes a restriction to maintain and preserve respect among humans for all of life. God remains the Lord of life. Second, human life is set apart. This prevents not only cannibalism but also homicide. Even animals that kill humans are held responsible.

(4) Fourth, human life is special and of priceless value and worth. God specifies two things concerning homicide. First, the human race is one family. We are all related. When a human life is wantonly taken, we are our brother's keeper. Genesis 9:5, in the Hebrew text, is the first time since the story of Cain and Abel that the word "brother" is used (cf. Gen. 4:2, 8 [2x], 9 [2x], 10, 11, 21). This is frequently obscured in modern translations. Genesis 9:5 can be literally translated, "and surely the blood of your lives I will require; from the hand of every creature I will require it and from the hand of humans, i.e., from the hand of the man's brother, I will require the life of humans." Thus the narrator reminds us of God's ordinance, given originally to the family of Adam (Gen. 4:9–10), that he would require an accounting of life from fellow family members. God holds the community responsible to exact a penalty from the offender. He demands an accounting from society. It is clear from the text that retribution is in the hands of government, and not left to the anger and vengeance of an individual; nor are blood feuds authorized. Second, God requires retributive justice. That is, the penalty for taking a life is paying with a life ("Whoever sheds the blood of mankind, his blood will be shed *in exchange for* the [murdered/slain] man"; 9:6).

(5) God holds the human family/society responsible to administer retribution when a human life is taken wantonly. This accounting principle is based on the fact that humans—men and women—are made in the image of God (v. 6). The mention of the image of God is significant. It reasserts the creation standard and the unique status of mankind and explains why human life is specially protected while animal life is not protected to the same extent. Humanity owns the animals and thus can kill them, but humans cannot be killed, because *they* are owned by God—stamped with his seal of ownership. Furthermore, as we shall see, the mention of the divine image is a direct reference to the covenant between God and creation and God and humanity established at creation.

Table 3.1 outlines the terms of the covenant with Noah and his family and shows how they correspond to, renew, and repeat the terms of God's covenant at creation with Adam and Eve and their family.

Table 3.1 Comparison of Covenant with Noah and Covenant with Creation

Covenant with Noah	Covenant with Creation
be fruitful and increase in number	Gen. 1:28: be fruitful . . .
fear of you	Gen. 1:28: rule over fish, birds, animals
animals given for food	Gen. 1:29: plants given for food
don't eat meat with blood	
your blood . . . his brother's life	See Gen. 4:8–24
in the image of God	Gen. 1:27: in his own image

Genesis 9:8–17 now describes the covenant promise, its parties, and its sign.

THE PARTIES OF THE COVENANT

In Genesis 6:18 the covenant is made between God and Noah and his family. In Genesis 9:8–17 there is an expansion. The partners of the covenant are referred to in six different ways:

vv. 9–10: "with you and with your seed after you and with every living being which is with you: birds, animals domesticated, animals wild . . ."

v. 12: "between me and you and every living being which was with you"

v. 13: "between me and the earth"

v. 15: "between me and you and every living being among all flesh"

v. 16: "between God and every living being among all flesh which is on the earth"

v. 17: "between me and all flesh which is on the earth"

The statements in verses 8–17 are highly repetitive and monotonous to Western ears. This repetition is like a cathedral bell ringing out again and again, reverberating into the future, that God is committing himself to all his living creatures while the earth lasts. There can be no mistaking of the parties specified in the covenant.

THE PROMISE OF THE COVENANT

Genesis 9:11 specifies the obligation that God places upon himself, the promise he makes to Noah and to the entire human race through him: "Never again will all life be cut off by the waters of a flood; never again will there be a flood to destroy the earth" (NIV). God reiterates his promise in verse 15 with stylistic variations. We first learn of this divine decision in 8:21:

> And Yahweh smelled the soothing smell and Yahweh said to himself, "I will never again curse the ground on account of mankind because the inclination of the heart of mankind is evil from his youth."

William J. Dumbrell aptly comments,

> The reference to the heart of man in Gen. 8:21 which remains unchanged by the experience of the flood refers initially to the eight who have been saved and thus throws into clear relief the nature of Noah's righteousness as something extrinsic to him. Since we are virtually being told that a deluge would be an appropriate response by God to the sin of any age, mankind has been preserved by grace alone. Until the end of time the continued existence of the created order will thus be grounded simply in the gracious nature of the divine character.[1]

The references to the "inclination of the heart of mankind" harks back to the previous instance of these words in Genesis 6:5, where we were informed of the cause of the great judgment: "The LORD saw how great the wickedness of the human race on the earth had become and that every inclination of the thoughts of their hearts was only evil all the time." The condition of humanity after the cataclysmic judgment remains the same as it was before; the judgment has not altered or changed the condition of the human heart. The implication is that God would be completely justified in wiping out every generation of humanity by means of a great judgment. There is

---

[1] William J. Dumbrell, *Covenant and Creation: A Theology of Old Testament Covenants* (Nashville: Thomas Nelson, 1984), 26–27.

only one reason why he does not do so: because of his own grace and mercy toward us. The earth is maintained and preserved in spite of the human situation. Thus the covenant made with Noah creates a firm stage of history where God can work out his plan for rescuing his fallen world.

Four of the eight occurrences of the word "covenant" in this narrative have the possessive pronoun "my" attached to it: "I will affirm *my* covenant with you" (Gen. 6:18; 9:9, 11, 15). We must pause for a moment and consider the force of the "my" in the expression "my covenant" in these texts. We have already noted that covenant, on any understanding of the term, has the notion of commitment or obligation built into it. Is this a covenant by which humans are obligated, or does God bind himself and thus make mankind the beneficiary of the obligation so undertaken? The "my" of "my covenant" indicates that the latter is the correct interpretation. This is a covenant in which God binds himself, God obligates himself, and he will maintain the covenant in spite of human failure.

In Genesis 9:18–29 we have the strange story of the drunkenness of Noah and his curse upon Canaan. Like the first Adam, the second Adam is also a gardener who plants a vineyard. Like the first Adam, the second Adam is also a disobedient *son* whose sin results in shameful nakedness. One of the points this episode is making is that once again the human partner has failed as a covenant keeper, and that the fulfillment of the promise will be due solely to the faithfulness and grace of God, who is always a faithful covenant partner. This is the parallel in the Noah story to the Fall in Genesis 3.

THE SIGN OF THE COVENANT

God gives to Noah and to all of his descendants, to the entire human race, a physical sign of the covenant. The sign of the covenant with Noah is a rainbow in the clouds. Actually, there is no word in Hebrew for "rainbow"; the word used here is the ordinary term for an archer's bow. The only other place where the Old Testament refers to a rainbow is Ezekiel 1:28, where a circumlocution such as "the bow which will be in the clouds" is required to indicate that a rainbow is in view and not an archer's bow. We like the comment of Warren Austin Gage: "The bow is a weapon of war, an emblem of wrath. God will now set it in the heavens as a token of grace. The Lord who makes his bow of wrath into a seven-colored arch of beauty to ornament the heavens is the one who will finally command the nations to beat their swords into plowshares and spears into pruninghooks (Mic. 4:3) for the Prince of

Peace takes pleasure in mercy (Mic. 7:18) and the Righteous Judge delights in grace."[2] The rainbow, then, is a physical picture that God has "laid his weapons down," as indicated in the promise, "never again will there be a flood to destroy the earth." It is interesting that the bow set in the clouds is always aimed or pointed up to the heavens, and never downward at us on the earth. Although not every covenant has a sign, this is the only covenant sign which can be given only by the divine partner. All of the other covenant signs are given by the human partner.

THE PLACE OF THE COVENANT WITH NOAH IN THE LARGER STORY

The covenant with Noah is in effect today. God's promises and statements about the future employ an emphatic negative, "never again," four times (8:21; 9:11 [2x]; 9:15). His commitment is throughout everlasting generations (9:12). And in 9:16 he calls the arrangement an everlasting covenant. Indeed the sign of this covenant, the rainbow, remains as a witness to God to the present time. It is still with us today. There is no evidence anywhere in the completed canon of Scripture as a whole that this covenant has been annulled or superseded.

SUMMARY

Later references to the covenant with Noah pick up on features clearly expressed within the text of Genesis 6–9. Two of the texts, Isaiah 54 and Jeremiah 33, note the emphatic "never again," so that God promises never again to employ floodwaters in judgment to destroy all flesh. Nonetheless there are stipulations and terms given to both animals and humans. God demands an accounting. Isaiah 54 picks up on the importance of human responsibility.

The covenant with Noah "affirms" the divine image. This is to be discussed next. As we shall see, it entails a covenant relationship between God and humans on the one hand and between humans and creation on the other. The human community must express obedient sonship in faithful, loyal love to the creator God and must rule over the creation with humble servanthood and responsible stewardship. Worship is a priority in achieving these purposes. The narratives of Genesis 6–8 begin by depicting Noah as an obedient

---

[2] Warren Austin Gage, *The Gospel of Genesis: Studies in Protology and Eschatology* (Winona Lake, IN: Carpenter, 1984), 135.

son and steward of animal life on the earth. He also offers significant worship in a sacrifice that appeases the anger of the Lord and turns away further
judgment. Nonetheless, like the first Adam, he ends up as a disobedient son
whose nakedness reveals shame rather than full integrity.

The covenant with Noah is instructive because it shows that being given
a fresh start and a clean slate is not a sufficient remedy for the human plight.

The unmerited favor and kindness of God in preserving his world in
the covenant with Noah creates a firm stage of history where God can work
out his plan for rescuing his fallen world. It also points ahead to the coming
deliverance in Jesus Christ.

Chapter 4

THE COVENANT WITH
CREATION IN GENESIS 1–3

Whether or not there is a covenant in Genesis 1–3 is debated. A recent work, *Sealed with an Oath*, by Paul Williamson, argues that a divine-human covenant is introduced for the first time in Genesis 6:18.

First, Williamson offers what many consider a strong argument: "prior to Genesis 6:18 there is not even a hint of any covenant being established—at least between God and humans."[1] The absence of the word for "covenant" in Genesis 1–5, however, cannot constitute an argument to demonstrate the absence of any covenant before Genesis 6:18. It is fully possible in biblical literature to speak of a covenant without actually using the word. Consider Isaiah 66:1 as an illustration:

> This is what the LORD says:
>
>> "Heaven is my throne,
>>   and the earth is my footstool.
>> Where is the house you will build for me?
>>   Where will my resting place be?" (NIV)

Although the word "king" does not occur in this verse, the text is loudly proclaiming the kingship of Yahweh. Just as one can speak of kingship without the word "king," so one can speak of covenant without using the word. Later we will see that the phrase "I will be their God and they will be my people" is a frequent method of referring to a divine-human covenant. Furthermore, the word "Torah" implies covenant as its reflex, just as faith implies repentance as its reflex. These are just a couple of examples. The absence of the word for "covenant" (*bĕrît*) in Genesis 1–3, then, is no argument at all against the

---

[1] Paul R. Williamson, *Sealed with an Oath: Covenant in God's Unfolding Purpose*, New Studies in Biblical Theology 23 (Downers Grove, IL: InterVarsity Press, 2007), 72.

notion that a divine-human covenant is established at creation, if exegesis can demonstrate that the idea is there.

It is legitimate to ask why the expression "to cut a covenant" does not occur in Genesis 1–3. Probably the answer is simply that the ceremony involving cutting an animal in half to symbolize a self-imprecatory oath would have been anachronistic and unsuitable as a communicative instrument for the covenant at creation established between God and humans on the one hand and humans and the creation on the other. Analysis of Genesis 1:26–28 will substantiate this.

Second, some have argued that covenants are necessary only after the Fall, in Genesis 3. Yet marriage is a covenant relationship that existed prior to the Fall, so neither is this an argument against a divine-human covenant in Genesis 1.

Third, Williamson's argument that there is no covenant in Genesis 1–3 results in a truncated biblical storyline that essentially begins with Noah and does not account for the parallels between Adam and Christ drawn by Paul from the larger story of Scripture. Jesus is the head of a new covenant community. Is Adam simply the physical progenitor of the human race?

Fourth, it is possible to exclude a covenant in Genesis 1 simply by defining the term "covenant" too narrowly. Covenants in both the biblical texts and the ancient Near Eastern culture vary widely, and a definition that is narrower than the evidence permits prejudges the situation in Genesis 1–3. It is interesting to note that Williamson speaks of "God's universal purpose" in creation, and that "God intended, through Noah, to fulfil his original creative intent."[2] These, in essence, are backdoor references to the (covenantal) *commitment* of the Creator to his creation, and they assume a covenantal relationship.

In the end, exegesis must show—an exegesis based not only on the cultural and linguistic data but also attuned to literary structures and techniques and a canonical metanarrative—whether or not there is a covenant in Genesis 1.

THE DIVINE IMAGE IN GENESIS 1:26–28

A covenant initiated at creation is indicated by the text of Genesis 1:26–28—particularly by the fact that humans are made as the divine image—as well as by elements in 2:4–3:24.

---

[2] Ibid., 51, 75.

Although the meaning of "image of God" in Genesis 1:26–28 has been debated for centuries, a contribution can yet be made to our understanding of this text by combining biblical theology and recent insights into the cultural setting and language of the text. The biblical-theological framework of Genesis 1:26–28 has already been provided from a consideration of the language used in the flood narratives, so now an exegesis of the text itself, with close attention to its cultural setting and linguistic and literary features, is appropriate.

Various literary techniques in the text point to the significance of the creation of humans. Human beings are the crown of God's creative work. The interpretation of the creation of man as the divine image will unfold this significance. First we survey the various views taken down through the years.

Survey of Views

Five views are deserving of mention:

(1) The terms "image" and "likeness" are distinct aspects of man's nature (from Irenaeus, c. A.D. 180 onward). The "image" denotes the natural qualities in man (personality, reason, etc.) that make him resemble God, while the "likeness" refers to the supernatural (i.e., ethical) graces that make the redeemed godlike. Study of "image" and "likeness" according to the cultural setting of the biblical text, however, shows that this distinction is foreign to Genesis.

(2) The divine image refers to the mental and spiritual qualities that man shares with his Creator. The fact that commentators cannot agree in identifying these qualities makes this approach suspect.

(3) The image consists of a physical resemblance. Before quickly dismissing this view, the Hebrew term *ṣelem* does refer to a physical image or statue in a majority of its occurrences. Moreover, in Genesis 5:3 Adam is described as fathering Seth "after his image," which most naturally refers to physical appearance. The Old Testament, however, emphasizes that God has no bodily form (Deut. 4:12). Also, if the language is related to Egyptian and Mesopotamian thinking, the image of God there refers to the function of the king and not to his appearance. Furthermore, the Old Testament does not sharply distinguish the material and spiritual realms in the way that we sometimes do. The image of God must characterize the whole man, not simply his mind or spirit on the one hand or his body on the other. Finally, the image of God is what separates man from the animals, and yet the practice

of sacrifice must have made the ancient people of Israel well aware of the physiological similarities between humans and animals.

(4) The divine image makes man God's representative on earth. Careful exegesis below indicates that the ruling function is a *result* of being made in the divine image and *not the image itself.*

(5) The image is a capacity to relate to God. The divine image means that God can enter into personal relationships with man, speak to him, and make covenants with him. Claus Westermann argued that the "image of God" is not part of the human constitution so much as it is a description of the process of creation which made man different. Although this view has something to commend it, in that relationship to God is fundamental to the image of God, nonetheless passages like Genesis 5:3 and Exodus 25:40 suggest that the phrase "in the image" describes the product of creation rather than the process.

Critique of the Traditional View

The majority of Christians have followed the second view, believing that "the image of God" refers to mental and spiritual qualities that humans share with the creator God. Since God is invisible (John 4:24), man does not resemble God physically but rather in terms of morality, personality, reason, and spirituality. This interpretation did not originate with the Christian church but can be traced back to Philo of Alexandria, a Jewish philosopher living in the time 30 B.C. to A.D. 45 (see his *On the Creation* § 69).

The traditional view, however, is inadequate. It does not rest on a grammatical and historical interpretation of the text; instead, it is based largely on theological conclusions. It does not account for the fact that "image" normally refers to a physical statue and therefore cannot be exegetically validated as the author's intended meaning or the first audience's natural understanding of the text in terms of the ancient Near Eastern cultural and linguistic setting.

Exegesis of Genesis 1:26–28

An attempt to determine the meaning of this text according to the historical setting and linguistic usage of the time in which it was written begins with the literary structure, consideration of grammatical and lexical issues, and ancient Near Eastern background.

THE STRUCTURE OF GENESIS 1:24–31

The paragraph in the creation narrative devoted to describing events of the sixth day is structured differently from the other paragraphs. The following outline shows this structure:

The Sixth Day—Genesis 1:24–31

A. Creation of the Animals 1:24–25
   1. Command for creation of animals . . . 24a
      Confirmation 24b
   2. Execution of creation of animals 25a
      Evaluation 25b
B. Creation of Mankind 1:26–31
   1. Decision for creation of man 26
      To make man 26a
      To give him a certain role 26b
   2. Execution of creation of man 27–28
      Creation of man 27
      Proclamation of his role 28
   3. Food regulations 29–30
      For man 29
      For animals 30
C. Conclusion 1:31
   Evaluation 31a
   Day notation 31b

For the creation of humans, instead of the normal pattern giving a command and indicating a result, there is first a divine decision followed by a divine execution of that decision. Note that the decision has two parts, and the execution of the decision has the *same two corresponding parts*. This observation leads to consideration of two separate grammatical issues before looking at the ancient Near Eastern setting.

KEY GRAMMATICAL ISSUES IN GENESIS 1:26–28

The sequence of verbs in verse 26 is inadequately represented in most modern translations. The first verb in the divine speech is a command form in Hebrew and is correctly rendered "let us make" in all of the English versions. The second verb in the sequence could be understood as a command form or as a future indicative. What is important, however, is that grammarians of Hebrew agree that this particular sequence marks purpose or result.

The correct translation, therefore, is "let us make man . . . *so that* they may rule . . ." Here, many modern versions fail to represent properly the grammar of the Hebrew text. An important exegetical point is at stake: the ruling is not the essence of the divine image, but rather a result of being made as the divine image.

Another grammatical issue concerns the clause patterns in verse 27. The verse contains three clauses or sentences: (1) and God created man in his image; (2) in the image of God he created him; (3) male and female he created them. The first sentence has a normal clause pattern: verb-subject-object. The conjunction *and* is used, and the verb is standard in Hebrew narrative. The remaining two sentences have a different clause pattern: modifier-verb-object. Neither begins with the conjunction "and," while the word order is what is usually used in clauses marking an aside from the narrative. This is a clear discourse signal: these clauses do not advance the narrative but digress and pause to comment on the first clause in the verse. These two short sentences are grammatically marked as circumstantial information or as parenthetical remarks. The author is *digressing from* the narrative in order to stress two particular aspects or features of the creation of man:

a) the creation of mankind entails male and female genders
b) mankind resembles God in some way

By pausing to stress these two things, the author prepares us for the two commands given to man in the very next verse:

a) be fruitful (three imperatives in Hebrew)
b) rule over the other creatures (two imperatives in Hebrew)

The actual literary presentation is chiastic in structure: The word *chiasm* comes from the letter in the Greek alphabet known as *chi* (χ). The top half of the letter has a mirror image in the bottom half. If, for example, a literary piece has four distinct units and the first matches the last while the second matches the third, the result is a mirror image, a chiasm. The following diagram illustrates the chiastic structure AB::B'A':

God created mankind in his image
    according to his likeness:
A   in the image of God he created him
B   male and female he created them

B'   be fruitful and increase in number
          and fill the earth
A'   and subdue it
          and rule over the fish/birds/animals

Thus, duality of gender is the basis for being fruitful, while the divine image is correlated with the command to rule as God's viceroy. These observations from the discourse grammar of the narrative are crucial. They are decisive in showing that the divine image is *not* to be explained by or located in terms of duality of gender in humanity.

THE CLAUSE "LET US MAKE MAN IN OUR IMAGE, ACCORDING TO OUR LIKENESS"

We are now in a position to explain the meaning of the clause in 1:26a, "Let us make man in our image, according to our likeness." The exegetical microscope will be focused on (1) the ancient Near Eastern background to the text, (2) the meaning of the nouns "image" and "likeness," and (3) the exact force of the prepositions "in" and "according to."

The Ancient Near Eastern Background

In biblical revelation, God communicates in the culture and language of the people. Yet, in employing language people understand, he also fills the terms with new meaning. The key to correct interpretation, therefore, is to *compare and contrast* the biblical text and the data from the contemporary cultures. One must notice not only the similarities between the Bible and the ancient Near Eastern background but also the differences, which show the new meaning being revealed by God.

This can be illustrated by considering the tabernacle (Exodus 25–40). If we consider the plan of the tabernacle or the plan of Solomon's temple, there is nothing unusual or unique. Its overall plan was just like any other temple in the ancient Near East. They all had an outer courtyard, an altar of sacrifice, and a central building divided into a "Holy Place" and a "Holy of Holies." What, then, made the faith of Israel different from the faith of the pagan religions surrounding her? If one were to enter a pagan temple, passing through the courtyard, and through the Holy Place into the Holy of Holies, what would one find there? An image representing one of the forces of nature. But that is not what one finds at the center of Israel's worship. What was in the Holy of Holies in the tabernacle? First of all, there was no image or statue there representing God. First, God is invisible spirit; and second, he has already made an official image of himself: humanity. All there is in the Holy of Holies is just a little box. And what is in that box? The Ten Commandments. Thus, what God is saying to the Israelites is that he cannot be manipulated by magic. If they want the good life, they must conform their lifestyle to his revealed standards of right and wrong. Standards of right and wrong guarantee the good life, not manipulation of the powers that be by magic.[3] The meaning is clear when one both compares and contrasts the biblical text with the ancient Near Eastern cultural setting. At the outset, the differences appear to be small and insignificant. Yet in the end, the differences are so radical that only divine revelation can explain the origin of the text.

The Meaning of Image and Likeness in the Bible and the Ancient Near East

We begin by looking at the ancient Near Eastern background to the image of God. In the ancient Near East we see the flourishing of plastic arts; they were part and parcel of religion. Statues and likenesses of all sorts have been preserved to the present time.

The epithet or descriptive title of the Egyptian king as a "living statue of such and such a god" was common in Egypt from 1630 B.C. onward and therefore was well known to the Israelites. In Egyptian thinking, the king is the image of god because he is the son of god. The emphasis or stress is not on physical appearance, e.g., a male king could be the image of a female goddess. Rather, the behavior of the king reflects the behavior of the god. The image reflects the character traits of the god. The image reflects the essential notions of the god.

Commonly associated with the image is the notion of conquest and power. A clear example is an inscription from the Karnak Temple marking the triumph of Thutmoses III at Karnak, c. 1460 B.C. In the following stanza, the god is speaking in the first person, and the second person refers to the king:

---

[3] The divine image is particularly revealed in the living out of the Ten Commandments. This is why there could be no image at the center of Israel's worship—God wanted the commands or instructions in the ark to be imaged in one's actions: this was the divine character embodied in human lives!

> I came to let you tread on Djahi's chiefs,
>> I spread them under your feet throughout their lands;
> I let them see your majesty as lord of light,
>> so that you shone before them in my likeness.[4]

The god Amen-Re, in giving victory to Thutmoses III, calls the king his son in the prologue of the poem and in this stanza indicates that the extension of the rule of the king entails his shining before his enemies in the likeness of his god.

In the thirteenth century B.C., Pharaoh Ramesses II had his image hewn out of rock at the mouth of the Kelb River, on the Mediterranean just north of Beirut. His image—displayed like the presidents at Mount Rushmore—meant that he was the ruler of this area. In the ancient Near East, since the king is the living statue of the god, he represents the god on earth. He makes the power of the god a present reality.

To sum up, the term "the image of god" in the culture and language of the ancient Near East in the fifteenth century B.C. would have communicated two main ideas: (1) rulership and (2) sonship. The king is the image of god because he has a *relationship* to the deity as the son of god and a *relationship* to the world as ruler for the god. In the ancient Near East these would have been understood as *covenant* relationships. We ought to assume that the meaning in the Bible is identical or at least similar, unless the biblical text clearly distinguishes its meaning from the surrounding culture.

Likeness and Image

Careful and exhaustive studies of the Hebrew terms "likeness" (*demût*) and "image" (*ṣelem*) indicate their possible range of meaning.

"Likeness" (*demût*) may refer to a physical entity, such as the model of the altar King Ahaz sent Uriah the priest (2 Kings 16:10b). It may also refer to a likeness that is real yet unspecific as to referent (Isa. 40:18). It can even be nonreferential, to express resemblance or relative similarity (Isa. 13:4). Ezekiel 1:26 is instructive since, opposite to Genesis 1:26, which speaks of humanity created in the likeness of God, Ezekiel's vision speaks of God appearing in the likeness of humanity. Either way, God and humanity are morphologically similar.

"Image" (*ṣelem*) frequently refers to an object in the real world that can

---

[4] Miriam Lichtheim, *Ancient Egyptian Literature: A Book of Readings* (Berkeley: University of California Press, 1976), 2:36–37.

have size, shape, color, material composition, and value. The image erected by King Nebuchadnezzar in the plain of Dura is an example (Dan. 3:1). Yet as Psalm 39:6–7 shows, *ṣelem* can also be abstract and nonconcrete. And like *demût*, "image" can simply be an imprint etched on a wall (Ezek. 23:14b, 15b).

Particularly instructive for Genesis 1:26–28 is the usage of the words "likeness" and "image" in the Tell Fekheriyeh Inscription. Inscribed on a large statue of King Hadduyithʿî of Gozan, a city in what is now eastern Syria, is an Akkadian-Aramaic bilingual text from the tenth or ninth century B.C. The text is divided thematically into two sections. The first half focuses on the role of the king as a supplicant and worshiper of his god and is headed in the Aramaic text by the same word as the Hebrew term for likeness. The second half focuses on the majesty and power of the king in his role in relation to his subjects. This is headed in the Aramaic text by the same word as the Hebrew term for image. While both terms can and do refer to the statue of the king, each has a different nuance.

Mesopotamian texts containing the cognate for the Hebrew word "image" support the force and meaning of the word in the Tell Fekheriyeh Inscription. One example will suffice to further clarify the use of the term "image":

> *LAS 125:14b–19 (K 595; from the time of Esarhaddon, 681–668 B.C.):*
> What the king, [my lord], wrote to me: "I heard from the mouth of my father that you are a loyal family, but now I know it from my own experience", the father of the king, my lord, was the very image of the god Bēl, and the king, my lord, is likewise the very image of Bēl.[5]

The author of the letter is a loyal subject. He proclaims that the king is the image of the god Bel because he is acknowledging the authority and majesty of the king in the king-subject relationship.

We must now compare and contrast the data in Genesis 1:26–28 with these ancient Near Eastern data.

SIMILARITIES

The grammar of the first sentence in Genesis 1:26a is unusual. Following the verb "let us make" and its object, "man," are two distinct prepositional

---

[5] Simo Parpola, *Letters from Assyrian Scholars to the Kings Esarhaddon and Assurbanipal, Part I: Texts* (Winona Lake, IN: Eisenbrauns, 2007), 98–99 (= LAS).

phrases which are not obligatory either grammatically or semantically. The exact force of each preposition will be discussed shortly. This much is clear: these nonobligatory phrases specify a divine-human relation in the creation of mankind, and the differential marking suggests each phrase has distinct meaning.

Given the normal meanings of "image" and "likeness" in the cultural and linguistic setting of the Old Testament and the ancient Near East, "likeness" specifies a relationship between God and humans such that *'ādām* can be described as the son of God, and "image" describes a relationship between God and humans such that *'ādām* can be described as a servant king. Although both terms specify the divine-human relationship, the first focuses on the human in relation to God and the second focuses on the human in relation to the world. These would be understood to be relationships characterized by faithfulness and loyal love, obedience and trust—exactly the character of relationships specified by covenants after the Fall. In this sense the divine image entails a *covenant relationship* between God and humans on the one hand, and between humans and the world on the other. In describing a divine-human relationship, the terms in Genesis 1:26–28 correspond precisely to the usage of the same words in the Tell Fekheriyeh Inscription.

Confirmation of this interpretation of "likeness" and "image" comes from both the context of Genesis 1 and interpretation of Genesis 1 found later in the Old Testament.

1) The term "likeness" indicates that *'ādām*, i.e., humanity, has a special relationship to God like that of father and son. This is clearly implied by Genesis 5:1–3:

> [1] This is the book of the generations of Adam. When God created man, he made him in the likeness of God.
> [2] Male and female he created them, and he blessed them and named them Man when they were created.
> [3] When Adam had lived a hundred and thirty years, he became the father of a son in his own likeness, after his image, and named him Seth (RSV).

The comment of Stephen Dempster is both adequate and succinct:

> By juxtaposing the divine creation of Adam in the image of God and the subsequent human creation of Seth in the image of Adam, the transmission of the image of God through this genealogical line is implied, as well as the

link between sonship and the image of God. As Seth is a son of Adam, so Adam is a son of God. Language is being stretched here as a literal son of God is certainly not in view, but nevertheless the writer is using an analogy to make a point.[6]

This can be further supported from later texts: (1) Luke 3:38 interprets the "likeness of God" in Genesis to indicate that Adam is the son of God; (2) Israel inherits the role of Adam and Eve and is specifically called the son of God (Ex. 4:22, 23). The Song at the Sea pictures Israel as a new Adam entering the Promised Land as a new Eden (Ex. 15:17). Later, the divine sonship devolves particularly upon the king in the Davidic covenant (2 Sam. 7:14–15): what was true of the nation will now be fulfilled specifically and solely by her king.

2) The term "image" indicates that *'ādām* has a special position and status as king under God. Humans rule *as a result of* this royal status. The term "to rule" (*rādâ* in Gen. 1:26, 28) is particularly true of kings, as Psalm 72:8 illustrates. Also, the term "to subdue" (*kābaš*) especially speaks of the work of a king (e.g., 2 Sam. 8:11).

Further confirmation comes from Psalm 8, in which verses 5–8 constitute a word-by-word commentary and meditation on Genesis 1:26–28. Verse 5, which says, "you have made him a little less than the gods; you have crowned him with glory and honor," is a commentary on 1:26a, "Let us make mankind in our image and according to our likeness." Verses 6–8 then detail and unfold the rule of mankind specified in 1:26b. It is clear and obvious that the psalm writer has the text of Genesis 1:26 before his mind word-by-word. Note in particular that the terms in Hebrew for "crowned," "glory," and "honor" are all royal terms. This shows that the psalm writer understood "image" to speak of royal status. Furthermore, the Hebrew word "rule" (*māšal*) used in Psalm 8:7 (8:6, English versions) is a broad term meaning "have dominion, reign, rule," but it usually speaks of a king (examples of royal uses are Ps. 103:19; Mic. 5:1; Isa. 14:5; 19:4; 2 Sam. 23:3; Prov. 29:26a). The phrase "place under his feet" is an image associated with royalty. This is clear from 1 Kings 5:17 (5:3, English versions), Egyptian texts like the Poem of Thutmoses III cited above, Phoenician inscriptions (Karatepe A.i.16), and Assyrian Royal Texts.

In verses 7–8 of Psalm 8, humans rule over the animals. Paul Dion ap-

---

[6] Stephen G. Dempster, *Dominion and Dynasty: A Biblical Theology of the Hebrew Bible*, New Studies in Biblical Theology 15 (Downers Grove, IL: InterVarsity Press, 2003), 58–59.

propriately suggests that the word "all" in Psalm 8:6b is restricted to the earthly sphere in the light of Genesis 1:14–19 and 26–28, where man rules only the earthly sphere.

DIFFERENCES

Correct interpretation requires one to contrast as well as compare the biblical text with the contemporary documents.

In Egypt, only the king is the image of god. In the Bible, all humans constitute the image of God, regardless of gender. The covenant relationship between God and man is not restricted to an elite sector within human society.

PRECISE MEANING OF THE PREPOSITIONS "IN" (*BĔ*) AND "AS/ACCORDING TO" (*KĔ*)

As already noted, the grammar of the first sentence in Genesis 1:26a is unusual. Two distinct prepositional phrases that are not obligatory either grammatically or semantically follow the verb "make" and the direct object (*'ādām*): "in our image, according to our likeness." The preposition "in" corresponds to the preposition *bĕ* in Hebrew, while "as" or "according to" corresponds to Hebrew *kĕ*. What is the exact value of each preposition?

The phrase "made in his image" has been construed in two different ways. First, the "in" has been interpreted to indicate the norm or standard. This is normal usage of the preposition "in" following the verb "to make." The statement that man is created "in" the image of God would then mean that man conforms to a representation of God. As Gordon Wenham explains, "man is made '*in* the divine image,' just as the tabernacle was made '*in* the divine pattern.' This suggests that man is a copy of something that had the divine image, not necessarily a copy of God himself."[7] The traditional view, however, does not do full justice to the meaning of the words "image" and "likeness," nor does Wenham's explanation account for the fact that the prepositions *seem* somewhat interchangeable. The phrase occurs in six places:

Genesis 1:26a	*in* our image, *according to* our likeness
Genesis 1:27aα	*in* his image
Genesis 1:27aβ	*in* the image of God
Genesis 5:1b	*in* the likeness of God

---

[7] Gordon J. Wenham, *Genesis 1–15*, Word Biblical Commentary 1 (Waco, TX: Word, 1987), 32 (emphasis his).

Genesis 5:3a   *in* his likeness, *according to* his image
Genesis 9:6b   *in* the image of God

It is possible to use "in" with "likeness" as well as "image," and Genesis 5:3a has the prepositions exactly the reverse of what we find in Genesis 1:26a. Indeed, in the example of the tabernacle used by Wenham, the expression "made *in* the pattern" in Exodus 25:40 is "made *according to* the pattern" in Exodus 25:9. James Barr has shrewdly observed, "that *bĕ*, commonly 'in' *when combined with nouns of the semantic function 'likeness'*, is thereby brought to have almost the same effect as the preposition *kĕ* 'like, as'. It is the semantics of the noun, not those of the preposition alone, which are here decisive."[8] Thus, when the verb "make" is followed by "in" (*bĕ*), *because it is used with nouns indicating likeness*, the "in" likewise receives a value almost identical to "as" (*kĕ*). This makes the expression in Genesis 1:26a differ somewhat from that in Exodus 25:9, where the object of the preposition is "pattern" (*tabnît*).

It is possible, then, that the preposition "in" could be translated "as" in Genesis 1:26a. The usage shows that *bĕ* (= "in") and *kĕ* (= "as") have roughly the same value in these texts. God indeed created man *as* the divine image. Humans do not conform to a representation of God; they *are* the divine image. This interpretation is supported by the New Testament. In 1 Corinthians 11:7, Paul says that man is the image of God. Why, then, is the statement in Genesis not more forthright in saying that man *is* the divine image? Why is this expressed in a slightly less direct manner? We suggest that a less direct expression is used in the cultural and linguistic setting of the ancient Near East to prevent man from being considered an idol and being worshiped as such.

In spite of the fact that the two prepositions are close in meaning, we must not assume that the meaning is identical. Thorough linguistic analysis reveals that the preposition *bĕ* (= "in") emphasizes proximity while the preposition *kĕ* (= "as" or "according to") emphasizes something similar, yet distinct and separate. Indeed exhaustive research showed that, in fundamental meaning, *kĕ* stands between the opposition pair *bĕ* (marking an equating relation) and *lĕ* (marking a non-equating relation) as an expression of partial

---

[8] James Barr, "The Image of God in Genesis—Some Linguistic and Historical Considerations," in *Proceedings of the Tenth Meeting (1967) of Die Ou-Testamentiese Werkgemeenskap in Suid-Afrika*, ed. A. H. van Zyl (Pretoria: Craft Press, 1971), 9 (emphasis his). Paul Dion discovered a linguistic phenomenon similar to this in the Elephantine Papyri of the fifth century B.C. Cf. P. E. Dion, "Ressemblance et Image de Dieu," in *Suppléments aux Dictionnaire de la Bible*, ed. H. Cazelles and A. Feuillet (Paris: Letouzey & Ané, 1985), 55:388–389.

equation (and so also partial non-equation) of the semantic characteristics of two quantifications.[9] Thus, *bĕ* indicates something close and near (in likeness) while *kĕ* indicates something similar but distal and distinct.

Although the words "image" and "likeness" share similar meanings, each has a different emphasis. In the Tell Fekheriyeh Inscription, the word "likeness" focuses on the king as a suppliant and worshiper of his god, and it communicates sonship. The word "image" focuses on the majesty and power of the king in relation to his subjects. These ancient Near Eastern data correspond to the use in the biblical text. The word "likeness" in Genesis is closely associated with the creation of the human race, human genealogy, and sonship. It occurs in Genesis 1:26 in the creation of humans and again in 5:1, when this event is recapitulated under the heading "Birth History of Humankind."[10] The third use is in 5:3, with the generation of Seth. The word "image" is consistently used of man representing God in terms of royal rule. Putting the nouns and prepositions together, humans closely represent God in image, i.e., they represent his rule in the world. Humans are also similar to God in performing the action of creating human life, but not in the same way. Thus *bĕ* emphasizes a way in which humans are closely like God, *kĕ* a way in which humans are similar but distinct. This interpretation also explains the reversal of the prepositions in Genesis 5:3. Seth shares precisely in the matter of generation and sonship, but is only similar and not identical in the representation of his father's image.

Summary

Genesis 1:26 defines a divine-human relationship with two dimensions, one vertical and one horizontal. First, it defines human ontology in terms of a covenant relationship between God and man, and second, it defines a covenant relationship between man and the earth. The relationship between humans and God is best captured by the term "sonship." The relationship between humans and the creation may be expressed by the terms "kingship" and "servanthood," or better, "servant kingship."

This interpretation best honors the normal meaning of *ṣelem* ("image") according to the cultural and linguistic setting. Hans Walter Wolff expressed the matter well as follows:

---

[9] Ernst Jenni, *Die hebräischen Präpositionen, Band 1: Die Präposition Beth* (Stuttgart: Kolhammer, 1992), 11–40; idem, *Die hebräischen Präpositionen, Band 2: Die Präposition Kaph* (Stuttgart: Kolhammer, 1994), 11–12.
[10] The Hebrew term *tôlĕdôt* ("generations") is construed as a heading in the text.

In the ancient East the setting up of the king's statue was the equivalent to the proclamation of his domination over the sphere in which the statue was erected (cf. Dan. 3.1, 5f.). When in the thirteenth century BC the Pharaoh Ramesses II had his image hewn out of rock at the mouth of the *nahr el-kelb*, on the Mediterranean north of Beirut, the image meant that he was the ruler of this area. Accordingly, man is set in the midst of creation as God's statue. He is evidence that God is the Lord of creation; but as God's steward he also exerts his rule, fulfilling his task not in arbitrary despotism but as a responsible agent. His rule and his duty to rule are not autonomous; they are copies.[11]

Thus the image is physical and yet goes far beyond being merely physical. This is an interpretation that allows for the physical aspect of "image" but results in an emphasis such that the character of humans in ruling the world is what represents God.

It is important to note that this definition of the divine image is not only functional but also *ontological* and *structural*. As Wenham points out, the phrase "in the image" describes the product rather than the process of creation, as suggested by the usage in Genesis 5:3 and Exodus 25:40.[12] The grammar reveals that man rules as a result of being made as the divine image; ruling is not the essence of the image itself. Thus those who define the image merely in functional terms are in error both linguistically and theologically.

Man *is* the divine image. As servant king and son of God, mankind will mediate God's rule to the creation in the context of a covenant relationship with God on the one hand and the earth on the other. Hence the concept of the *kingdom of God* is found on the first page of Scripture. Indeed, the theme is *kingdom through covenant*. No wonder the Mosaic covenant, which seeks to implement this in Abraham's family, can be summarized as providing divine direction concerning (1) a right relationship to God, (2) how to treat each other in genuinely human ways, and (3) how to be good stewards of the earth's resources.

Theologians have debated the extent to which the divine image was marred or even lost by the fall into sin (Genesis 3). Normally it is argued that the divine image was marred but not lost through the Fall (Gen. 9:6; James 3:9). The interpretation given here of the divine image as God establishing his rule in the world through covenant clarifies the matter. The human rebellion described in Genesis 3 violated the love, loyalty, obedience, and trust

---

[11] Hans Walter Wolff, *Anthropology of the Old Testament* (Philadelphia: Fortress, 1974), 160–161.
[12] Wenham, *Genesis 1–15*, 31.

at the heart of the covenant. God sought to confirm and reestablish this relationship in the covenant with Noah; hence the expression *hēqîm běrît*. The story of the drunkenness of Noah (Gen. 9:20–27) shows once more the inability of the human partner in the covenant relationship. God makes a new start with Abraham and his family in the covenant made with Abraham. The Abrahamic covenant is implemented in the Iron Age, with Israel as Abraham's family through the Mosaic covenant. Israel, or more particularly, Israel's king, as the Davidic covenant later makes plain, will be the instrument for renewing the covenant relationship and establishing the instruction and will of Yahweh (i.e., *tôrâ*) in the hearts and lives of his people and, through them, to the nations. In a long history of apparent failure, Jesus of Nazareth came as Israel's King to renew the relationship by inaugurating a new covenant and bringing about the rule of God in the lives of those who are part of his new creation. Thus Jesus' proclamation of the kingdom is nothing less than the message we already find in Genesis 1:26–27.

When we look at the New Testament and the references there to the renewal of the divine image brought about by the work of Jesus Christ, terms are used that emphasize man's *relation* to God. This is clear in the parallel texts in Ephesians and Colossians:

Ephesians 4:24
and put on the new humanity created according to God in righteousness and holiness which derives from the truth

Colossians 3:10
and have put on the new humanity that is being renewed to a true knowledge according to the image of the One who created it

God has planned a new creation—a new heavens and a new earth. Unlike the first creation, where he first made the place and afterwards the people to live there, in the new creation he is first making the people and afterwards the place where they will live. The new creation begins in the midst of the old: when God raised Jesus from the dead, he was the first man in the new creation. And anyone who is joined to Jesus Christ by faith *is* new creation (2 Cor. 5:17; frequently incorrectly translated as "is a new creation"). This happens first in the inner person and later at the resurrection, in the outer person. The passages in Ephesians 4:24 and Colossians 3:10 call believers to adopt in daily lifestyle all that is entailed in the new creation life within them. The phrase "accord-

ing to God" in Ephesians 4:24 may be ambiguous by itself, but is clarified by
the parallel in Colossians 3:10 and means that the new creation is, like the
old, according to the image and likeness of God. The words that Paul uses in
connection with this are "righteousness" and "holiness" in Ephesians 4 and
"knowledge" in Colossians 3. This has been misconstrued in past studies on
the divine image. Paul mentions holiness, knowledge, and righteousness, not
because one can identify ethical or mental or spiritual qualities as *elements*
of the divine image, but because these terms are *covenantal* and describe a
covenant relationship. Thus the New Testament supports the explanation of
the divine image in Genesis 1:26 advanced here. The divine image indicates
man's relationship and spiritual fellowship with God.

THE GOAL OF THE COVENANT: REST

Day Six is the climax of the creation week, but not the consummation. The
conclusion is Day Seven. Thus the account of creation does not conclude
with man and his mandate, for humankind is not the consummation of all
things, even though he is the agent through whom the aims of creation will
be realized. Dumbrell aptly says,

> The symmetry of the eight creative acts spread over the preceding six days,
> and set in what seems to be an inner parallelism and progression between
> days one to three and four to six, receives its real significance from the ad-
> dition of the seventh day. By the divine rest on the seventh day the goal of
> creation is indicated, a goal which will be maintained notwithstanding sus-
> tained human attempts to vitiate it. Not only does the seventh day rest note
> the goal to which creation points, but it is the call to man to begin history
> holding firmly to the view that the "goal of creation, and at the same time
> the beginning of all that follows, is the event of God's Sabbath freedom,
> Sabbath rest and Sabbath joy, in which man, too, has been summoned to
> participate."[13]

GENESIS 1:26–27 IN THE CONTEXT
OF GENESIS 2:8–17

The interpretation advanced here for the creation of humans as the divine
image and according to the divine likeness is corroborated by Genesis 2:8–17
and developed further there. Indeed, Genesis 2:4 begins an explanation and

---

[13] William J. Dumbrell, *Covenant and Creation: A Theology of Old Testament Covenants* (Nashville: Thomas
Nelson, 1984), 34–35. Dumbrell is citing Karl Barth, *Church Dogmatics*, 3/1 (Edinburgh: T. & T. Clark, 1958), 98.

exposition of Genesis 1:26–28 in which the creation of man as a species is related, and royal rule over the world is conferred upon man. Chapter 2, in effect, tells us how this royal rule that is given to humankind within the covenant structure is to operate. The writer indicates that man was created outside Eden and then placed within the garden. The garden is presented as a center of blessing in the world. In it arose the world river that divided outside the garden into four systems. The garden also functions as a divine sanctuary, the point where the divine presence was experienced and enjoyed in a close and immediate way. Gordon Wenham, followed by William Dumbrell, has described the garden in Eden as a sanctuary and Adam as a priest worshiping there. This may be briefly summarized and connected to the divine image.

The Garden as Separate Space

The Hebrew word for "garden" (*gan*) comes from a root meaning to "enclose," "fence off," or "protect." The garden envisioned in Genesis 2:8–17 is an enclosed or protected space. In the Old Testament, walls surrounded both royal gardens (2 Kings 25:4; Neh. 3:15; Jer. 39:4; 52:7) and vineyards (Prov. 24:30–31; Isa. 5:5). In Genesis 2, the Greek translation of the Old Testament used a loanword from Persian that ended up as "paradise" in English. This meant a pleasure garden surrounded by an earthen or stone wall like *The Secret Garden* of Frances Hodgson Burnett. In our culture and society today we normally think of gardening as a lowly task, a job or vocation for a blue-collar worker or someone lower on the ladder of success. While gardeners could be from the lower strata of society in the culture of the ancient Near East, *kings* in Mesopotamia nonetheless created and kept extravagant gardens. In fact, "gardener" was a descriptive title or epithet for monarchs in Mesopotamia. This use reminds us of Louis XIV's gardens in Versailles, which showed that he was able to control nature and form entire trees into topiaries. So "gardener" was a royal vocation. The role of Adam as gardener further portrays him as a royal figure.

The role of Adam as gardener comes up much later in Scripture. After the crucifixion of Jesus, on that first Easter Sunday, the disciples (Peter and John) ran to the tomb. They found it empty and returned to their homes:

> But Mary stood weeping outside the tomb. . . . She turned around and saw Jesus standing there, but she didn't know that it was Jesus. . . . *Supposing him to be the gardener*, she said to him, "Sir, if you have carried him somewhere, tell me where you have laid him, and I will take him away."

Jesus said to her, "Mary!" She turned and said to him in Aramaic, "Rabbouni!" (which means Teacher). (John 20:11–16)

As N. T. Wright notes, "it wasn't, after all, such a silly mistake for Mary to think that Jesus, the true Adam, *was the gardener.*"[14]

The Garden as Sacred Space/Sanctuary

Creation accounts in the ancient Near East commonly connected creation and temple building. For example, the temple Esagila was built for Marduk in *Enuma Elish*. Genesis 2:8–17 portrays the first man as a kind of priest in a garden sanctuary. In terms of literary structure, 2:8a describes the creation of the garden and 2:8b the placing of the man there. In what follows, 2:9–15 elaborates on 2:8a, and 2:16–17 elaborates on 2:8b.

Parallels between the description of the garden in Eden and descriptions of sanctuaries elsewhere in the Old Testament and ancient Near East reveal that the garden is being portrayed as a sanctuary. Some of the evidence is summarized as follows:

1. The garden in Eden is characterized by the presence of God. There God comes to meet man at the cool of the day. The *hithpael* stem of the verb *hālak* is iterative, meaning "to walk back and forth" (Gen. 3:8). The same form is employed to describe the divine presence in the later tent sanctuaries (Lev. 26:12; Deut. 23:15 [23:14, English versions]; 2 Sam. 7:6–7).

2. When humans were cast out of Eden, *kĕrûbîm* ("cherubim," i.e., guardian creatures) were stationed east of the garden to guard the way to the tree of life (Gen. 3:24). This clearly indicates that the entrance to the garden was on the east side. Like the garden in Eden, the entrances to the later tabernacle and temple were also on the east and were guarded by *kĕrûbîm* (1 Kings 6:23–28; Ex. 25:18–22). Two guarded the inner sanctuary of Solomon's temple, and two more the mercy seat of the ark in the inner sanctuary. Pictures of *kĕrûbîm* decorated the curtains of the tabernacle and the walls of the temple (Ex. 26:31; 1 Kings 6:29).

3. In the center of the garden in Eden is the tree of life. Similarly, in the center of the tabernacle and temple is the menorah (i.e., the branching lampstand), which, as Carol Meyers has shown, is a stylized tree of life.[15]

---

[14] N. T. Wright, *Following Jesus: Biblical Reflections on Discipleship* (Grand Rapids, MI: Eerdmans, 1995), 57–59 (emphasis ours).
[15] Carol L. Meyers, *The Tabernacle Menorah: A Synthetic Study of a Symbol from the Biblical Cult*, American Schools of Oriental Research Dissertation Series 2 (Missoula, MT: Scholars Press, 1976).

The idea that fullness of life can be found in the sanctuary is basic to the instructions for the sacrifices in the Torah and is a recurrent theme in the Psalms.

4. The responsibility and task given to Adam in the garden is "to serve/work it and to keep it." The only other passages in the entire Torah where the same two verbs occur together are Numbers 3:7–8; 8:26; and 18:5–6, which describe the duties of the Levites in guarding and ministering in the sanctuary. These words are also commonly used in the Old Testament for worship. Thus Adam is portrayed as a kind of Levite who fulfills his role or task by maintaining the priority of worship.

5. According to Genesis 2:10, "A river flows out of Eden to water the garden." This river brings fertility and life to the entire world, as we see in verses 11–14. Similarly, in Psalm 46:4 we read of "a river whose streams make glad the city of God," and Ezekiel 47 describes a great river flowing out of the temple in the new Jerusalem to sweeten the Dead Sea. Such a source of fertility and life is an indication that the divine presence is there. One of these rivers was called the Gihon, which was also the name for the spring under the Jerusalem temple (1 Kings 1:33, 38, 45).

6. The river giving life to the garden divides into four as it issues from Eden. Since water flows downhill, this fact clearly indicates that Eden was an elevated place. In the ancient Near East, temples were situated on mountains because that is where the heavens meet the earth. In Ezekiel 28:13–14, Eden is also described and portrayed as a mountain sanctuary. Interestingly, there are passages in the Old Testament that portray Canaan, the Promised Land given to Israel, as a new Eden. These texts speak of the "new Eden" as a mountain sanctuary, the dwelling place of God (Ex. 15:17; Ps. 78:54). After divine judgment brings devastation to the land of Israel, God's plan of renewal involves restoring the desert so that it is like Eden (Isa. 51:3; Ezek. 36:35). The future new Jerusalem/Zion is likewise a mountain sanctuary (Isa. 2:2–4; 4:5; 11:9; 25:6–8; 56:7; 57:13; 65:11, 25).

7. The garden is the place of divine decrees. After placing man in the garden (Gen. 2:8, 15), God gave commands to the man there. The Lord daily met the man there, and as Judge and King he called him to account for his sin in one of these daily meetings. Similarly, the tabernacle (and later Solomon's temple) is the place from which God rules as King: "then make for me a sanctuary so that I may dwell among them" (Ex. 25:8). The ark in the center of the inner room of the sanctuary is a kind of footstool of God's throne: "the

LORD sits enthroned above the cherubim" (1 Sam. 4:4; 2 Sam. 6:2 = 1 Chron. 13:6; 2 Kings 19:15; Ps. 99:1).

8. The tree of knowledge in the garden in Eden was recognized as "pleasant to the sight, good for food and to be desired to make one wise" (Gen. 3:6). These characteristics are echoed by Psalm 19, where the covenant/Torah/law is described as "making wise the simple, rejoicing the heart, and enlightening the eyes." Referred to as the "testimony," the covenant/Torah was kept in the ark in the Holy of Holies, the inner sanctuary (Ex. 25:16; Deut. 31:26). Touching the ark brought death, just as eating from the tree of knowledge did (2 Sam. 6:7; Num. 4:20).

There are also parallels between Genesis 1–3, the account of creation, and Exodus 25–40, the account of the building of the tabernacle. There are six commands for building the tabernacle, just as there are six days in the creation narrative. The pattern of six days plus a seventh is the structure not only of the creation narrative but also of Exodus 25–40. Just as God rested on the seventh day of creation, so also he rested in Exodus 40, as he began his dwelling in the tabernacle.

We find in Genesis 1–2 the recursive, resumptive, and holographic pattern characteristic of Hebrew literature. Genesis 1 goes around the topic of creation, and Genesis 2 goes around the topic again from a different perspective. Put the two together and you have a hologram of the creation.

Genesis 2:8–17 pictures Adam as a kind of king-priest worshiping in a garden sanctuary. This passage explains how the royal rule given to humankind within the covenant structure established in 1:26–27 is to operate. Dumbrell begins to draw out the implications of this as follows:

> In short, created in the world with dominion over it, man is immediately abstracted from the world and placed directly in the divine presence. What is being said in all this is surely how the dominion mandate was to be exercised. . . . Man was to control his world, not primarily by immersing himself in the tasks of ordering it, but by recognizing that there was a system of priorities by which all of life was to be regulated. If he were rightly related to his Creator, then he would rightly respond to creation.[16]

Included in the covenant was an ordering of male/female relationships and family life so that part of responding rightly to creation was true humanness defined in proper ways of treating each other.

---

[16] Dumbrell, *Covenant and Creation*, 35–36.

The relationship between Genesis 2:8–17 and Genesis 1:26–27 is significant. Genesis 2:8–17 explains the relationship between "likeness" and "image" in the covenant relationship between man and God. Only when the father-son relationship is nurtured through worship, fellowship, and obedient love will humankind appropriately and properly reflect and represent to the world the kind of kingship and rule intrinsic to God himself. Kingship is effected *through* covenant relationship.

THE DEMAND OF THE COVENANT AND ITS BREACH

There was a real and vital element of condition in the covenant relationship in the garden. Eating the fruit of the tree of the knowledge of good and evil was prohibited. We know that the conditions for maintaining love, loyalty, and trust in the covenant relationship were not met. When the fruit of the forbidden tree was eaten, we were all involved somehow, as Romans 5:12–21 makes plain.

A brief comment is necessary to discuss the breaking of the covenant. Just what was involved in this initial transgression? Was the prohibition against eating the fruit of the forbidden tree an arbitrarily imposed means for testing loyalty and obedience? This is surely true, but it does not do justice to what was offered by the snake, and confirmed by God after the Fall: that they would be "like gods, knowing good and evil" (see Gen. 3:5, 22).

Some have explained knowing good and evil as reflecting sexual understanding of each other. This is inadequate because it does not make plain how the acquisition of such knowledge would make one like God.

Others have explained good and evil as a way of expressing the totality of knowledge by describing opposite poles. But certainly neither Adam and Eve nor any subsequent humans can claim the totality of knowledge.

The best explanation to date is that of W. M. Clark,[17] who carefully analyzed all the occurrences of the phrase in the Hebrew Bible and showed that the "knowledge of good and evil" has to do with the exercise of absolute moral autonomy. That is to say, knowing good and evil means choosing or determining for oneself what is right and wrong independently of God. The decision of Adam to be self-legislating did make him like God in one sense, but also unlike God in that he would not be able to foresee the consequences of his choices long term or always be certain of the issues before him.

---

[17] W. M. Clark, "A Legal Background to the Yahwist's Use of 'Good and Evil' in Genesis 2–3," *Journal of Biblical Literature* 88 (1969): 266–278. See also Henri Blocher, *In the Beginning* (Downers Grove, IL: InterVarsity Press, 1984), 126–133.

SUMMARY

Careful exegesis of Genesis 1–3 has shown that, at creation, God made humankind as his image and according to his likeness. In the cultural and linguistic setting of the fourteenth century B.C., and according to the literary techniques embedded in the text and the framework provided by the metanarrative, this speaks of man's relationship to God as son and his relationship to creation as servant king. In the ancient Near East, both the context of the family and the relationship of king and people is covenantal, requiring loyal love, obedience, and trust.

Chapter 5

THE COVENANT WITH ABRAHAM (I)

At creation humans are hardwired for a covenant relationship with God on the one hand and for a covenant relationship with creation on the other. The covenant with Noah affirms the original plan and purpose established at creation.

Next in the grand story comes the covenant with Abraham. Brian Walsh, Christian Reformed chaplain at the University of Toronto in Canada, wrote some time ago of the importance of this grand story to the challenges facing the church in a postmodern age:

> Postmodern culture is deeply suspicious of all grand stories. Again, The Smashing Pumpkins prove to be insightful in this regard. In their infinitely sad song, "tales of a scorched earth," they sing, "we're all dead yeah we're all dead/inside the future of a shattered past." We live inside the future of a shattered past because that "past" told grand stories of Marxist utopia, technological freedom, or capitalist paradise. Yet we have come to see not only that these stories are unfinished, but that they are also fundamentally unfinishable, for the simple reason that they are fundamentally lies. The postmodern ethos insists that stories such as these that have so shaped our lives are not stories of emancipation and progress after all, but stories of enslavement, oppression and violence. And on such a view, any story, any world view, that makes grand claims about the real course and destiny of history will be perceived as making common cause with such violence and oppression. This characteristic of the postmodern shift is, I think, the most challenging to Christian faith. If there is one thing that Christianity is all about it is a grand story. How else can we interpret the cosmic tale of creation, fall, redemption and consummation that the Scriptures tell? Yet it is precisely this story that we must tell in a postmodern culture. In the face of the dissolution of all grand stories, Christians have the audacity to proclaim, week after week, the liberating story of God's redemption of all creation. It is, we insist, the one story that actually delivers on what it promises.[1]

---

[1] Brian Walsh, "The Church in a Postmodern Age: Ten Things You Need to Know," in *Good Idea! A Resource Sheet on Evangelism and Church Growth* 3/4 (Toronto: Wycliffe College Institute of Evangelism, 1996), 1–5.

ABRAHAM IN THE GENESIS PLOT STRUCTURE

If we are to construct a metanarrative that is, in fact, the metanarrative of Scripture and not a marriage of biblical data and secular worldviews, we must pay attention to the shape of the text and the literary techniques used by the narrator to locate the narratives concerning Abraham within the larger plot structure of Genesis, the Pentateuch, the Old Testament, and the Bible as a whole. Afterwards we can reckon with the internal movement and literary structure within the Abraham narratives.

N. T. Wright, a British evangelical scholar, describes the story of Abraham this way:

> Abraham emerges within the structure of Genesis as the answer to the plight of all humankind. The line of disaster and of the 'curse', from Adam, through Cain, through the Flood to Babel, begins to be reversed when God calls Abraham and says, 'in you shall all the families of the earth be blessed'.[2]

Here, after Adam and Noah, God is making another new start. Abram and his family constitute another Adam. Notice the parallels in the biblical narrative: Adam and Eve had three sons (besides other children who are not named in the text; Gen. 5:4). Similarly, the genealogy in Genesis 5 ends with a man who also had three sons (Shem, Ham, and Japheth). The genealogy in Genesis 11 ends in the same way: with a man who had three sons (Abram, Nahor, and Haran). This parallel is a literary technique inviting the reader to compare Abram with Noah and Adam.

There are other parallels between Genesis 1–3 and Genesis 12 which suggest that we should view Abram as a new Adam, and we will now explore some of them.

GENESIS 12 AS A NEW CREATION

According to the apostle Paul, the choosing of Abram by God involved calling into existence that which is nonexistent. Paul says,

> [16] That is why it depends on faith, in order that the promise may rest on grace and be guaranteed to all his offspring—not only to the adherent of the law but also to the one who shares the faith of Abraham, who is the father of us all, [17] as it is written, "I have made you the father of many nations"—in the presence of the God in whom he believed, who gives

---

[2] N. T. Wright, *The New Testament and the People of God* (Minneapolis: Fortress, 1992), 262.

life to the dead and calls into existence the things that do not exist. (Rom. 4:16–17, ESV)

When Paul speaks of Abraham believing in the God who calls into existence the things that do not exist, what does this language bring to mind? Paul can have only one passage of Scripture foremost in mind: Genesis 1. Over and over again in the creation narrative we read the words, "And God said, 'Let x be.' And x was." God simply speaks his word and calls into existence things that do not exist. Therefore, according to the New Testament, as we read Genesis 12–25, we are to view the call of Abram as a kind of "new creation." Just as the divine word in Genesis 1:3 brings into being and existence things that are not, so in Genesis 12:3 it is the divine word that brings into existence a new order out of the chaos resulting from the confusion and curse of Babel—the condition of the world just prior to Genesis 12. Note that Genesis 10 and 11 are not presented in chronological order. Genesis 10 constitutes a "Table of Nations," showing the various families and peoples of the world lost and scattered over the face of the earth. Genesis 11 presents the narrative of the Tower of Babel, which explains how the nations had been scattered in this way. Just as the first Adam failed as a covenant keeper and his family line through Cain ended up with the corruption and violence displayed by Lamech—a polygamist who murdered a boy and promised severe vengeance for any who would redress his heinous act (4:18–24)—so the second Adam, Noah, also failed to produce a covenant community practicing social justice, resulting in the humanistic hubris of Babel. The earth returned once more to chaos before God began anew by calling Abram. As Dumbrell notes, "in this way the absolutely free and unconditioned nature of the choice of Abram is emphasized, and thus the presence of the divine will as the power which shapes and directs all history is at this point made perfectly clear."[3]

ISRAEL AS ANOTHER ADAM

Other parallels are established by the use of key words. Let us now notice how the language of the commission to Adam is repeated throughout the book of Genesis by following the use of "bless," "be fruitful," and "multiply" in the narratives subsequent to the creation narrative:

---

[3] William J. Dumbrell, *Covenant and Creation: A Theology of Old Testament Covenants* (Nashville: Thomas Nelson, 1984), 58.

1:28: And God *blessed* them, and God said to them, "Be *fruitful* and *multiply*, and fill the earth, and subdue it; and have dominion over the fish of the sea and over the birds of the air, and over every living thing that moves upon the earth."

12:2f.: "And I will make of you a great nation, and I will *bless* you, and make your name great; and be a *blessing*! And I will *bless* those who *bless* you . . .

17:2, 6, 8: "I will make my covenant between me and you, and will *multiply* you exceedingly. . . . I will make you exceedingly *fruitful*, . . . and I will give to you and to your seed after you, . . . all the land of Canaan, . . ."

22:16ff.: "Because you have done this, . . . I will certainly *bless* you, and I will greatly *multiply* your descendants as the stars of heaven and as the sand which is on the seashore. . . . and in your seed all the nations of the earth shall be *blessed*, because you have obeyed my voice."

26:3f.: [The LORD said to Isaac] "I will be with you and will *bless* you; for to you and to your descendants I will give all these lands, and I will fulfill the oath which I swore to your father Abraham. I will *multiply* your descendants as the stars of heaven, and will give your descendants all these lands; and by your descendants all the nations of the earth shall be *blessed* . . ."

26:24: "Fear not, for I am with you. I will *bless* you, and *multiply* your descendants, for the sake of my servant Abraham."

28:3: [Isaac blessed Jacob and said,] "God Almighty *bless* you and make you *fruitful* and *multiply* you, that you may become a company of peoples. May he give you the blessing of Abraham, to you and to your descendants with you, that you may possess the land of your sojournings, which God gave to Abraham."

35:11f.: And God said to [Jacob], "I am God Almighty: be *fruitful* and *multiply*; a nation and company of nations shall come from you, . . . and the land which I gave to Abraham and Isaac I will give to you, and I will give the land to your descendants after you."

47:27: Thus Israel lived in the land of Egypt, . . . and they gained possessions in it, and were *fruitful* and *multiplied* exceedingly.

48:3f.: Jacob said to Joseph, "God Almighty appeared to me . . . and said to me, 'Behold, I will make you *fruitful*, and *multiply* you, . . . and will give this land, to your seed after you . . .'"

From tracing this trail of the terms "bless," "be fruitful," and "multiply" through Genesis, Wright concludes as follows:

> Thus at key moments—Abraham's call, his circumcision, the offering of Isaac, the transition from Abraham to Isaac and from Isaac to Jacob, and in the sojourn in Egypt—the narrative quietly makes the point that Abraham and his family inherit, in a measure, the role of Adam and Eve. The differences are not, however, insignificant. Except for 35.11 f., echoed in 48.3 f., the command ('be fruitful . . .') has turned into a promise ('I will make you fruitful . . .'). The word 'exceedingly' is added in ch. 17. And, most importantly, possession of the land of Canaan, and supremacy over enemies, has taken the place of the dominion over nature given in 1.28. We could sum up this aspect of Genesis by saying: Abraham's children are God's true humanity, and their homeland is the new Eden.[4]

Question #1

The last point made by Wright is forcefully illustrated by Exodus 15:17. At the end of the song sung by Israel after crossing the Red Sea we read,

> You will bring them in and plant them on your own mountain,
> the place, O LORD, which you have made for your abode,
> the sanctuary, O Lord, which your hands have established. (ESV)

32 words

In this verse the establishment of Israel in Canaan is pictured as the planting of a tree in a *mountain sanctuary*, exactly the picture of Eden presented in Genesis 2 and Ezekiel 28. Thus Abraham and his family, later called Israel, are, as it were, another Adam. God made a major new start with Noah. Now he is making another new start with Abraham. There are no major new beginnings after this in the narrative of Scripture (until we come to the new creation at the end of the story).

When we see that Israel is, according to the Old Testament, another Adam—and, as later Jewish tradition understood it, the one undoing the sin of Adam—we see the background for Paul's understanding of Christ as the last Adam, because as history unfolds, Jesus accomplishes in his person and work what God intended for Israel as a people to accomplish.

OVERVIEW OF GOD'S DEALINGS WITH ABRAM

It was over a period of forty years that God had dealings with Abram, later called Abraham. During this time there was a call to leave his homeland and

---

[4] N. T. Wright, *The Climax of the Covenant* (Minneapolis: Fortress, 1991), 21–23.

journey to a country unknown to him. Initially God made promises to Abram (Genesis 12) that were later enshrined in a covenant (Genesis 15 and 17) and confirmed finally by an oath (Genesis 22). All throughout this period of time, one can perceive development and growth in the character and life of Abram in terms of faith in God's promises and obedience to his instructions revealed to him (frequently by means of visions).

As far as the covenant God made with Abraham is concerned, three or four episodes in the Abram narrative are particularly prominent. First, in Genesis 12, God makes incredible promises to Abram involving progeny and land (i.e., a place where his progeny can live and that they can call home). Then, in chapter 15, both of these promises are enshrined in a covenant. Later on, in chapter 17, after Abram and Sarai's attempt to fulfill the promise of progeny through Hagar and Ishmael, God repeats his promises and affirms his covenant, this time adding the rite of circumcision. Some ten to fifteen years afterwards, according to chapter 22, God "tests" Abraham and, upon his obedience, swears by himself in another mighty confirmation of the promises.

Key Points in the Abraham Narratives
1. The Giving of the Promise: the Call of Abram (Genesis 12)
2. Making the Covenant: the Promise of Descendants and Land (Genesis 15)
3. Affirming the Covenant: the Sign of Circumcision (Genesis 17)
4. Abraham's Obedience and Confirmation of the Promises by Oath (Genesis 22)

We might compare the relationship between God and Abraham to a marriage. The giving of the promises in chapter 12 would then represent the betrothal or engagement. The covenant making in chapter 15 and affirmation in chapter 17 would correspond to the wedding vows of the marriage covenant. After testing Abraham, God reiterates his promises by a mighty oath.

OUTLINE OF GENESIS 12

Careful consideration of key grammatical issues and the literary structure of Genesis 12 are necessary for a correct interpretation of the promises made by God to Abram and the covenant ensuing from them. In fact, interpretation at this key point affects how one understands the rest of the Bible.

The Giving of the Promise: The Call of Abram (Genesis 12)

The divine word: command and promise   **12:1–3**

Go (Command)

1. I will make you into a great nation	(Promise)
2. I will bless you	(Promise)
3. I will make your name great	(Promise)

Be a Blessing (Command)

1. I will bless those who bless you	(Promise)
2. I will curse him who curses you	(Promise)
3. In you all nations will be blessed	(Promise)

Abram's response: obedience   **12:4–9**

1. Obedience	(vv. 4–6)
2. Confirmation	(v. 7)
3. Obedience	(vv. 8–9)

The passage divides into two sections: verses 1–3 constitute the divine word to Abram, and verses 4–9 indicate his response to that word. Noting the literary structure of verses 1–3 is crucial. In the Hebrew text, there are two commands (i.e., verbs in Hebrew marked as imperatives): "go" and "be." Each of these two commands is followed by three verbs that mark purpose or result. Thus three promises flow from each of the two commands.

The promises given to Abram as an individual focus on nationhood, blessing, and a great name. First, Abram will become a great nation. Now, you cannot have a great nation without land, without territory, without a place for a large number of people to live in and call home. So the idea of land is implied in this promise, and the Lord makes this explicit in verse 7: "The LORD appeared to Abram and said, 'To your offspring I will give this land.'" The promise of land is also implicit in the first command: "Go from your country!" One cannot become a great nation and inhabit territory without first becoming distinct from the land and nation where one starts out. The confirmation and promise of land or territory for the future nation in verse 7 is in a chiastic structure, showing Abram's response to the divine promises. On either side of the confirmation by divine revelation in verse 7 is the obedience and worship of Abraham. Verses 8 and 9 speak of Abram building an altar and calling out in the name of Yahweh and pitching his tent. The altar and the tent characterize Abram's activities in Canaan. Note that the altar is mentioned only in connection with sojourning in Canaan (Gen. 12:7, 8; 13:4, 18; 22:9 [2x]). There is no altar during his sojourns in Egypt or in Gerar—only half-truths, lies, and troubles. We saw above that Canaan is depicted in Edenic language as a mountain sanctuary. Now we see Abram fulfilling *an Adamic role*: he offers sacrifice as a priest and worships God in this mountain sanctuary. The only occurrence of the word "altar" prior to Genesis 12 is in Genesis 8:20, where Noah, the second Adam, offers sacrifice to the Lord after the judgment of the flood. This reinforces the activity of Abraham as another Adam in his role of offering sacrifice in the mountain sanctuary of Canaan. The tent simply emphasizes that the fulfillment of the promises and the permanent situation has not yet arrived.

The second promise given to Abram as an individual is blessing. As the narrative unfolds, we will see what blessing means and will return again to this topic. The third promise is that God will make Abram's name great. There are possible royal overtones to this promise. The promise to Abram is similar to the one given to David when God makes a covenant with him: "Now I will make your name great, like the names of the greatest men of the earth" (2 Sam. 7:9). This fits with the clear and direct reference to kings coming from Abraham and Sarah (Gen. 17:6, 16). It also matches the fact that Abram is a royal figure due to his Adamic role. Although Abram is never called a king, the King of Gerar treats him as an equal, the inhabitants of Hebron designate him a "prince of God" (Gen. 23:6), and his military exploits in Genesis 14 place him on a par with kings.

Genesis 14, in fact, presents a surprising figure, Melchizedek, who is a king-priest, and the narrator describes Abram as identifying with him. The events of Genesis 14 are important to the depiction of Abram and his role as "king-priest." The narrative introduces four major rulers of the east who come to punish Canaanite rulers who have refused to pay the required tribute exacted in conquests fourteen years earlier. They defeat various groups, including five kings ruling cities in the plain south of the Dead Sea. The defeat involves the abduction of Lot, who by this time was living in Sodom. Abraham stages a dramatic rescue, attacking the four kings at night with only 318 men from his household and his Amorite allies, Mamre, Aner, and Eschol. As Abram returns from his victory over the four kings, he is met by two kings: the king of Sodom and the king of Salem (= Jerusalem).

The two kings represent two different types of kingship. The king of Sodom represents the notion that one acquires goods and rules by might: might makes right. It is the normal pattern of kingship in Canaan—an absolute ruler uses his position to aggrandize himself. Melchizedek, king of Salem, represents a different kind of kingship. He acknowledges a supreme God who is Creator/Possessor of everything. Therefore all rule must acknowledge the sovereignty of the Most High God and must consider that everything one owns is a gift from him. He is a servant of the Most High God; his kingship is based on the *worship* of this God. Abram does three things: (1) he identifies the Most High God as Yahweh, (2) he gives a tenth to Melchizedek, and (3) he refuses to accept from the king of Sodom any of the goods that are his by right as the spoils of war. In other words, he identifies with the kind of king-priest rule that Melchizedek represents. Abram is thus adopting a king-priest role originally given to Adam and now given to him.

The second group of three promises offer blessing (or cursing) for the nations of the world through their relation to Abram (and his family). First, God promises to bless those (plural) who bless Abram. Second, the same promise is stated negatively: God will curse the one who slights or treats Abram lightly. Then, in a summary statement, Abram is told that all the clans of the earth would be blessed through him. Blessing both begins the three promises and ends them. Note also that God will bless the ones who bless Abram but will curse the one who treats him lightly. Why the shift from plural to singular? God is hoping that there will be *many* who bless and *few* who curse Abram. The shift from plural to singular emphasizes the generosity of God in his plan of rescuing and saving a world that has reverted to chaos and death.

Debate exists concerning the last promise, "in you all the clans of the earth will be blessed." The exact function of the *niphal* form of the verb "bless" is in question. Two main options are advanced by scholars. One construes the *niphal* form as passive (i.e., "in you all the clans of the earth will be blessed"); the other reckons the *niphal* form to be reflexive (i.e., "in you all the clans of the earth will bless themselves"). Both interpretations are grammatically possible.

The best scholarship shows that the *niphal* forms are passive ("they shall be blessed") and the *hithpael* are estimative-declarative reflexive ("they shall consider/declare themselves as blessed"). There is overlap in meaning, but each has a slightly different emphasis in the context where it is used.

Blessing

In the first three verses of Genesis 12, the word "blessing" occurs five times. As Dumbrell notes, the choice and use of the term is doubtless deliberate, playing on the notion of the power of the word. His comment is apt:

In Gen. 12:2a God blesses Abram and here the notion of blessing is bound up with nationhood and fame. As a result Abram is thus to be the embodiment of blessing, the example of what blessing should be (v. 2b). God will bless those who rightly recognize the source of Abram's blessing (3a), and then finally in 12:3b Abram becomes the mediator of blessing for mankind.[5]

What is actually meant by "blessing"? Blessing is connected with life, just as cursing brings death. So what would blessing mean in the ancient Near East in Abraham's time? Does blessing mean a full, long life, the good life in the sense of having good health, having a big family to look after one as a senior, business success (i.e., having big flocks and herds or crops that are abundant and successful), acquiring land, having power and victory over your enemies? If we convert these ideas into our modern society, what would blessing mean? Does blessing mean health, business success, being surrounded by a circle of friends (on Facebook?), having influence and power, having a big house and car, having better sex? The term "to bless" (*brk*) in Hebrew with God as subject denotes having a big family and victory, accompanied by a sense of loyalty to the future generations (Gen. 1:28; 26:24; 27:27–29). It also connotes redemption, a relationship with God that transforms the beneficiary and provides security. As Abraham's life unfolds, we begin to see what blessing means. Blessing operates in the context of a covenant relationship with God. Blessings are the manifestation of a faithfulness, fidelity, and solidarity in relationships whereby one's natural and personal capacity to fulfill God's intention and purpose is advanced and furthered. God's word to Abram is powerful, enabling the calling to be fulfilled.

Curse and Blessing

In our study of Genesis 12:1–3 we just noted that the word "blessing" occurs five times in that text (Gen. 12:2 [2x], 3 [3x]). What is interesting and noteworthy is that the antonym "curse" (*'ārar*) occurs precisely five times in Genesis 1–11 (3:14; 3:17; 4:11; 5:29; 9:25). The curse in 3:14 brought the loss of freedom and power as well as certain defeat and humiliation (for the serpent). In 3:17 the curse effected an alienation between humans and the soil. Further, in 4:11, Cain was cursed from the land, resulting in

---

[5] Dumbrell, *Covenant and Creation*, 67–68.

estrangement from human society as he became a nomad and wanderer. Noah's curse of Canaan brought further degradation and shame, as Canaan was to be the lowest of slaves. Cumulative deprivation and increasing loss are therefore associated with the word "curse," bringing man from Eden to Babel. The fivefold repetition of the word "blessing" in Genesis 12:1–3 indicates that the call of Abram will change this situation: broken relationships are to be potentially and progressively repaired. The ruptured relationships that had developed between man and God and between man and man are eventually to be restored. The new, powerful word calling Abram out of Ur is to annul the curse of chapters 1–11.

There is, then, in Genesis 12:1–3 a causal relationship between the first group of three promises and the second group of three promises. God's plan to bless Abram and his family is a means to bring blessing and salvation to all the nations. Paul House comments appropriately on the divine choice of Abram and the decision to bless him and his family: "Election here does not exclude or condemn anyone. Rather it works exclusively as a benefit to a world that has no intention of doing what is right."[6]

Abram and the City of God

The call of Abram in Genesis 12:1–3 consists of two commands ("go" [v. 1] and "be" a blessing [v. 2]). Each command is followed by three promises. The first promise is, "I will make you into a great nation," and the last promise is, "all the clans/families of the earth will be blessed in you" (12:1, 3). We need to pay attention to the terms used here to describe both the people of God and the other peoples of the world. God promises to make Abram into a great *nation*; this is the word *gôy* in Hebrew. The other people groups of the world are called *clans* or *families*; here the Hebrew term is *mišpāḥâ*.

First, consider the term *gôy*, or "nation." It is highly unusual for this term to be applied to the people of God. There is in the language of the Old Testament a completely consistent usage: the word *'am* is almost always reserved for Israel. It is a *kinship* term that expresses effectively the closeness of the family/marriage relationship between God and Israel established by the covenant made at Sinai (Exodus 24). On the other hand, the word *gôy* is the standard term for the communities or other societies in the world excluding Israel. So consistent is this use that when we see something different, we need to ask why. For example, there are instances where the term *gôy* is

---

[6] Paul R. House, *Old Testament Theology* (Downers Grove, IL: InterVarsity Press, 1998), 73.

applied to Israel in a pejorative sense. Sometimes Israel is called "nation" and not "people" because the author may wish to communicate that, because of her wickedness, she is behaving as if she were *not* the people of God. Her actions and attitudes indicate she is like those communities who have no special status as the chosen people of God (e.g., Judg. 2:20).

Why, then, in Genesis 12 does God speak of Abram becoming a great *gôy*, or nation? The basic meaning of *gôy* is an *organized* community of people having *governmental*, *political*, and *social structure*. This contrasts with the fact that the other nations are derogatorily termed *mišpāḥâ* in Genesis 12. This word refers to an amorphous kin group larger than an extended family and smaller than a tribe.

The background of Genesis 12 is chapters 10 and 11. There we have the history of Babel, where we see a complete confidence and naive optimism about human achievement and effort. Man is at the center of his world, and he can achieve anything. This philosophy comes under divine judgment in Genesis 11 and results in the nations being lost and scattered over the face of the earth. By contrast, Genesis 12 presents a political structure brought into being by the word of God, with God at the center and God as the governmental head and ruler of that community. In other words, we have the kingdom of God brought into being by means of the covenant (i.e., the covenant between God and Abram). Hence, we have *kingdom through covenant*.

The promise in Genesis 12:3 is cited or quoted several times in later texts of the Old Testament. In Genesis 28:14 the nations of the world are also called *mišpaḥôt* to form an *inclusio* with Genesis 12:3 and mark off a literary section. In Genesis 18:18, 22:18, 26:4, Psalm 72:17, and Jeremiah 4:2 (the five other texts directly referring to Genesis 12:3), however, the nations of the world are called by the more common and normal term, *gôyim*. This shows that the author has a real purpose in Genesis 12:3 in using the term *mišpaḥôt*: he wants to indicate that the kingdoms of this world will never amount to anything; only the kingdom of God will last forever. The author's choice of terms emphasizes that the family of Abram is a real kingdom with eternal power and significance, while the so-called kingdoms of this world are of no lasting power or significance. In fact, Abram is portrayed as a king, because what Abram is promised in Genesis 12 was the hope of many oriental monarchs (cf. 2 Sam. 7:9; Ps. 72:17).

The word in Hellenistic Greek which best conveys this meaning is *polis*, or "city." In our modern world we tend to think of cities as great centers of population in contrast to the rural areas, which by definition are sparsely populated. In contrast to the modern notion, in the first century the term "city" conveyed the idea of an organized community with governmental headship and appropriate political and social structure—what we normally convey by the English word *state*. Thus the promises of God to Abram really did entail the *city of God*, and the author of Hebrews is accurately explaining for his readers the author's intended meaning in Genesis 12. Abraham was to go to a country God would indicate to him and reside there—even if as an alien and a stranger: he was awaiting "the city that has foundations, whose architect and builder is God" (Heb. 11:10).

In Genesis 15 and 17 the great promises to Abram will be enshrined in a divine-human covenant between God and Abraham. For now, in chapter 12, we note that although the context, expressions, idioms, and language are completely different from the creation narrative and the image of God in Genesis 1:26–28, the *ideas* are identical. Abram (and the nation that comes from him) constitutes an *Adamic* figure. God intends to establish his rule over all his creation through his relationship with Abram and his family: *kingdom through covenant*. Through blessing Abram and his descendants, the broken relationship between God and all the nations of the world will be reconciled and healed. As we will soon see, the covenant entails not only a relationship with God that can be described as sonship, but also a relationship to the rest of creation that entails kingship in establishing the rule of God.

Chapter 6

THE COVENANT WITH ABRAHAM (II)

SUMMARY OF THE LARGER STORY TO THIS POINT

The larger story of Scripture begins with a creator God who is the maker of our world and all that is in it. Humans are the crowning glory of his work. There is a difference, moreover, between human creatures and all other creatures: we alone have been made as the image of this creator God, resulting in a covenant relationship with God and with all creation that entails a particular role and special tasks in the world. The first humans, however, decided to act independently of the creator God. As a result, there is chaos and discord in the creation at every level, bringing destruction and death.

The destructive path chosen by the first humans led continually downward until divine intervention was required. God judged the human race and made a new beginning with Noah and his family. Noah is portrayed as a new Adam. As soon as the dry land appears out of the chaos of waters, Noah is placed there and is commanded to be fruitful and multiply (Gen. 9:1); i.e., he is given Adam's blessing and commission. Eventually, however, the family of Noah ends up in the same chaos and corruption as the family of the first Adam.

So God makes another new start, with Abram and his family. Abraham and his family, called Israel, is another Adam, who will be God's true humanity. Israel is, in fact, the "last" Adam because there will be no major new starts for the human race as a whole from this point on. Israel will display to the rest of the world within its covenant community the kind of relationships—first to God and then to one another, as well as stewardship of the ecosystem—that God originally intended for all of humanity. In fact, through Abraham's family God plans to bring blessing to all the nations of the world. In this way, through Abraham's family, through Israel, he will bring about a resolution of the sin and death caused by the first Adam. The fact that the blessing to the nations through Abraham and his family included dealing with the sin and death caused by the first Adam is not *plainly* stated until much later, such as in the passages relating to the suffering servant in Isaiah (Isa. 42:1–9; 49:1–13; 50:4–9; 52:13–53:12).

We have considered the call of Abram and the promises given to him, recorded in Genesis 12. Now, in Genesis 15, the divine promises are enshrined in a covenant between Yahweh and Abram that is affirmed and upheld in Genesis 17. We need to trace the development of the covenant relationship between God and Abram and the progress of Abram's faithfulness and love in this relationship.

THE MAKING OF THE COVENANT (PROMISE OF DESCENDANTS AND LAND)—GENESIS 15

The literary structure of Genesis 15 is clear. The text is divided in half (vv. 1–6 and vv. 7–19), and each half has an identical pattern and structure. First, the Lord reveals himself to Abram (by vision) and makes promises. Second, Abram responds in complaint, asking about the fulfillment of God's promises. Third, God expands and extends his revelation a second time, confirming and reiterating his promises. Each half, then, has a (chiastic) three-part structure in which the first and last parts are matching. The promises in the first half are centered on the gift of descendants; the promises in the second half are centered on the gift of land. The covenant, therefore, enshrines the promises given in Genesis 12, with a focus on fulfillment of the first three promises in Genesis 12:1–3, i.e., a focus on the divine promises particularly to Abram himself.

Outline of Genesis 15

Part 1—Seed/descendants .15:1–6
A. God reveals himself and makes promises. . . .1
B. Abram's complaint and question 2–3
A'. God's revelation and confirmation 4–6
Part 2—Land 15:7–21
A. God reveals himself and makes promises. . . .7
B. Abram's complaint and question 8
A'. God's revelation and confirmation 9–19

Genesis 15 begins with the words "After these things," referring to the victory over the four kings from the east recorded in chapter 14. Thus, sometime following the defeat of these kings, Yahweh communicates to Abram by means of a vision. The translation in the King James Version, followed by such newer versions as the NKJV and NIV (1984, 2011), can be greatly improved upon at this point. The KJV rendering is as follows:

> After these things the word of the LORD came unto Abram in a vision, saying, Fear not, Abram: I *am* thy shield, *and* thy exceeding great reward. (Gen. 15:1)

First, the italicized "am" indicates the verb "to be" lacking in Hebrew, and the italicized "and" denotes a word not in the original text. The KJV construes as one sentence with "I" as subject and "thy shield" and "thy exceeding great reward" as the predicate. This is not a likely or plausible reading of the Hebrew text. The fact that "and" is also not in the text signals a new, separate sentence in which "your reward" is subject and "very great" is the predicate. The lack of a clause connector ("and") is not unusual in such a sequence of nominal sentences. God commands Abram not to be afraid. This is backed up by two statements: (1) God will protect him, and (2) God will reward him. Both the command and the promises relate directly to the events of chapter 14. Will the "Four Big Bad Guys from the East" be back next year to take their vengeance on Abram? Certainly the fear of reprisal is both real and significant. But Yahweh will be Abram's shield. He will protect Abram from possible reprisal. Second, at the end of Genesis 14, Abram took none of the spoils of the victory which were his by right. He wanted his sources of wealth to come from the Lord and not from the king of Sodom. So Yahweh promises Abram that he will reward him. He is not saying that he, Yahweh, is Abram's reward instead of the spoils of victory. He is saying that he will give something to Abram that will compensate for the fact that he took none of these spoils. The correct rendering is now provided by the ESV: "Fear not, Abram, I am your shield; your reward shall be very great." That this is the correct interpretation is clear from Abram's response. He says, "What will you *give* me?" not "How will you be my reward?" Abram is exasperated: Yahweh has made big promises, but he is anxiously waiting for the beginning of this great nation to reveal itself by the birth of at least *one baby*.

Yahweh responds to Abram's complaint with another night revelation. Asking Abram to count the stars, if he is able, he promises that Abram's descendants will be as numerous as the sand on the seashore or the stars of the night sky. At this point, all the Lord is doing is repeating the promise in grandiose terms. Yet Abram is hanging on to this. The rendering of verse 6 is debated: "Now Abram *was believing* in Yahweh, and he credited it to him as righteousness," or "Now Abram *believed* in Yahweh, and he credited it to him as righteousness." It is not necessary to decide this fine point, but an illustration may be useful to explain the meaning. Among our neighbors is an older couple. The husband smokes cigars, but always outside. One can imagine his wife saying to him, "If you want to be married to me, you smoke your cigars outside." It is important to recognize that the word "righteousness" usually operates in a covenant relationship. In a marriage, there must be trust. When one person makes a promise, righteousness requires the other person to believe him or her. Imagine a marriage where one person doubts the truth of more than half of what his or her partner promises or says. Abram simply accepts the promises of Yahweh and the stipulations he lays down for the relationship. That is what righteousness means here. We should not read the entire New Testament doctrine of justification from sin back into the life of Abram at this point.

Verse 7 begins the second half of Genesis 15, and again Yahweh communicates to Abram, repeating the promise of land made clear and explicit in Genesis 12:7. Again, Abram is exasperated: How will he know for sure that this promise will be fulfilled? So far in his experience, there is no evidence of its reality. Again Yahweh repeats his promise, but he does so by enshrining it within a covenant.

The ceremony or ritual described here is somewhat strange. Nonetheless, as 15:18 clearly states, this ceremony formalizes a covenant between God and Abram. The normal or standard terminology "to cut a covenant" (*kārat bĕrît*) is used. The interpretation of this mysterious rite is much discussed. The ceremony of covenant making involves an oath in which the covenant partners bring the curse of death upon themselves if they are not faithful to the covenant relationship and promises. Walking between the animals cut in half is a way of saying, "May I become like these dead animals if I do not keep my promise(s) and my oath." Scholars describe this as a self-maledictory oath, i.e., an oath where one brings the curse of death upon oneself for violating the covenant commitments. The details with which covenant making ceremonies are narrated vary from text to text. The covenant making in Jeremiah 34:18–20 is also explicit about walking between the pieces of the animal sacrificed for the rite:

[18] The men who have violated my covenant and have not fulfilled the terms of the covenant they made before me, I will treat like the calf they cut in two and then walked between its pieces. [19] The leaders of Judah and Jerusalem, the court officials, the priests and all the people of the land

who walked between the pieces of the calf, [20] I will hand over to their enemies who seek their lives. Their dead bodies will become food for the birds of the air and the beasts of the earth. (Jer. 34:18–20, NIV)

In the vision given to Abram, a "smoking firepot and a blazing torch" pass between the dead pieces. What would these represent? When we remember that Genesis was a book given to the Israelite people at the time of entering the land of Canaan, we can see from that perspective—i.e., after the exodus event—that smoke and fire are symbols of God's presence. The angel of the Lord first appeared to Moses in the flames of a burning bush (Ex. 3:2). During the desert journey, God appears as cloud and fire (Ex. 13:21). At Mount Sinai, his presence is manifested by smoke and fire (Ex. 19:18; 20:18). The fact that only God passes between the pieces is quite remarkable and shows that the promise depends upon him and him alone.

CONCLUSION

Ray Vander Laan has nicely expressed the powerful communication of the covenant making ritual in Genesis 15:

> What an awesome God we have! What incredible love he has for his creatures!
>
> Imagine! The Creator of the universe, the holy and righteous God, was willing to leave heaven and come down to a nomad's tent in the dusty, hot desert of Negev to express his love for his people.
>
> "Bring me a heifer, a goat and a ram . . . along with a dove and a young pigeon," God told Abraham. Then, when those animals had been sacrificed and laid out on both sides of their shed blood, God made a covenant. To do that, he walked "barefoot," in the form of a blazing torch, through the path of blood between the animals.
>
> Think of it. Almighty God walking barefoot through a pool of blood! The thought of a human being doing that is, to say the least, unpleasant. Yet, God, in all his power and majesty, expressed his love that personally. By participating in that traditional, Near Eastern covenant-making ceremony, he made it unavoidably clear to the people of that time, place and culture what he intended to do.
>
> "I love you so much, Abraham," God was saying, "and I promise that this covenant will come true for you and your children. I will never break My covenant with you. I'm willing to put My own life on the line to make you understand."
>
> Picturing God passing through that gory path between the carcasses of animals, imagining the blood splashing as he walked, helps us recognize the faithfulness of God's commitment. He was willing to express, in terms

his chosen people could understand, that he would never fail to do what he promised. And he ultimately fulfilled his promise by giving his own life, his own blood, on the cross.

Because we look at God's dealings with Abraham as some remote piece of history in a far-off land, we often fail to realize that we, too, are part of the long line of people with whom God made a covenant on that rocky plain near Hebron. And like those who came before us, we have broken that covenant.

When he walked in the dust of the desert and through the blood of the animals Abraham had slaughtered, God was making a promise to *all* the descendants of Abraham—to everyone in the household of faith. When God splashed through the blood, he did it for *us*.

We're not simply individuals in relationship to God, we're part of a long line of people marching back through history, from our famous Jewish ancestors David, Hezekiah, and Peter to the millions of unknown believers; from the ancient Israelites and the Jewish people of Jesus' day to the Christian community dating from the early church. We're part of a community of people with whom God established relationship in the dust and sand of the Negev.

But there's more. When God made covenant with his people, he did something no human being would have even considered doing. In the usual blood covenant, each party was responsible for keeping only his side of the promise. When God made covenant with Abraham, however, he promised to keep *both* sides of the agreement.

"If this covenant is broken, Abraham, for whatever reason—for My unfaithfulness or yours—I will pay the price," said God. "If you or your descendants, for whom you are making this covenant, fail to keep it, I will pay the price in blood."

And at that moment, Almighty God pronounced the death sentence on his Son Jesus.[1]

AFFIRMING THE COVENANT: THE SIGN OF CIRCUMCISION—GENESIS 17

The covenant between God and Abraham made in Genesis 15 is affirmed in Genesis 17. The precise relationship between Genesis 15 and 17 is debated. Before this relationship can be discussed, we must consider the literary structure of Genesis 17, the exegetical details of the text, and how and where it fits in the flow of the narratives dealing with Abraham.

As in the case of Genesis 15, the literary structure of Genesis 17 is clear. Again, the text is divided in half, and each half has an identical pattern and structure. Again the Lord communicates to Abram, presumably in a vision,

---

[1] Ray Vander Laan with Judith Markham, *Echoes of His Presence: Stories of the Messiah from the People of His Day* (Colorado Springs: Focus on the Family, 1996), 8–9.

although this is not explicit in the text as it is in Genesis 15. Yahweh begins by expressing his intention to confirm his covenant promise concerning descendants. Abram responds by falling on his face. God speaks further about his promises of both descendants and land. He prescribes circumcision to Abram as a covenant sign. Then the pattern is repeated. Yahweh expresses his intention to bless Sarah with progeny. Again, Abram falls on his face. God speaks further and announces in particular the birth of a son to Sarah in about a year's time. The section ends with Abraham obeying the instructions concerning circumcision for himself, Ishmael, and his entire household:

Outline of Genesis 17
A. Yahweh's intention to affirm his oath about progeny 1–2
B. Abram falls on his face 3
C. God promises descendants and the gift of land 4–8
D. The sign of circumcision given 9–14

A'. Yahweh's intention to bless Sarah with progeny 15–16
B'. Abraham falls on his face 17–18
C'. God promises a son from Sarah 19–22
D'. The sign of circumcision practiced 23–27

Just as the covenant making in chapter 15 came in response to the preceding events in chapter 14, so the covenant affirmation in chapter 17 comes in response to the events in chapter 16 (where Sarai and Abram seek descendants through Hagar).

Our attention is focused on several things in this text. Yahweh appears to Abraham and says, "I am God Almighty; walk before me and be blameless" (ESV, NIV). First, Yahweh reveals himself as *El Shaddai* ("God Almighty"). This is the first occurrence of this divine name in the Scriptures. In an attempt to determine the meaning of the Hebrew term *Shaddai*, scholars have argued over the origin of the word and have come to a stalemate. Its meaning, however, can be determined quite well from the way the word is used. This name for God is associated especially and particularly in the Old Testament with the lives of the patriarchs, Abraham, Isaac, and Jacob. It seems that this name was given to encourage faith because of the disparity between the covenant promises and the reality of the situation in which they found themselves at that time. Thus, in this context, Yahweh is the God who intervenes powerfully. It is customary in the Greek Old Testament to translate *El Shaddai* by "Almighty," and this expresses the meaning very well. As noted previously, the Abram narratives are presented as a new creation. Out of the post-Babel chaos portrayed by the nations and peoples of the world lost and scattered in the earth, and by the deadness and infertility of Abram and Sarai's bodies, the word of God to Abram is a powerful word bringing something out of nothing.

Second, *El Shaddai* commands Abram, saying, "Walk before me!" What does it mean to walk before someone? Careful study of the use of this expression throughout the Old Testament may be summarized as follows. When God walks before someone, this expression means to give guidance and protection. Conversely, when people walk before God, it means that they serve as his emissary or diplomatic representative. In Genesis 17:1 God commands Abram to walk before him. So Abram is to be God's agent or diplomatic messenger and representative in the world. When the world looks at Abram, they will see what it is like to have a right relationship to God and what it is to be what God intended for humanity. To see the significance of the geographical location of the land promised to Abraham and grasp its importance for the promises given to Abram in Genesis 12, consider a map of the ancient Near East (fig. 6.1), showing travel routes.

Travel Routes of the Ancient Near East

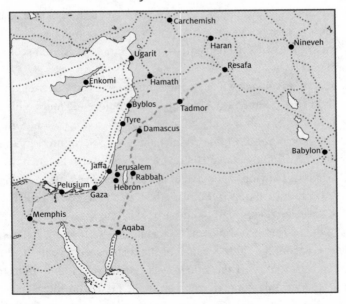

Fig. 6.1

Canaan, the land promised to Abram, is a minuscule piece of property about 30 miles wide and 100 miles long. The superpowers of the ancient world were on either side: Egypt to the west and Mesopotamia (Assyria and Babylon) to the east. Most of the area between Canaan and Mesopotamia is desert. The only functional route for commerce and travel between the great superpowers of the ancient world was the tiny country given to Abram. In modern terms, Abram and his family are to be settled along the *central spine of the Internet* in the ancient world. All of the communication, commerce, and trade back and forth between Egypt and Mesopotamia will pass through Canaan. And when it does, what are they supposed to see? They are supposed to witness a group of people who demonstrate a right relationship to the one and only true God, a truly human way of treating each other, and a proper stewardship of the earth's resources. God calls Abram to be a light to the nations. This is the beginning of his method and plan to bless all the nations through Abram and his family. Thus the command "walk before me" correlates directly with the command in 12:3 to be a blessing to the nations.

The divine command to Abram in Genesis 17:1 is actually twofold: (1) walk before me and (2) be blameless. The Hebrew word rendered "blameless" is *tāmîm*. This adjective comes from a root meaning "complete," "entire," or "whole." Although the adjective *tāmîm* and the closely related adjective *tām* are not infrequent in the Old Testament, use in reference to humans is uncommon since most of the instances concern animals that could be used for sacrifice. In fact, in all of Genesis, *tāmîm* is found only here (17:1) in reference to Abram, and in 6:9 in reference to Noah—both Adamic figures according to the literary techniques of the narrator.

The adjective *tāmîm* is also associated with "righteous" in Job 12:4, where Job protests that he, a completely righteous man, has become a laughingstock (cf. 2 Sam. 22:24–25 = Ps. 18:23–24; Prov. 11:5). Moreover, *tāmîm* is collocated with "upright" in Deuteronomy 32:4 and Proverbs 2:21; 28:10. Thus, God is calling Abram to be morally blameless and impeccable, honest and sincere in the covenant relationship.

As a matter of fact, however, when we consider the narratives concerning Abram to this point, we note that Abram has been less than honest and sincere in his dealings with others. Already in 12:17–20, when Abram and Sarai sojourned in Egypt during a period of famine in Canaan, Pharaoh complained that Abram's ruse of calling Sarai his sister was less than truthful. Again, in chapter 16, when the plan to have an heir through Sarai's maidservant Hagar results in contempt for Sarai, Abram tells his wife that this is her problem, and she can deal with Hagar however she wants. So Hagar and Ishmael are driven away into the wilderness. This conduct, too, is far from impeccable. And the command of God given in chapter 17 does not remove this trait from Abram's subsequent behavior. In chapter 20, when he sojourns in the country of the Philistines, again he represents Sarah in public as his sister, and Abimelech, the king, charges him with being deceptive in this matter. In chapter 21 Abraham and Abimelech make a treaty. Abraham complains that he has been mistreated by Abimelech's people over the matter of a well he had dug, but Abimelech counters that this is the first he has heard of it. This, too, is not impeccable behavior among the nations. God must have been embarrassed to own Abraham as his ambassador and prophet (Gen. 20:7), the one who would intercede for Abimelech so that he would not die as a penalty for his adultery. The author of Genesis is at pains to show that, in the course of time and in the passing of generations, little things become big things. So later, in Genesis 26:6–11, Isaac also represents his wife Rebekah as his sister; only this time, what was a "white lie" or half-truth in the mouth of his father (Sarah was in fact a half sister of Abram) becomes a black lie in his mouth. In the third generation, Isaac's son Jacob, in turn, is a complete deceiver and shyster. And Jacob, who deceived his father by means of a coat and a goat, was in turn deceived by his sons by means of a coat and a goat. To be sure, Abram has had an altar in Canaan and has called out (i.e., proclaimed) in the name of Yahweh. He has been an ambassador for his God, but he has not represented his God with complete integrity.

Thus the circumstances of chapter 16 are important motivation for the covenant affirmation in chapter 17. Genesis 17:2 begins with a modal verb, which in direct sequence with the commands of the previous verse marks a purpose or result clause: "Walk before me and be blameless so that I may make my covenant between me and you." Obedience is expected of Abram in the covenant relationship. Already in Genesis 12, when Yahweh called Abram and gave him such great promises, there were commands: "Go . . ." and "Be a blessing!" Chapter 15 reiterated the great promises and enshrined them in a covenant. Abram has not demonstrated full integrity, and so, in chapter 17, God comes to affirm his covenant and emphasize, among other things, the need for an obedient son in Abram's Adamic role.

Notice that, in Genesis 17, three times we have the expression *hēqîm bĕrît* (vv. 7, 19, 21) and never once the expression *kārat bĕrît*. This is an absolutely clear indication that Genesis 17 is an event not initiating a covenant but rather affirming one that has been initiated earlier, i.e., in chapter 15. In 17:2 the expression "give a covenant" (*nātan bĕrît*) is a synonym for the more specific term in context, i.e., *hēqîm bĕrît*. So the expression "give a covenant" in 17:2 indicates that God is affirming his covenant and does not mean a new and separate covenant is being initiated.

Williamson is helpful in discussing the relationship of Genesis 15 and 17. He correctly notes the prominence of the nations in this text; the focus on "becoming nations" is, in fact, in both halves of the chapter, in relation to both Abraham and Sarah:

> [4] As for me, this is my covenant with you: You will be the father of many nations. [5] No longer will you be called Abram; your name will be Abraham, for I have made you a father of many nations. [6] I will make you very fruitful; I will make nations of you, and kings will come from you. (Gen. 17:4–6, NIV)

> I will bless her and will surely give you a son by her. I will bless her so that she will be the mother of nations; kings of peoples will come from her. (Gen. 17:16, NIV)

Even Ishmael is promised both nationhood and royalty:

> And as for Ishmael, I have heard you: I will surely bless him; I will make him fruitful and will greatly increase his numbers. He will be the father of twelve rulers, and I will make him into a great nation. (Gen. 17:20, NIV)

In Genesis 17, the royal ideology of the promises in Genesis 12:1–3 comes to the fore, and it seems that not only will Abraham be a blessing to the nations but he will become more than one nation—in fact, a *multitude* of nations. No wonder Paul speaks of "the promise to Abraham and to his seed that he would be the inheritor of the *world*" (Rom. 4:13). He would inherit more than the land of Canaan; he would inherit the world.

Nonetheless, the exegesis of Williamson is faulty because he argues in the end that chapters 15 and 17 are two separate but related covenants.

The pronominal suffix on *bĕrît* in Genesis 17 ("my covenant") pointing to an already established covenant is noteworthy. The noun *bĕrît* has a first person singular pronominal suffix in 47 instances in the Old Testament. It is remarkable that 13 of these, i.e., more than one-quarter, occur in two texts: Genesis 6–9 and 17. Linguistically, a pronominal suffix makes the noun definite, and the grammatical function may be an anaphoric (i.e., a backward-pointing) reference. Careful examination of all instances in the Old Testament shows that in every case but one the reference is anaphoric and refers to an already established covenant.

Williamson's argument that the covenant in chapter 15 is unilateral and the one in chapter 17 is bilateral is based on a misunderstanding. The traditional language describing covenants as being either unconditional or conditional is inadequate. We would argue that God guarantees the faithfulness of both partners in the Abrahamic covenant, but still requires faithful obedience on the part of Abraham to bring the blessing to the nations promised in the covenant. The biblical metanarrative is about God seeking in Adam an obedient son from beginning to end. Chapters 15 and 17 are one and the same covenant, and together these texts present a full-orbed, three-dimensional idea of the one covenant.

There are also difficulties in reading chapter 17 as a separate covenant. If the covenant in chapter 17 is not the one in chapter 15, then the occurrences of the word "covenant" in chapter 17 are referring to the covenant God is about to establish. In 17:9 God asks Abraham to keep his covenant. In verse 10 he explains that the covenant involves circumcision. Then in verse 11 he says that this is for a covenant sign. This approach reduces the covenant keeping to a covenant sign. But if chapter 17 is affirming the covenant in chapter 15, then a sign is supplied for the Abrahamic covenant in general. If, however, chapter 17 is instituting a separate covenant, then the human obligation is reduced to being a covenant sign. Such a reading does not provide a satisfactory understanding.

Williamson's approach is flawed because later texts in both Old and New Testaments never refer to God's dealings with Abraham as "covenants"—*in the plural*. Never in all the historical summaries in the Old Testament (e.g., Nehemiah 9) is there a reference to two Abrahamic covenants. There is only one covenant with Abraham, affirmed to Isaac and Jacob (Ex. 6:4).

We may be confident, then, that just as Genesis 6–9 is an affirmation of God's covenant with creation in Genesis 1–3, so Genesis 17 is an affirmation of God's covenant with Abraham initiated in Genesis 15. Genesis 15 and Genesis 17 correlate respectively with the first three promises and the second three promises of 12:1–3. Abraham has shown a great deal of interest in God's promises to bless him personally with fame and nationhood, but these promises are foundational to the second three promises, to bless all the nations through Abram, and Abraham has not shown any interest in being a blessing to the nations. So Williamson is quite right to note the international emphasis in Genesis 17. Abraham's response to the revelation in Genesis 17 is clear:

> [17] Then Abraham fell on his face and laughed and said to himself, "Shall a child be born to a man who is a hundred years old? Shall Sarah, who is ninety years old, bear a child?" [18] And Abraham said to God, "Oh that Ishmael might live before you!" (Gen. 17:17–18, ESV)

Abraham is quite skeptical about the divine plan and urges God to consider his own attempt to implement God's plan in Genesis 16: "If only Ishmael might live under your blessing!" There is room, indeed, in the blessings promised for Abraham's son Ishmael to develop into a nation that entails great chieftains, but the covenant will be upheld with a son born only to Abraham and Sarah in about a year's time. Abraham laughs at this. He can see how the divine plan would work through Ishmael, but how would life come out of a couple whose bodies are both dead? Yet this is precisely the theme of chapter 17—"I am God *Almighty.* Walk before me and be blameless." The reason for the fourteen-year lapse between chapter 15 and chapter 17 is that Yahweh wants a covenant relationship in which Abraham really knows and understands who he is, and is faithful and loyal precisely at that level of understanding. Not until Abraham has tried everything in his own strength and is completely powerless will he know God as *El Shaddai.*

The narrator is at pains to portray both Noah and Abraham as Adamic figures. The command to Adam to "be fruitful and multiply" is passed on to Noah and becomes for Abraham a promise with the adverb "exceedingly" added to it.

The scope of chapter 17 is bigger than chapter 15 because it is characteristic of the Abraham narrative as a whole for God to answer every question with bigger promises. God also uses cultural means to communicate to his people who he is and what he wants in the relationship, such as a covenantal name change (17:5). But this need not be seen as any reason to consider Genesis 15 and 17 different covenants.

Third, in verses 7b and 8b of chapter 17, note that the covenant is with Abraham and his descendants:

> [7] And I will establish my covenant between me and you and your offspring after you throughout their generations for an everlasting covenant,

to be God to you and to your offspring after you. [8] And I will give to you and to your offspring after you the land of your sojournings, all the land of Canaan, for an everlasting possession, *and I will be their God.* (ESV)

Yahweh will be the God of Abraham and the God of his descendants. He will be their God. The italicized words constitute the first instance in Scripture of the Covenant Formula (at least the first half of it). We find the full formula in Exodus 6:7:

> I will take you as my own people, and I will be your God. Then you will know that I am the LORD your God, who brought you out from under the yoke of the Egyptians. (NIV)

Sometimes only the first half of the formula (A) is found, sometimes only the second half (B), and sometimes the entire formula (C):

Formula A: I will be your God
Formula B: You will be my people
Formula C: I will be your God and you will be my people = A + B

Whenever this phrase is used in Scripture, the author is emphasizing covenant in a highly conscious manner. At the heart of the covenant is this relationship: "I will be their God, and they will be my people." Although this phrase occurs here in Genesis 17 where the term *bĕrît* abounds, in many passages of the Bible the identical phrase or words occur where the term "covenant" is not found, and it always signals covenant as the subject and topic of discussion. Significant examples are 2 Corinthians 6:16 and Revelation 21:3:

> What agreement is there between the temple of God and idols? For we are the temple of the living God. As God has said: "I will live with them and walk among them, and I will be their God, and they will be my people." (2 Cor. 6:16, NIV)

> And I heard a loud voice from the throne saying, "Behold, the dwelling place of God is with man. He will dwell with them, and they will be his people, and God himself will be with them as their God." (Rev. 21:3, ESV)

Neither Paul nor John employ the word "covenant," but the Covenant Formula communicates this idea powerfully as they describe and discuss the new covenant in these texts.

Fourth, Abraham is given a covenant sign. In the Old Testament, it is common for a covenant to be accompanied by a physical sign, although by no means is a physical sign a necessary or obligatory part of covenant making. We saw that the rainbow was the sign of the covenant with Noah, and later the Sabbath is the sign of the covenant with Israel at Sinai. Abraham is commanded to practice circumcision as the physical sign of the covenant God was affirming between him and his descendants (Gen. 17:9–14).

The central question here is, what does circumcision indicate or signify? According to Genesis 17:14, this sign defines membership in the covenant community:

> Any uncircumcised male, who has not been circumcised in the flesh, will be cut off from his people; he has broken my covenant. (NIV)

The question remains, however: How does circumcision signify or symbolize belonging to the covenant community? Unfortunately the Christian church has had largely mistaken ideas and understandings of the rite of circumcision, mainly because the proper background to the meaning of this rite was not adequately researched. Some cultures circumcised children at puberty as a rite of passage from childhood to manhood. Abraham and his descendants are to circumcise children at eight days old. Correct understanding must be illuminated by the background of the ancient Near East and, in particular—in view of the connection between Abraham and Egypt and Israel and Egypt—the Egyptian background.

First, Egyptian circumcision was an initiation rite for priests, showing that they were completely devoted to the service of their gods.

Second, just as the king-priest was the son of the god in Egypt, and was consecrated to him through circumcision, Israel as the firstborn son of Yahweh (Ex. 4:22–23) has undergone and will undergo circumcision (Josh. 5:2–9) in order to be consecrated to his service. The Egyptian background would reveal to Israel that they indeed belonged to Yahweh as his firstborn son, since they had undergone circumcision just as the Pharaoh had.

Third, only the priests were obligated to be circumcised in Egypt, but in Israel *every* male was to be circumcised on the eighth day (Gen. 17:12), signifying that Abraham's family consists of priests. Later in the story, Israel is called a *kingdom of priests* and a holy nation (Ex. 19:6). The phrase "holy nation" also means consecrated to God or belonging to God and would complement the meaning of "kingdom of priests." Because they are a kingdom of priests, circumcision is the appropriate sign for the people of Israel, for it will remind every male Israelite that he is a priest, specially consecrated to Yahweh and his service. The family of Abraham and Sarah were to be signified as the priesthood of Yahweh from birth.

Contrary to the culture in the ancient Near East, where, as noted, males were circumcised as adults or at puberty, males in Abraham's family were to be circumcised just after birth, at eight days old. The eighth day derives its significance from the account of creation, where God made the world in six days and rested on the seventh. Since the seventh day is indefinite, the eighth day is the beginning of the new creation, and this fits with the new creation imagery connected with Abraham as a new Adam.

There is also a negative meaning for this rite. Like the dismembering ritual in Genesis 15:7–18 (cf. Jer. 34:17–20), circumcision graphically portrayed the covenant curse of excision and threatened the cutting off of descendants (Gen. 17:14). Although other nations besides Israel practiced circumcision, the Israelites were the only nation to completely cut off and remove the foreskin. Thus the negative meaning is that circumcision symbolizes being cut off from the covenant community for disloyalty to the covenant demand to "walk before me and be blameless" (Gen. 17:1). This negative aspect of circumcision is clearly supported in the text by verse 14, already cited.

Circumcision, then, was a ritual required of Abraham and his family, signifying membership in the covenant community. Negatively, the person who remained uncircumcised would be cut off from the covenant community. Positively, the rite of circumcision symbolized complete devotion to the service of God as a priesthood. The covenant sign underlines Abraham's Adamic role as a priest in his calling to bring blessing to the nations. Paul in Romans 4:11 rightly sees the obedience of Abraham described in Genesis 17:23–27 as an expression of the righteousness of faith which, according to 15:6, characterized his relation to Yahweh.

ABRAHAM'S OBEDIENCE AND GOD'S MIGHTY OATH
Genesis 18–19

A short time—no more than two to four months—after the covenant affirmation in Genesis 17, Abraham is visited by three men at Hebron. Turns out the mysterious strangers are Yahweh and two of his agents or messengers; the text describes this visitation in the same way that we find in earlier communications from God ("the Lord appeared to Abram"). In Genesis 15, the communication came by way of a vision. In Genesis 12:1, 7, and 17:1, the manner of divine revelation is left unspecified. Here, in 18:1, God appears to Abraham as a human.

Abraham urges the strangers to accept hospitality, and they accede to his request. While the men are eating and Abraham is serving them, they ask him where Sarah, his wife, is at that moment. Abraham answers curtly, "Here in the tent." No doubt cultural protocol in the ancient Near East would not allow men to address a man's wife directly. A conversation of sorts can be arranged with her behind the door of the tent. Suddenly the verb of speaking switches from third person plural to third person singular, and the speaker repeats the promise (of becoming [a] great nation[s]) made particular and specific in Genesis 17—of a *son* being given *through Sarah* within a year. Sarah laughs at this. The narrator informs us that she is not only postmenopausal but is no longer enjoying physical relations with her husband: they are just that *old*. Yahweh asks Abraham why Sarah laughed, since nothing is impossible for him, and again he repeats his promise of a son being born through her. Although the question is directed to Abraham, it is really intended for Sarah, who, out of fear, denies that she laughed. Thus, here, Sarah lies out of fear just as her husband, Abraham, lied out of fear when he entered Egypt and falsely declared that Sarai was only his sister.

The interchange between the Lord and Sarah is important background to the next scene in this episode. The visitors depart, heading for an "overlook" of Sodom with a Scots send-off by Abraham (i.e., he walks with them partway). Again Yahweh opens the conversation, this time with these words:

[17] The Lord said, "Shall I hide from Abraham what I am about to do, [18] seeing that Abraham shall surely become a great and mighty nation, and all the nations of the earth shall be blessed in him?" (Gen. 18:17–18, esv)

Yahweh opens with a rhetorical question—should he hide (lit., cover) his plan (of judging the cities of the plain) from Abraham? Of course not! Verse 18 expresses the motivation or reasons why Yahweh needs to be open and transparent. First, the statement that Abraham will become a great nation corresponds to the first set of promises in Genesis 12:1–3; and second, the statement that all the nations of the earth shall be blessed in him corresponds to the second set of promises in Genesis 12:1–3. The first set of promises was enshrined and solemnized in the covenant made in Genesis 15, while the second set was emphasized in the covenant affirmation of Genesis 17. Thus these two statements circumscribe the fact that God has a covenant relationship with Abram, and this type of relationship especially requires integrity, i.e., openness and transparency in the context of faithfulness and loyal love. These are precisely characteristics that Abraham and his wife, Sarah, have not shown in relationship with fellow humans or with God, as is evidenced by the call to be blameless in Genesis 17:1 and by the lie of Sarah in Genesis 18:15. The rhetorical question, then, shows that Yahweh is modeling for Abraham and Sarah the kind of covenant relationship he would like to have with them. This is clear as Yahweh goes on to explain his motivation for revealing to Abraham his plan (still veiled, as far as the reader is concerned):

> [19] "For I have chosen him, that he may command his children and his household after him to keep the way of the LORD by doing righteousness and justice, so that the LORD may bring to Abraham what he has promised him." [20] Then the LORD said, "Because the outcry against Sodom and Gomorrah is great and their sin is very grave, [21] I will go down to see whether they have done altogether according to the outcry that has come to me. And if not, I will know." (Gen. 18:19–21, ESV)

Several points in these verses must be either clarified or stressed. Normally in prose, when the words "justice" and "righteousness" are coordinated, they form a single concept or idea: social justice. This is a figure of speech known as a "hendiadys," one concept expressed through two words. The word pair becomes an idiom expressing a single thought that is both different from and greater than just putting the two words together. Just as one cannot analyze the idiomatic expression in English "by and large" by studying "by" and "large," so one cannot determine the meaning of this expression by analyzing "justice" and "righteousness" individually. Later on in the Old Testament, this word pair becomes a way of summarizing the requirements and stipulations of the Mosaic covenant, which in turn are an expression of the character of Yahweh. This defines the content of what is meant here by social justice in contrast to how the term might commonly be used today.

According to the grammar in Genesis 18:19, "practicing social justice" is the manner in which Abraham and his family are "to keep the way of Yahweh." And this "way of Yahweh" has already been clearly shown to Abraham. Yahweh began by modeling for Abraham the openness and transparency that is necessary in a covenant relationship, i.e., what it means to be blameless ("Shall I hide from Abraham what I am about to do?").

It seems in the flow of the narrative plot structure that as Abraham begins to plead with Yahweh not to destroy the righteous with the wicked in an attempt to avert destruction of the cities of the plain—and save Lot—he is taking his very first steps in practicing social justice, and this is also the beginning of being a blessing to the nations. Thus the instruction of Genesis 17 is effective in shifting his focus from the first three promises of Genesis 12:1–3 to also give attention to the second three: "in you all the nations of the earth will be blessed."

The reader is invited to compare and contrast Genesis 14 and 18, since in both of these events Abraham is seeking to rescue his nephew Lot, who is in trouble. Genesis 18, however, differs significantly from Genesis 14, where Abraham with his 318 household servants rescues Lot from the marauding kings. Here Abraham faces not the Big Bad Boys from the East, but Yahweh himself, God Almighty. It is God who is determined to judge the wicked cities. To rescue Lot this time, Abraham must abandon his own shrewd schemes of subterfuge (surprise attack by night; Gen. 14:15). Instead he must buy into the "way of Yahweh," i.e., the character of Yahweh himself, in the covenant relationship. He must embrace "the way of Yahweh" and practice social justice. He cannot call for mercy upon Lot solely on the basis that he is a relative. He must plead for "the righteous" as a group and call upon God as a just judge who would not destroy the righteous along with the wicked. Thus he intercedes *as a priest for the nations* on the basis of God's own character. Yahweh is patient as he intercedes and gradually reduces the required number of righteous people in the city six times, from fifty to just ten. Apparently, there were only six people who might deserve to be called righteous: Lot, his wife, his two daughters, and their fiancés (for the divine agents of judgment sought to extract them from the city before the destruction). As the sorry story of Lot at the end of Genesis 19 shows, Abraham succeeded in saving two entire (future) nations: Moab and Ammon. Abraham is beginning to be a blessing to the (other) nations.

In Genesis 22 the promises given to Abraham in Genesis 12, enshrined in a covenant in chapter 15 and in the covenant affirmed in chapter 17, are now *further* confirmed by a mighty oath—the first time in the narrative that Yahweh *swears* an oath:

[15] And the angel of the LORD called to Abraham a second time from heaven [16] and said, "By myself I have sworn, declares the LORD, because you have done this and have not withheld your son, your only son, [17] I

will surely bless you, and I will surely multiply your offspring as the stars of heaven and as the sand that is on the seashore. And your offspring shall possess the gate of his enemies, [18] and in your offspring [seed] shall all the nations of the earth be blessed, because you have obeyed my voice." (Gen. 22:15–18, esv)

Note that in this text—as well as in four further texts (Gen. 26:3, 5, 24 [2x])—the fulfillment of the promises is directly tied to Abraham's obedience. Once again we see that the categories of conditional covenant versus unconditional covenant are not satisfactory. And a solution that separates Genesis 15 and 17 into two separate covenants is clearly a case of imposing one's system on the flow of the biblical narrative. What we must conclude from the narratives as a whole is that Yahweh completely guarantees fulfillment of the obligations for both partners/sides of the covenant, but in the end, this will also entail an obedient son.

TENSIONS IN THE METANARRATIVE

Significant tensions have been introduced into the plot structure of the metanarrative in the course of the unfolding of the story of Abraham. The larger story began with creation and the first man in covenant with the Lord God as obedient son and royal vice-regent over the world. Human disobedience brought chaos and death. God made a new start after the flood with a brand-new world and a second Adam. Here, too, we saw that the human partner was not faithful in the covenant relationship. Divine grace alone preserves the world.

So out of the chaos leading to Babel, God begins another new creation with another new Adam, Abraham and his family. Abraham is depicted in the narratives as a new Adam placed in Canaan, a new Eden. From the metanarrative to this point, we now know that the human partner not only will not but *cannot* be faithful in the covenant relationship. We also now know that a fresh, new start is a nonsolution to the original problem of human disloyalty and disobedience that resulted in the arrival of death in the creation.

Nevertheless, God calls Abram and makes huge promises concerning blessing in his life and salvation for the entire world through him. Later, in Genesis 15, these big promises are strengthened by a covenant, although Abram still has nothing to show from God's word. Although this covenant is patterned in general after ancient Near Eastern treaties, strangely God undertakes the self-maledictory oath for both partners in the covenant. This is completely unheard of in Abraham's world and introduces another tension. Since we know that the human partner will not demonstrate complete devotion and full obedience within the covenant relationship, God seems to be guaranteeing only his own death at this point. How can God die? We understand how this works from the end of the story, but at this stage, we must allow this tension in the narrative.

Yet as Genesis 17:2 shows (as well as subsequent texts such as Gen. 18:19; 22:18; and 26:5, where God affirms his covenant [later confirmed by a mighty oath]), God still requires an obedient son in the covenant relationship and bases fulfillment of the promises not only upon himself but also upon Abraham's obedience and, indeed, upon the future obedience of Abraham's family, Israel. In sum, Abraham was not a perfect covenant partner and badly represented Yahweh to the world of that time in a number of ways. His lack of complete devotion and obedience points to the fact that another is coming who will be obedient in every respect.

There are theological tensions as well as tensions in the narrative plot structure. We wonder how another divine-human covenant relationship can survive, given that disloyalty is *endemic* in the human partner, i.e., the human partner is unfaithful *by nature*. The narrative assures the reader that this covenant is undergirded by the mighty promises of the Almighty. God guarantees the covenant promises and yet he also requires an obedient son in the covenant relationship.

All of these tensions are important to the later plot structure of the metanarrative, and we must not attempt to remove them through defending our systems of theology and reading things into the text. These tensions must be allowed to stand. We must let the text stand over us; we must not stand over the text to judge what can and cannot be allowed in the story.

THE PURPOSE OF THE ABRAHAMIC COVENANT— HOW THE GRAND STORY UNFOLDS

Why did God make a covenant with Abraham? And how is this covenant, made so long ago, relevant to us today? Exegesis of the relevant texts has shown that, although the cultural-historical setting and language of Genesis 12–26 differ from Genesis 1–3 or Genesis 6–9, the main idea is still that God is establishing his rule in the context of a covenant relationship. Abraham and his descendants will be a light to the nations in this matter.

Looking backward and forward in the canon of Scripture, two things must be said about the covenant with Abraham. First, the covenant with Abraham is the basis for all of God's dealings with the human race from this point on, and the basis for all of his later plans and purposes in history. Thus the covenants (with creation, with Noah, with Abraham) are the backbone of the metanarrative plot structure of the Bible. A quick overview of the Old Testament demonstrates this.

The book of Genesis ends with Israel, the family of Abraham, becoming a great and numerous people. The promise of descendants is being fulfilled.

The point of the book of Exodus will be to add, by way of redemption from slavery, the gift of the land. So the covenant with Abraham is the basis for delivering Israel from slavery in Egypt. Israel becomes a great nation, and God makes a covenant with the nation at Sinai (Deut. 7:7–9).

The Mosaic covenant at Sinai is, in turn, the basis for God's covenant with David. The king of Israel is the administrator and mediator of the Mosaic covenant, representing God's rule to the people and representing the people as a whole (2 Sam. 7:22–24).

As the story unfolds, however, it is marked by divine faithfulness on the one hand and human unfaithfulness on the other. At every point along the way, it seems that God's plan is doomed to failure. Israel is a major bottleneck in the plan of God to bless the nations. How can blessing flow through her to the world when she is just as riddled with sin? Paul explains this in Galatians 3:

> [8] The Scripture foresaw that God would justify the Gentiles by faith, and announced the gospel in advance to Abraham: "All nations will be blessed through you." [9] So those who have faith are blessed along with Abraham, the man of faith.
>
> [10] All who rely on observing the law are under a curse, for it is written: "Cursed is everyone who does not continue to do everything written in the Book of the Law." [11] Clearly no one is justified before God by the law, because, "The righteous will live by faith." [12] The law is not based on faith; on the contrary, "The man who does these things will live by them." [13] Christ redeemed us from the curse of the law by becoming a curse for us, for it is written: "Cursed is everyone who is hung on a tree." [14] He redeemed us in order that the blessing given to Abraham might come to the Gentiles through Christ Jesus, so that by faith we might receive the promise of the Spirit. (Gal. 3:8–14, NIV)

When we come to the time of Jesus, Israel is under a curse because they have been unfaithful to the Israelite covenant. Do they want to be an instrument of blessing to the nations? No, they want to raise an army of guerrillas who will conquer and smash the might of Rome, drive the nations away, and bring glory to Israel by setting her over the world. And so God sent Jesus to fulfill his promises. First, Jesus had to deliver Israel from the curse and put her back into a right relationship with God. Then, as King of Israel, he had to do what the nation as a whole had failed to do: bring blessing to the nations. He accomplished both by dying on the cross. Several texts in the New Testament specifically connect the coming of Jesus Christ with the Abrahamic covenant. First, Luke 1:54–55:

> [54] He has helped his servant Israel,
>   remembering to be merciful
> [55] to Abraham and his descendants forever,
>   even as he said to our fathers.

Mary's Song of Praise in Luke 1 describes the birth of her son as God "remembering mercy." Behind the Greek word that is rendered "mercy" is the Hebrew term *hesed,* which has to do with fulfilling covenant obligations. The covenant promises being fulfilled are the ones made to Abraham, according to Mary.

Then, in verses 69–75, at the birth of John the Baptist, Zechariah, the father, regains speech and opens his mouth in a prophecy:

> [69] He has raised up a horn of salvation for us
>   in the house of his servant David
> [70] (as he said through his holy prophets of long ago),
> [71] salvation from our enemies
>   and from the hand of all who hate us—
> [72] to show mercy to our fathers
>   and to remember his holy covenant,
>   [73] the oath he swore to our father Abraham:
> [74] to rescue us from the hand of our enemies,
>   and to enable us to serve him without fear
>   [75] in holiness and righteousness before him all our days.
>   (Luke 1:69–75, NIV)

He speaks here of God fulfilling his promises to Abraham in bringing help to Israel.

Then, in Acts 3:24–26, after the beggar is healed in the Porch of Solomon, Peter preaches at the temple and announces good news through God's servant Jesus, crucified and risen from the dead:

[24] Indeed, all the prophets from Samuel on, as many as have spoken, have foretold these days. [25] And you are heirs of the prophets and of the covenant God made with your fathers. He said to Abraham, "Through your offspring all peoples on earth will be blessed." [26] When God raised up his servant, he sent him first to you to bless you by turning each of you from your wicked ways (NIV).

The good news is that God has fulfilled his promises to Abraham and sent Jesus "to bless you by turning each of you from your wicked ways." Thus it is clear, from even a few texts in the New Testament, that the covenant with Abraham is the basis and foundation for the gospel message announcing forgiveness of sins and justification through Jesus Christ.

No doubt the claim that the covenants, and in particular the Abrahamic covenant, form(s) the backbone of the metanarrative will be criticized. One problem faced by many biblical theologies is that they comprehend the history and the prophets, but where do the Psalms and Wisdom texts fit in the picture? Yet books like the Psalms are founded on the Abrahamic covenant and the Mosaic and Davidic covenants flowing from it. Two examples will suffice.

Psalm 47 is a brief psalm inviting the nations to rejoice because Yahweh is supreme sovereign over all peoples and has subdued them under Israel. At the end, we read:

[8] God reigns over the nations;
    God sits on his holy throne.
[9] The princes of the peoples gather
    as the people of the God of Abraham.
For the shields of the earth belong to God;
    he is highly exalted! (Ps. 47:8–9, ESV)

Note how "the princes of the peoples [plural] gather as the people [singular] of the God of Abraham." Non-Israelite nations are included in the one people of God. The mention of the "God of Abraham" is sufficient to remind those singing this psalm that the inclusion of the Gentiles into the one people of God can be possible only through Abraham becoming father in a spiritual sense, i.e., the model of faith, for a company of nations, as Genesis 35:11 intends.

Psalm 117, although the shortest in the entire Psalter, the Hymnal of ancient Israel, is perhaps the most profound because it functions like a dissertation abstract, encapsulating in as few words as possible the burden of the entire book of Psalms:

[1] Praise the LORD, all nations!
  Extol him, all peoples!
[2] For great is his steadfast love toward us,
  and the faithfulness of the LORD endures forever.
  Praise the LORD! (ESV)

The word pair "steadfast love" (*ḥesed*) and "faithfulness" (*'ĕmet*) is actually a summary of the behavior required of both parties in the Mosaic covenant/Torah. This shortest psalm sums up the whole Psalter: Yahweh is to be praised by the nations for his covenantal faithfulness and love. The exegetical issue debated is the identification of the referent of the pronoun "us" in verse 2. Does it refer only to Israel, or to Israel and the nations? If, however, the standard view is taken, the command to the nations to praise the Lord is given *by* Israel. The "us" could then be taken to refer to Israel. Faithfulness and loyal love is what Israel has experienced in covenant relationship with God. But then, due to God's faithful, loyal love, the blessing flows to the nations by virtue of the Abrahamic covenant. This indeed seems to be Paul's point in Romans 15:11. Thus, in the end, there hardly seems to be much difference between the two positions.

Second, the purpose of the covenants is for God to reveal himself. After the covenant with Noah, we know that everything depends on divine favor. Humans will not and cannot demonstrate faithfulness in the covenant relationship with God that is fundamental to life in this world. So, a friend, Don Wood, asked, "If everything depends on God's grace, then why such a long story?" Why doesn't God just zap us with his grace in Genesis 12? We know for sure by this point in the metanarrative that chaos and death will be overcome only by divine grace. The answer to this question is that God wants to reveal himself. John Walton explains:

> God has a plan in history that he is sovereignly executing. The goal of that plan is for him to be in relationship with the people whom he has created. It would be difficult for people to enter into a relationship with a God whom they do not know. If his nature were concealed, obscured, or distorted, an honest relationship would be impossible. In order to clear the way for this relationship, then, God has undertaken as a primary objective a program of self-revelation. He wants people to know him. The mechanism that drives this program is the covenant, and the instrument is Israel. The purpose of the covenant is to reveal God.[2]

---

[2] John H. Walton, *Covenant: God's Purpose, God's Plan* (Grand Rapids, MI: Zondervan, 1994), 24.

Pentateuch: the first five books of the
Bible

Sinai: ②Mount, the moutain, in ~~the~~ S. Sinai,
of uncertain identity, on which Moses
received the law. Ex.
A desert and a mountain

Chapter 7

THE MOSAIC COVENANT—
EXODUS/SINAI

Central to the book of Exodus—and indeed to the entire Pentateuch—is the covenant made between Yahweh and Israel at Sinai, comprised in chapters 19–24. The eighteen chapters preceding describe the release of Israel from bondage and slavery in Egypt and the journey through the wilderness to Sinai. Chapters 25–40 are devoted to the construction of a place of worship as the appropriate recognition of the divine kingship established through the covenant.

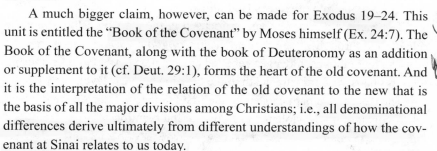

A much bigger claim, however, can be made for Exodus 19–24. This unit is entitled the "Book of the Covenant" by Moses himself (Ex. 24:7). The Book of the Covenant, along with the book of Deuteronomy as an addition or supplement to it (cf. Deut. 29:1), forms the heart of the old covenant. And it is the interpretation of the relation of the old covenant to the new that is the basis of all the major divisions among Christians; i.e., all denominational differences derive ultimately from different understandings of how the covenant at Sinai relates to us today.

Where and how Exodus 19–24 fits into the larger story of Scripture will be briefly detailed at both the beginning and the end of this chapter—framing as bookends our analysis of the covenant at Sinai. In between, attention will be given to the literary structure of Exodus 19–24, and afterwards exegesis will be focused on the divine purpose of the covenant in Exodus 19:5–6, the first four of the Ten Commandments, and the ceremony of covenant ratification in Exodus 24:1–11.

EXODUS 19–24 WITHIN THE LARGER
STORY OF SCRIPTURE

As noted at the beginning of chapter 6, the biblical narrative begins with a creator God who is the maker of our world and, indeed, of the entire universe. We humans are the crowning achievement of his creative work. There is a difference, moreover, between humans and animals, in fact, between us and all other creatures: we alone have been made as the image of this creator God and have been given special tasks to perform on behalf of the Creator.

Exegesis of Genesis 1:26–28 shows that the divine image is functional, relational, and structural and speaks of human life in terms of a covenant with God on the one hand, and with the creation on the other hand. The former relationship may be captured by the term "sonship," while the latter finds its reflex in the terms "kingship" and "servanthood." We noted previously that in the ninth-century Aramaic Tell Fekheriyeh Inscription, *ṣalmā'* ("image") refers to the king's majestic power and rule in relation to his subjects, while *demûthā'* ("likeness") refers to the king's petitionary role and relation to the deity. The ancient Near Eastern data confirm, correspond to, and illustrate precisely the terms used in the biblical text.

Furthermore, as Genesis 2:4–25 shows, the Adamic son is like a priest in a garden sanctuary. He must first learn the ways of God in order to display and exercise the rule of God as God himself would.

The biblical narrative, then, is focused at the start on establishing the rule of God through covenant relationship: *kingdom through covenant*.

The first humans, however, rebelled against the creator God. As a result, there is chaos, discord, and death in the creation at every level.

The destructive path chosen by the first humans led to a downward spiral of corruption and violence until divine intervention was required. God judged the human race by a flood and made a new beginning with Noah and his family. Noah is presented in the narrative as a new Adam. As soon as the dry land appears out of the chaos of the floodwaters, Noah is placed there and is commanded to be fruitful and multiply (Gen. 9:1); i.e., he is given Adam's commission or mandate. The correspondence to Genesis 1 is striking. Eventually, however, the family of Noah ends up in the same chaos and corruption as the family of the first Adam. With the Tower of Babel, the nations are lost and scattered over the face of the earth.

So, God made another new start, this time with Abraham. Abraham and his family, called Israel, is another Adam, who will be God's true humanity. God makes great promises to Abraham in Genesis 12. These promises are enshrined eventually in a covenant made with him and his descendants in chapters 15 and 17 and confirmed by a mighty oath in chapter 22.

The first of God's promises to Abram, "I will make you into a great nation," employs the term *gôy* in Hebrew, while the last of God's six promises, "all the clans/families of the earth will be blessed in you," employs instead the term *mišpāḥâ*. This contrast in terms carries forward the focus on kingdom through covenant.

Thus, Abraham and Israel have inherited an Adamic role. Yahweh refers to the nation as his *son* in Exodus 4:22–23. The divine purpose in the covenant established between God and Israel at Sinai is unfolded in Exodus 19:3–6. As a kingdom of priests, they will function to make the ways of God known to the nations and also to bring the nations into a right relationship to God. Israel will display to the rest of the world within its covenant community the kind of relationships, first to God and then to one another and to the physical world, that God intended originally for all of humanity. In fact, through Abraham's family, God purposes and plans to bring blessing to all the nations of the world. In this way, through the family of Abraham, through Israel, his "last" Adam, he will bring about a resolution of the sin and death caused by the first Adam. Since Israel is located geographically on the one and only communications link between the great superpowers of the ancient world (Egypt and Mesopotamia), in this position she will show the nations how to have a right relationship to God, how to treat each other in a truly human way, and how to faithfully steward the earth's resources. This is the meaning of Israel's sonship.

The promises of God to Abraham focused on two things: descendants and land. When we come to the books of Exodus to Deuteronomy, which constitute the Mosaic covenant or covenant with Israel, we have the fulfillment of these promises. First, God has greatly increased the descendants of Abraham so that they are innumerable, like the sand upon the seashore or the stars of the night sky. Second, he has given them the land of Canaan.

God's plan and purpose, however, has not changed. He wants to bless the descendants of Abraham and, through them, all the nations. In fact, his plan is to restore his broken and ruined creation through Israel. As they come out of Egypt and before they enter the land, God makes an agreement with Israel. The purpose of this agreement or covenant is to enable them to enjoy the blessings he wants to give them and to be the blessing to the other nations. This covenant will show them how to be his true humanity. It will direct, guide, and lead them to have a right relationship with God and a right relationship with everyone else in the covenant community. It will also teach them how to have a right relationship to all the creation, to be good stewards of the earth's resources. We might say, then, that the Mosaic covenant is given at this time to administer the fulfillment of the divine promises to Abraham and to the nation as a whole, and through them to the entire world.

LABELING COVENANTS

Frequently this covenant is entitled "the covenant at Sinai," but what is the biblical terminology? From the point of view of the New Testament, i.e., Latinized English for "new covenant," it is called the "old covenant" in 2 Corinthians 3:14 (and compare v. 15). Hebrews 8–9 also uses the term "first" for this covenant. In the Old Testament, however, it is commonly called the Torah (law) or the Torah (law) of Moses (Ex. 24:12).

In Scripture, covenants are normally named according to the human partner. The covenant in Genesis 6–9 is between God and Noah. This is expanded to include his family and, through them, all of humanity. It is fair to call this "the covenant with Noah." The covenant in Genesis 15 and 17 is called the "covenant with Abram" in 15:18. Since it is passed directly on to Isaac and Jacob, it is called the covenant with Isaac and also the covenant with Jacob in Leviticus 26:42. Later we find the phrase "the covenant with the fathers" (Deut. 4:31), referring to Abraham, Isaac, and Jacob. Note that the term "covenant" is always singular. It is never "the covenants with the fathers." We can conveniently and legitimately call it the "covenant with Abram/Abraham." The covenant made at Sinai is simply called "the Book of the Covenant" in Exodus 24:7. In Exodus 34:27 this same covenant is with Moses and with Israel. Hence some scholars have called it the Mosaic covenant. It could just as well be called the Israelite covenant or covenant with Israel. In Deuteronomy 29:1 it is called the covenant made at Horeb (= Sinai). Later, when God makes a covenant with David, it is called just that, his "covenant with David" (2 Chron. 13:5; 21:7; Ps. 89:3; Jer. 33:21). Finally, God makes what is called a "new covenant" in Jeremiah 31:31.

THE LITERARY STRUCTURE OF EXODUS 19–24

One of the reasons why both popular and scholarly discussions of the relation between the Old Testament and the New have resulted in futile debates over false dichotomies and issues is *a failure to consider properly the literary shape of this text*. Instead, what is foisted upon the text is a framework or structure it does not clearly indicate itself or possess.

Outline of Exodus 19–40

The broad outline and shape of the text is indicated by headings and the use of specific terms. At the heart of the text are two sections: (1) the "Ten Words" in chapter 20 and (2) the "Judgments" (or "laws"/"ordinances") in chapters 21–23. *These are the actual headings in the text.* Exodus 20:1 introduces the matter simply: "And God spoke all these words." While Christians commonly refer to this section as the "Ten Commandments," the commands that form the basis of the covenant are simply referred to as the "Ten Words" in Exodus 34:28 and Deuteronomy 4:13; 10:4. The precise expression "the Ten Commandments" occurs nowhere in the Old Testament, although in a general way the Ten Words are included when reference is made to the commands of Yahweh. They are frequently referred to as commandments in the New Testament (Matthew 5; Matt. 19:17; Mark 10:19; Luke 18:20; Rom. 7:7–8; 13:9; 1 Tim. 1:9–10), and that is why the preferred term today is the Ten Commandments. So first we have just "the Words." Then, in Exodus 21–23, we have the "Judgments": 21:1 is clearly a heading for this entire section.

Not only the headings but also the contents clearly distinguish the two sections. The Ten Words are presented as absolute commands or prohibitions, usually in the second person singular. They are general injunctions not related to a specific social situation. They could be described as prescriptive law, since no fines or punishments are specified. As an example, "You [singular] shall not steal!" The construction in Hebrew is durative and nonspecific. You shall not steal today, not tomorrow, not this week, not this month, not this year—as a general rule, never! By contrast, the Judgments are presented as case laws. These are presented as if they were court decisions functioning as precedents. They are normally in the format of conditional sentences. Here the fundamental principles embodied in the Ten Words are applied in particular to specific social contexts. They could be described as descriptive law, since they impose fines and punishments. As an example, Exodus 21:28–32 addresses the case where a bull gores a human and considers whether or not this was the animal's habit. More will be said about these case laws later. So chapter 20 and chapters 21–23 constitute specific sections of the covenant, simply labeled "the words" and "the judgments":

The Ten Words (Ex. 20:1; 34:28; Deut. 4:13)
- absolute commands, usually second person singular prohibition
- general injunctions not related to a specific social situation
- prescriptive law—no fines or punishments mentioned

The Judgments (Ordinances, NASB; Laws, NIV)
- case decisions, case laws, judicial precedents
- the fundamental principles embodied in the Ten Commandments are applied in particular to a specific social context
- descriptive law imposing fines and punishments (usually in the form of "if . . . then" statements or conditional sentences)

These two distinct sections to the covenant are clearly referred to in chapter 24, where the covenant ratification ceremony is described. Note carefully the particular terms used in verses 1–8 of chapter 24 as follows. Chapter 24:1, according to the clause pattern in the Hebrew text as well as the topic, connects and directly follows 20:21–22. In verses 21–26 of chapter 20 and verses 1–2 of chapter 24, Yahweh speaks to Moses from the cloud on Mount Sinai and gives instructions concerning altars and who will ascend the mountain for the covenant ratification meal. In 24:3 Moses comes and gives a report to the people: "And Moses came and reported to the people all the words and all the judgments, and all the people responded with one voice, 'All the words which Yahweh has spoken we will do.'" Note that Moses reported "all the words" and "all the judgments." These two terms clearly refer to the "Ten Words" in chapter 20:2–17 and the "Judgments" in chapters 21–23. When the people say, "All the words which Yahweh has spoken we will do," the term "the words" is an abbreviated form of the expression "all the words and all the judgments" occurring earlier in the verse. Similarly in the next verse, 24:4, we read, "And Moses wrote all the words of Yahweh." Here, again, "the words of Yahweh" is a short way of saying "the words and the judgments." The shortening of long titles is typical in this culture. Much later, the Hebrew Canon, whose full title is "the Law and the Prophets and the Writings," may be simply shortened to "the Law." For example, Paul says that he is quoting from "the Law" and then cites a passage from Isaiah (1 Cor. 14:21). So "Law" must be short for "Law and Prophets."

Alternatively, since "the judgments" are simply unfolding "the ten words" in practical situations, the expression "the words" in 24:3 and 4 may refer to the whole (words and judgments) by specifying just "the words." So the two parts or sections of the covenant are written down by Moses. And this is called "the Book of the Covenant" in 24:7.

Chapters 19 and 24 form the bookends to this "Book of the Covenant." At the beginning, chapter 19 provides the setting in space and time, the divine purpose of the covenant, and the preparation of the people for the revelation of Yahweh at Mount Sinai. At the end, chapter 24 describes the ceremony of covenant ratification. Following this, chapters 25–40 describe the construction of a place of worship, showing the proper response to the divine kingship established among the people by means of the covenant. Just as Genesis 1 establishes divine rule via covenant, followed by the priority of worship in sanctuary in Genesis 2, so the book of Exodus establishes God as King in the midst of Israel, followed by the priority of worship for the nation as God's Adamic son.

The shape and structure of Exodus 19–24, then, is clearly marked in the text. Chapters 20–23 constitute "the Book of the Covenant" consisting of "the Words" (chapter 20) and "the Judgments" (chapters 21–23). Chapters 19 and 24 frame the Book of the Covenant as bookends, with chapter 19 providing the background and setting and chapter 24 describing the ceremony of covenant ratification.

THE DIVINE PURPOSE OF THE COVENANT (EXODUS 19:5–6)

As already stated, chapter 19 provides the background to the Book of the Covenant (Exodus 19–24) and acts as a bookend on the opening side of the covenant document. Israel arrives at Mount Sinai in her travels through the desert to the Promised Land. Central to the chapter is the flurry of movement by Moses going up and down the mountain. Three sequences of up and down dominate the section: (1) up (19:3) and down (v. 7); (2) up (v. 8) and down (v. 14); and (3) up (v. 20) and down (v. 25). These three sequences form the boundaries of three sections within the chapter delimiting (1) the divine purpose of the covenant, (2) the preparation of the people to meet Yahweh and receive his revelation and Torah (a word simply meaning direction or instruction), and (3) the actual epiphany of God on the mountain. The literary structure of the chapter, then, is as follows:

Literary Structure of Exodus 19

1. The setting in time and space . . . . vv. 1–2
2. The divine purpose in the covenant . . . . vv. 3–8
3. The human preparation for the covenant . . . . vv. 9–15
4. The revelation of Yahweh at Sinai . . . . vv. 16–25

The constant ascending and descending provides a vivid portrayal of the distance between the people and God, and thus the need for a mediator. It then emphasizes the miracle of a covenant relationship of love, loyalty, and trust between parties such as these:

> [3] Then Moses went up to God, and the LORD called to him from the mountain and said, "This is what you are to say to the house of Jacob and what you are to tell the people of Israel: [4] 'You yourselves have seen what I did to Egypt, and how I carried you on eagles' wings and brought you to myself. [5] Now if you obey me fully and keep my covenant, then out of all nations you will be my treasured possession. Although the whole earth is mine, [6] you will be for me a kingdom of priests and a holy nation.' These are the words you are to speak to the Israelites."
>
> [7] So Moses went back and summoned the elders of the people and set before them all the words the LORD had commanded him to speak. [8] The people all responded together, "We will do everything the LORD has said." So Moses brought their answer back to the LORD. (Ex. 19:3–8, NIV)

Thus, after verses 1–2 specify the place and time in history, verses 3–8 detail the purpose of the covenant from God's point of view. What we have in these verses is a proposal of the covenant in a nutshell: (1) verse 4 describes the past history of relationship between the two covenant partners; (2) verses 5 and 6 propose a relationship of complete loyalty and obedience of Israel as a vassal to Yahweh as the great King, and promise certain blessings; and (3) in verses 7 and 8 the people agree to the proposal. Thus, even in this covenant proposal in verses 3–8, the form and structure corresponds to the formulae of ancient Near Eastern covenants and treaties.

Verse 4 is a marvelous encapsulation of the past relationship between the people and the Lord, using the imagery of being carried out of trouble on the wings of an eagle: "You yourselves have seen what I did to Egypt, and how I carried you on eagles' wings and brought you to myself." This brief statement summarizes the abject condition of the people in slavery in Egypt and the signs and wonders performed by Yahweh, in both the ten plagues and the crossing of the Red Sea, that delivered and freed them from slavery.

It also speaks of the way in which God had directed them through the mazes and mirages of the desert using a pillar of cloud by day and of fire by night. This form of leadership also protected them from extreme heat by day and cold by night. Every day, bread rained from heaven for their nourishment and water gushed from the rock to satisfy their thirst. Our culture today can picture this from the movie world in the miraculous rescue of Gandalf by the eagles in *The Lord of the Rings*. God had protected the people and provided for them during the difficult desert journey, bearing them on eagles' wings, so to speak, and had so arranged their itinerary as to bring them to himself, that is, to the place already prepared as a meeting place between God and men—to Sinai, the mountain of God (Ex. 3:1).

Verses 5–6 of chapter 19 are constructed in the form of a conditional sentence: "if you do this . . . then you will be . . . and you will be. . . ." The "if clause," or protasis, specifies absolute obedience to the covenant stipulations. The "then clause," or apodosis, defines the result in terms of relationship to Yahweh; they will belong to him in two ways: (1) as a king's treasure, and (2) as a kingdom of priests and a holy nation.

Before explaining the meaning of the terms defining the divine goal in the covenant relationship, the relation of verses 5–6 to verse 4 must be stressed. Perhaps a diagram may be used to picture this:

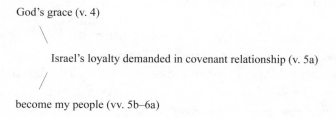

God's grace (v. 4)

Israel's loyalty demanded in covenant relationship (v. 5a)

become my people (vv. 5b–6a)

Verse 4 shows that the motivation for concluding and keeping a covenant with Yahweh is sovereign grace. The creator God has chosen to display favor and kindness to Israel and has acted in history to redeem them and make them his people. A lot of misunderstanding has been caused by contrasting the old covenant with the new in terms of "law" versus "grace." This text is clear: the old covenant is based upon grace, and grace motivates the keeping of the covenant, just as we find in the new covenant. God had protected the people and provided for them during the difficult desert journey, bearing them on eagles' wings, so to speak, and had so arranged their itinerary as to bring them to himself, that is, to Sinai, the mountain of God. This passage teaches, then, that the basis for the covenant from the point of view of the human partner was confidence and trust in, as well as gratitude to, Yahweh as established by the events of the exodus. (What is unlike the new covenant is that covenant keeping depends on Israel's promise to obey.)

Verses 5 and 6, then, describe the purpose, from God's point of view, for which the covenant was given to the people, and the nature of the relationship between God and Israel that will result from ratifying the covenant proposed by Yahweh.

Scholars have debated the logic of the conditional sentence in verses 5–6. Some have considered the situation similar to biblical passages that offer a reward based on obedience. Others argue that the "if clause" does not so much lay down a condition for benefits as define the content and nature of the status in the apodoses or "then clauses." These options can be illustrated by the following two sentences:

> 1. If you accept my offer to teach you, and you devote yourself to learning Hebrew and other cognate languages, you will get a well-paid university position and a rewarding superannuation package.

> 2. If you accept my offer to teach you, and you devote yourself to learning Hebrew and other cognate languages, you will have the satisfaction of being a Semitics scholar.

The second sentence is a conditional definition where the "then clause" spells out what is inherent in the "if clause." Strong support for this latter understanding may be found in recent linguistic research. Thus the conditional sentence (19:5–6) is proclaiming the privileged status of Israel inherent in the covenant relationship. Important parallels in Deuteronomy such as 7:6–11; 14:2; and especially 26:18–19 also substantiate this view.

1. Personal Treasure (1 Chronicles 29:3; Ecclesiastes 2:8)

The meaning of the terms defining the divine plan for the role and status of Israel in the covenant relationship may now be explained. It is crucial to note the literary structure of Exodus 19:5–6 in explaining the terms "personal treasure," "kingdom of priests," and "holy nation." Two clauses joined by the conjunction "and" constitute the content of the declaration by Yahweh. The first is, "you will be my treasured possession more than/out of all the nations, for the whole earth is mine." The second is, "and you will be for me a kingdom of priests and a holy nation." The relationship of these two statements is best understood by recalling the description given earlier of the approach in ancient Hebrew literature of taking up a topic and developing it from a particular perspective and then stopping and taking up the same theme again from another point of view. This pattern is repetitive and is pursued recursively at both the macro and micro levels.

One begins a conversation on a topic and then closes that conversation down and begins another. Taken together, both conversations are like the left and right speakers of a stereo sound system: each differs slightly, and together they produce Dolby Surround Sound or a three-dimensional idea. In other words, both statements are saying the same thing, but each does it in a different way and looks at the topic from a different perspective. Once the terms are explicated, it will become clear that "royal priesthood" and "holy nation" taken together constitute another way of saying "God's personal treasure." In other words, the terms "royal priesthood" and "holy nation" constitute the right and left speakers of a holographic image, and then, together, they form the left speaker for which the term "personal treasure" is the right speaker.

The first purpose of the covenant is that these chosen, redeemed people might become God's own possession and private treasure. The word *segullâ* in Hebrew that is translated "possession" is the same word used in 1 Chronicles 29:3 for King David's own private cache or vault of gold and silver, his personal store of all things precious and valuable. If we were to travel back in time to the ancient Near East, we would find at capital cities such as Hattusa (Boğazkale, Turkey) and Ugarit (Syria) the rich treasure-vaults of the kings. It is difficult for us to imagine, since we have no monarchy such as the monarchs of Europe in the nineteenth century. Perhaps something comparable today would be the Crown Jewels in London. The use in Ecclesiastes 2:8 is also of a king's personal treasure. These two are the only nonmetaphorical occurrences of the word in the Old Testament.

John Davies's discussion of the meaning of *segullâ* is most illuminating. Although the word is not common in biblical Hebrew, it is common in the postbiblical literature of the Mishna as a commercial-legal term, where it refers to the personal property of a social inferior (such as a wife or slave). There is a connection between the Hebrew word and Akkadian *sikiltu*: found in Old, Middle, and Standard Babylonian, at Nuzi, and also in Middle Assyrian texts, the Akkadian word refers to "acquisition" or "possession," first of illegally acquired goods, then of private possessions in distinction from those possessions which form part of an estate. In the Old Babylonian period, there is a metaphorical usage that casts light on the passage in Exodus. It is used no later than the fifteenth century B.C. by a god to refer to an honored king. Davies cites the following designation of King Abban:

> Abban, the mighty king, son of Šarran, the servant of the god . . . the beloved of the god . . . the treasure of the god.[1]

Thus a royal figure is seen as a devoted servant of the god. A similar usage is found in Ugaritic, as Davies explains:

> Text 60 (18.38) of *PRU* 5 dates from the early twelfth century BCE and is a copy of a letter (no doubt a translation of the original Akkadian) from the Hittite suzerain to Ammurapi, the last king of Ugarit. It describes the vassal king in relation to the suzerain as both his 'servant ([']*bdh*) and *sglth*'. This spelling out of the relationship between the two kings is a preface to a reproach by the suzerain for the failure of the Ugaritic vassal king to pay the customary visits of homage.[2]

Note that the use of the Ugaritic word for "personal treasure" is paired with the notion of servant, as in the above example in Akkadian from Alalakh. "Personal treasure" is used in the context of devoted service in a relationship defined by a treaty. The same pairing of service and personal treasure is found in the Bible, in Malachi 3:17:

> "They shall be mine," says the LORD of hosts, "in the day when I make up my treasured possession (*segullâ*), and I will spare them as a man spares his son who serves him." (ESV)

What is parallel here to "personal treasure" is "son," qualified by the concept of devoted *service*. This biblical passage, corroborated by the Akkadian and Ugaritic parallels, casts enormous light on Exodus 19:5. When Yahweh calls Israel to be his personal treasure, he is speaking of the kind of devoted service given by a son. With this, we are back to the divine image in Genesis 1:26–28. Israel has inherited an Adamic role, giving the devoted service of a son and honored king in a covenant relationship.

---

[1] John A. Davies, *Royal Priesthood: Literary and Intertextual Perspectives on an Image of Israel in Exodus 19:6*, Journal for the Study of the Old Testament: Supplement Series 395 (London: T. & T. Clark, 2004), 53.
[2] Ibid.

A causal-explanatory clause explains that the whole world belongs to Yahweh. In one sense, the king is owner or possessor of the entire country, but in addition to this, he may also have a personal/private treasure. The whole world is like a ring on God's hand, and his chosen people are the jewel in that ring.

2. Kingdom of Priests

Although some expositions consider the meaning of "kingdom of priests" and "holy nation" separately, in a real sense they should be taken together. The text clearly divides the goal of the covenant relationship into two statements. The first is supported by an explanation or reason. A second statement combines the phrases "kingdom of priests" and "holy nation" either as a hendiadys or at least as an expression similar to Hebrew poetry, where a pair of parallel lines allows one to consider a topic from two slightly variant but similar viewpoints to create a full-orbed perspective on some proposition. These phrases will be explained here, each in turn, but with the meaning of the other phrase kept in mind. In turn, we should keep in mind that both phrases together are unpacking the full meaning of "personal treasure."

First, consider the phrase "kingdom of priests." The full sentence is, "You will belong to me as a kingdom of priests" (*tihyû lî mamleket kōhanîm*). The *lamed* preposition in the phrase *lî* ("to me") clearly indicates possession. The Hebrew word "kingdom" may refer to the domain or realm that is ruled, or to the exercise of kingly rule and sovereignty. According to the main options, then, the phrase "kingdom of priests" could mean a domain of priests whom God rules or, alternatively, the exercise of royal office by those who are in fact priests, i.e., a royal priesthood. It is difficult to decide between the two main options since the *lamed* preposition suggests the former reading, while the term "priests" modifying "kingdom" suggests the latter. Yet in the latter option, understanding "priests" as a genitive of apposition after the collective "kingdom" (royalty, royal body, royal house) would be a more natural reading than to construe it as an attributive genitive. Thus we may view in "priests" a collective reference to all Israel as being in some sense "priests" rather than as being a "priestly kingship" or "priestly royalty." Perhaps both meanings are intended, so that both the relationship between God and Israel and the relationship between Israel and the world is indicated. This ambiguity would serve the theme "kingdom through covenant."

What is the function of a priest? This is also important in the interpretation. Some readings focus on the priest as an intermediary, so that the function of a priest is to bring others into the presence of God by offering sacrifices on their behalf. Alternatively, Davies focuses on priesthood as access to the divine presence. He argues that Exodus 19 itself provides an all-important clue to the significance of priesthood in verse 22:

> Also let the priests who come near to the LORD consecrate themselves, lest the LORD break out against them. (ESV)

This passage offers a virtual definition of what it is to be a priest: priests are those who approach or come near to Yahweh and who are consecrated and devoted to him.

The emphasis and focus for which Davies argues is correct because the arguments are based solidly on the text. Nonetheless, the focus on Israel's priesthood as access to the divine presence and a priority in the worship of Yahweh alone as God does not exclude the function of priest as intermediary. The metanarrative is the context for Exodus 19:5–6. Just as in Genesis 1–2 God establishes his rule through a covenant relationship between himself and man and between man and the creation (wherein Adam's priority, according to Genesis 2, is to spend time in the divine presence to order his perspectives and role in the world), so through the covenant with Abraham (Genesis 12–22), promising blessing to the nations in relationship to Abraham and now through the covenant with his family Israel (Exodus 19–24) as a royal priesthood (with a priority on worship that results in being a light to nations), God is extending his rule. Since Israel is settled at the navel of the world, the nations of the world will see displayed a right relationship to God, social justice in human interaction, and good stewardship of the earth's resources.

We see, then, that Israel, as another Adam, will belong to God as a people under his rule, and will exercise royal rule by spending the time in the worship of God so necessary for display of the divine rule in one's thoughts, words, and ways. The tabernacle, the construction of which is the topic of the literary unit following Exodus 19–24, is in form a miniaturized and portable reproduction of God's heavenly sanctuary, of which Israel has caught a glimpse in the covenant ratification ceremony in Exodus 24:9–11. The cloud denoting the divine presence on Mount Sinai settles on the tabernacle in Exodus 40. Thus Israel carries the divine presence with them. Moreover, the tabernacle is also a replica of the garden of Eden and a representation of the universe, so just as Adam was to fulfill his mandate by devoting himself to worship as a priest in the garden sanctuary, so Israel as a new Adam is to fulfill her mandate by devoting herself to worship as a priest in the tabernacle, and later the temple. Since, in the Bible and the ancient Near East, kings are the ones who build temples, Israel as a nation building the tabernacle, in Exodus 25–40 also depicts her royal status. She is a king-priest. This, in fact, is the point of the debated passage in Hosea 6:7: "But they [i.e., Israel], like Adam, have transgressed the covenant." Israel's covenant violation was in her role as king-priest, thus making her sin precisely like that of Adam.

Israel is also a vehicle for bringing the nations to the divine presence and rule. Israel would be a people completely devoted to the service of God. The rite of circumcision as practiced in Israel is an excellent illustration of this. As noted, the background for understanding circumcision is Egypt, where only the aristocracy, the highest order of priests, and the noblest elite warriors, along with the Pharaoh and his family, were circumcised, because only they were completely devoted to the service of the gods. In Deuteronomy 10:16 the command to Israel, "Circumcise your hearts," is an exposition of the earlier command "to fear the LORD your God, to walk in all his ways, to love him, to serve the LORD your God with all your heart and with all your soul, and to observe the LORD's commands and decrees that I am giving you today for your own good" (Deut. 10:12–13, NIV). Thus circumcision is an apt expression for the idea: be completely devoted to Yahweh.

In a work on biblical theology entitled *Dominion and Dynasty*, Stephen Dempster analyzes the phrase "kingdom of priests" in a way similar to the exposition given here:

> The final phrase designates Israel as a particular type of kingdom. Instead of being a kingdom of a particular king, it will be a kingdom marked by priesthood; that is, service of God on behalf of people and *vice versa*. It will be 'a kingdom run not by politicians depending upon strength and connivance but by priests depending upon faith in Yahweh, a servant nation instead of a ruling nation' (Durham 263). Israel will thus redefine the meaning of dominion—service. This will be its distinctive task, its distinguishing characteristic among the world of nations.[3]

In sum, the call of Israel to be a royal priesthood connects the Israelite covenant to the Abrahamic. Psalm 67 draws this out very well:

---

[3] Stephen G. Dempster, *Dominion and Dynasty: A Biblical Theology of the Hebrew Bible*, New Studies in Biblical Theology 15 (Downers Grove, IL: InterVarsity Press, 2003), 101–102.

[1] May God be gracious to us and bless us
and make his face to shine upon us, *Selah*
[2] that your way may be known on earth,
your saving power among all nations.
[3] Let the peoples praise you, O God;
let all the peoples praise you! (ESV)

In verse 1 we see Israel praying as a priest, since the nation as a whole is invoking the Aaronic blessing of Numbers 6. The goal or purpose of invoking this blessing is so that salvation may come to the nations. This is none other than the goal of the Abrahamic covenant.

3. Holy Nation

The parallel phrase to "kingdom of priests" is "holy nation" (*gôy qādôš* in Hebrew). As already mentioned, this phrase is not necessarily identical in meaning to "kingdom of priests," but both phrases function as a pair, like parallel lines in Hebrew poetry, to paint a three-dimensional picture in one's mind.

The term *gôy* or "nation" is the parallel term to "kingdom." It is an economic, political, and social structure in which a final governmental headship operates. It therefore clearly reminds us of Genesis 12:2, as explained earlier. This is the city of God, the kingdom of God. In fulfillment of the promises to Abraham, Israel, by virtue of the Mosaic covenant, will provide under the direct rule of God a model of God's rule over human life, which is the divine aim for the entire world.

"Nation" is modified by the adjective "holy." What is a "holy" nation? Unfortunately the term "holy" is one that is not very well understood by the church today. Definitions commonly given are "pure" or "set apart." Such definitions are erroneous because the meaning is being determined by etymology rather than usage, and the etymology is completely speculative. The idea that "holy" means set apart can be traced to the influence of W. W. Baudissin, who proposed in 1878 that the root of "holy" in Hebrew, i.e., *qdš*, is derived from *qd-*, "to cut."[4] Recently, exhaustive research by a French evangelical scholar, Claude-Bernard Costecalde, has cast better light on the meaning of this term since his analysis was based on the way the word is used rather than on hypothetical origins.[5] Costecalde discovered that the

---

[4] W. W. Baudissin, "Der Begriff der Heiligkeit im Alten Testament," in *Studien zur semitischen Religionsgeschichte* (Leipzig, Germany: Grunow, 1878), 2:1–142.

[5] Claude-Bernard Costecalde, *Aux origines du sacré biblique* (Paris: Letouzey et Ané, 1986).

basic meaning of *qdš* is not "separated" but rather "consecrated to" or "devoted to." This is also the basic meaning of the counterpart in Greek.[6]

Noteworthy is the passage in Exodus 3 where Moses encounters Yahweh in the burning bush and is asked to remove his sandals because he is standing on "holy ground." This is the first instance in the Old Testament of the root *qdš* in either an adjectival or a noun form. In the narrative, Moses is commanded to stay away from the bush, that is, from the place from which God speaks, but he is not commanded to stay away from the holy ground. There is nothing inaccessible or set apart about the holy ground. Moreover, his fright and shock come from a revelation of God, not from the holiness of the place. The "holy ground" (Ex. 3:5) encompasses a larger space than just the bush from which God speaks and is equivalent to "the mountain of God" in 3:1. The act of removing one's sandals, like the act of the nearest relative in Ruth 4:7, is a ceremony or rite of de-possession well known in the culture of that time. Moses must acknowledge that this ground belongs to God and must enter into an attitude of consecration. Thus, rather than marking an item as set apart, "holy" ground is ground prepared, consecrated, or devoted to the meeting of God and man.

A holy nation, then, is one prepared and consecrated for fellowship with God and one completely devoted to him. Instructions in the Pentateuch are often supported by the statement from Yahweh, "for I am holy." Such statements show that complete devotion to God on the part of Israel would show itself in two ways: (1) identifying with his ethics and morality, and (2) sharing his concern for the broken in the community. The commands and instructions in Leviticus 19 and 20 are bounded by the claim that Yahweh is holy (19:2; 20:26) and include concern against mistreating the alien and the poor, the blind and the deaf. In the "Judgments" of the Book of the Covenant (Exodus 19–24), some instructions relate to the oppression of orphans and widows (Ex. 22:22–23). God was concerned about the rights of the slave (e.g., Ex. 21:2–11) and the disenfranchised in society. Over the past thirty years we have heard the strident voice of the feminist, of the anti-nuclear protest, and of the gay rights movement. But God hears the voice of those who are broken in body, in economy, and in spirit. If we are in covenant relationship with him, we must, like him, hear the voice that is too weak to cry out.

---

[6] See H. G. Liddell, R. Scott, and H. S. Jones, *A Greek-English Lexicon*, 9th ed. with revised supplement (Oxford: Oxford University Press, 1996), s.v. ἅγιος, who give as the fundamental meaning, "devoted to the gods."

God also jealously protects what is devoted to him. His anger flares when his holiness is violated, as in the case of Uzzah (2 Sam. 6:7), who extended his hand to touch the ark of the covenant. Also in Psalm 2, when the kings and princes of the earth gather to touch the Anointed of the Lord, he flares out in anger to protect his King. Also in the case of Paul, in the New Testament, who in persecuting the church was reaching up to heaven, as it were, to shake his rebellious fist at Jesus, the Anointed One (= the Christ), and slap him in the face: Paul therefore rightly called himself the chief of sinners (1 Tim. 1:15).

Explanation of the terms "personal treasure," "kingdom of priests," and "holy nation," then, shows the goal and purpose of the Sinai covenant for Israel. Although the language is different from that of Genesis 1:26–28 and 12:1–3, we can clearly see that the covenant at Sinai achieves and administers in the Iron Age, through the nation as a whole, the purposes of the promises given to Abraham. God is establishing his kingdom through covenant. The covenant entails relationship with God on the one hand and relationship with the world on the other hand. Israel will model to the world what it means to have a relationship with God, what it means to treat each other in a genuinely human way, and what it means to be good stewards of the earth's resources. As priests, they will mediate the blessings of God to the world and will be used to bring the rest of the world to know God.

The new covenant succeeds where the old covenant failed. The purposes of the Mosaic covenant are now being fulfilled in the church. The apostle Peter calls the church God's special treasure, a kingdom of priests, and a holy nation (1 Pet. 2:9–10). God has forged both Jews and non-Jews into his new humanity [man, i.e., Adam], according to Ephesians 2:15. And as we shall see later on, this cannot rightly be called "replacement theology."

THE TEN WORDS (EXODUS 20)

A brief explanation of the Ten Words will support our contention that the Mosaic covenant entails a right relationship to God and social justice in human relationships. Some general observations on the Ten Words are fundamental to a proper understanding of this covenant.

The Ten Words form the heart of the covenant between God and Israel at Sinai. The Book of the Covenant, as we have seen, consists of the Ten Words and the Judgments. The former constitute the basic and fundamental requirements of the covenant. The latter are detailed stipulations based on the Ten Words, which apply them in practical ways to specific social situations and demonstrate their meaning in various circumstances.

Attention has already been drawn to the fact that the earliest tradition in the biblical text refers to these requirements as the "Ten Words" (Ex. 34:28; Deut. 4:13; 10:4) and not as the "Ten Commandments" as we now know them. There is, in fact, a particular reason for this and for why there are precisely ten instructions. A connection is being made between the covenant at Sinai and the creation. In the creation narrative, God creates the universe by simply speaking, i.e., by his word. In the Hebrew text, the verb *wayyō'mer*, "and he [= God] said" occurs ten times. In a very real way, the entire creation depends or hangs upon the word of God. Here, the Book of the Covenant is what forges Israel into a nation. It is her national constitution, so to speak. And it is also the Ten Words that brings about the birth of the nation. Like the creation, Israel as a nation hangs upon the Ten Words for her very being.

Although the biblical text explicitly tells us that there are *ten* words, we do not *seem to be told* exactly how to number them. Jewish, Catholic-Lutheran, and Protestant traditions have differed in the way they number them. Analysis based on discourse grammar has clarified the issue decisively. If one pays close attention to the presence or absence of the word "and" in the Hebrew text, the numbering intended is clear:

    (1) No other gods/no images
    (2) No bearing the name deceitfully
    (3) Sabbath
    (4) Honor parents
    (5) No murder
    (6) No adultery
    (7) No theft
    (8) No false witness
    (9) No coveting wife
  (10) No desiring household members/objects

In the version of the Ten Words in Deuteronomy 5:6–21, the enumeration is clarified because commands 5–10 are joined by the conjunction "and," while commands 1–4 are set off from the last six by the absence of the conjunction. Moreover, the fact that only one reason in both Exodus 20:3–6 and Deuteronomy 5:7–10 supports commands 1 and 2 in the enumeration of the

Protestant tradition provides further corroboration that they should be considered a single command.

The biblical text, then, divides the Ten Words into three commands defining Israel's relationship to Yahweh and six commands dealing with human interpersonal relationships within the covenant community. In the middle is the fourth command, which supports how the basic human community, the family, is to function. The last seven commands, then (the fourth through the tenth), define a genuinely human way to treat each other.

Note in particular that a reason or rationale is given for keeping the first three commands, introduced by *kî* (= "because" or "for" [Ex. 20:5, 6, 11]). Yet no reason is given for keeping the last seven commands. These entail the basic and inalienable rights of every human and have been recognized by the customs and laws of every society. These "laws" can be paralleled in legal documents from other societies in the ancient Near East:

Legal Treatises of the Ancient Near East[7]

The Laws of Ur-Nammu . . . . 21st century B.C.
The Laws of Lipit-Ishtar . . . . 19th century B.C.
The Laws of Eshnunna . . . . . 18th century B.C.
The Code of Hammurabi . . . . 18th century B.C.
The Old Hittite Laws . . . . 17th century B.C.
The Middle Assyrian Laws . . 12th century B.C.

Although the Ten Words expresses these laws negatively, they could also be expressed positively in terms of the inalienable rights of every human person:

Thou shalt not murder . . . . = the right of every person to their
own life
Thou shalt not commit adultery . . . . = the right of every person to their
own home
Thou shalt not steal . . . . = the right of every person to their
own property
Thou shalt not bear false witness . . = the right of every person to their
own reputation

No society can endure that does not respect the basic inalienable rights of every human person. Since the last seven commands can be paralleled in

---

[7] John H. Walton, *Ancient Near Eastern Thought and the Old Testament: Introducing the Conceptual World of the Hebrew Bible* (Grand Rapids, MI: Baker, 2006), 69–71.

the law treatises of other societies in the ancient Near East and were well known to the Israelites, no rationale for keeping them need be supplied in the text. The first three commands, however, are unparalleled in the ancient Near East. Certainly the command to worship only one God, the command not to manufacture or worship idols, and the command to observe the Sabbath are absolutely unique. In fact, the seventh day in Mesopotamia was considered unlucky. These commands constitute a new revelation, and God graciously supplies a rationale for keeping them, so that Israel may grasp an adequate motivation for following a practice that was unprecedented.

The question must also be raised as to why the commands are given as prohibitions and why they are formulated in the second person singular. Why not express them positively as inalienable rights? Why not indicate by a second person plural that they are addressed to all? The reason for this is simple. God wants each and every individual person to think first of the inalienable rights of the other person and not first about their own inalienable rights. This explains both the negative formulation and the second person singular.

From the start and throughout the entire history of Israel, attempts were made to boil down, digest, and summarize the instructions of the covenant—both the many Judgments that elaborate the Ten Words in practical situations as well as the Ten Words themselves. For example, Leviticus 18–20 contains a collection of instructions that develop further in particular the last six of the Ten Words. It is interesting to note that at the mid- and end-points of Leviticus 19 we find the instruction, "You shall love your neighbor as yourself" (vv. 18, 34), which means to give help or be useful to your neighbor. Jesus and other rabbis of the first century demonstrated exegetical insight to observe that this was a summary statement of the various instructions in this section of Leviticus, and indeed of the last portion of the Ten Words that they elaborate. Later on, the prophets and poets used two pairs of words as summaries of the Torah. One is the pair "lovingkindness and truth," and the other is "justice and righteousness." Each pair of words is a hendiadys—communicating a single idea through two words. The first pair speaks of faithful, loyal love and the second speaks of social justice. These are attempts to boil down the covenant stipulations into a single "sound bite." They are important because they show that the instructions represent faithful love as well as social justice in human interrelationships.

Space permits in this brief treatment of the Mosaic covenant only a short explanation of each of the first three of the Ten Words, as these have been more troublesome for Christians to understand than the last seven.[8]

First Command A: No Other Gods before Me

The first command has two parts, one relating to how Yahweh is perceived in the heavenly realm and one relating to how he is perceived in the earthly realm.

The Reformers and the creeds following them interpret the first part of the first commandment to mean that we should not have any other gods before the Lord, i.e., *in preference* to the Lord. The prohibition is understood in terms of priorities. According to the Westminster Confession, God must be the highest priority in our attitudes, thoughts, words, and ways. Others have interpreted the prohibition philosophically and argued that the main point is to establish absolute monotheism and rule out the existence of other deities.

The command, however, does appear to acknowledge the existence of other gods. In courses taught in the history of religion at universities in the Western world, the suggestion is frequently made that, at an earlier stage of the history of Israel, the people were henotheists—that is, they believed in the existence of many gods but consciously chose to worship only one. At a later point in the development of Israel's religion, henotheism gave way to monotheism, i.e., the belief that there *is* only one god.

Some scholars alleviate this problem by distinguishing between religious command and theological statement. Theological statement says there is only one God (Deut. 4:39), but our hearts are idol factories, and the religious command assumes the depravity of the human heart.

This distinction is helpful but assumes that the exegesis in terms of priorities is correct. Yet this exegesis is difficult to maintain. There are clear ways to express in Hebrew the notion of priority. An exhaustive study of the use of the Hebrew preposition "before" plus personal object in the Hebrew Bible shows that the meaning is *consistently spatial*. The linguistic data, then, demand that a spatial sense be considered as the main option.

In the past, students of the text have avoided this interpretation because they could not understand how it could make any sense. Evidence from the ancient Near Eastern culture now illuminates how a spatial sense is eminently suitable. In that time, the gods operated within a pantheon, a divine assembly

---

[8] For further discussion, see the longer treatment in our larger work, *Kingdom through Covenant* (Wheaton, IL: Crossway, 2012).

or assembly of gods. Having this image as background suggests that the Isra-elites were not to imagine any other gods in the presence of Yahweh:

> In view of the information provided from outside the Bible, this spatial sense gains credibility. In the ancient Near East the gods operated within pantheons and decisions were made in the divine assembly. Furthermore, the principal deities typically had consorts. For the gods life was a com-munity experience. The destinies of the gods were decreed in assembly, as were the destinies of kings, cities, temples and people. The business of the gods was carried out in the presence of other gods. . . .
>
> Accordingly, by a comparative interpretation of the first command-ment the Israelites were not to construe Yahweh as operating within a com-munity of gods. Nor were they to imagine Him functioning as the head of a pantheon surrounded by a divine assembly, or having a consort. In short, He works alone. The concept of a pantheon/divine assembly assumed a distribution of power among many divine beings. The first commandment declared simply and unequivocally that Yahweh's authority was absolute. Divine power was not distributed among other deities or limited by the will of the assembly. . . .
>
> Although this text does not explicitly deny the existence of other gods, it does remove them from the presence of Yahweh. If Yahweh does not share power, authority, or jurisdiction with them, they are not gods in any meaningful sense of the word. Thus, the first commandment does not insist on the non-existence of other gods; only that they are powerless. In so doing it disenfranchises them, not merely by declaring that they should not be worshiped; it leaves them with no status worthy of worship.[9]

In the progressive revealing and unfolding of God in history and Scrip-ture, the completed Canon shows that God has revealed himself completely and fully in Jesus Christ. Jesus said, "All authority in heaven and on earth has been given to me" (Matt. 28:18). Our lives, our service and work, our worship must recognize his authority alone. This disenfranchises all gods and idols worshiped in our culture. There is no one else I am living my life for than Jesus Christ.

First Command B: No Images/Idols

The second part of the first command is as follows: "You shall not make for yourself an image and form which is in the heaven above and which is in

---

[9] John H. Walton, "Interpreting the Bible as an Ancient Near Eastern Document," in *Israel: Ancient Kingdom or Late Invention? Archaeology, Ancient Civilizations, and the Bible*, ed. Daniel I. Block (Nashville: B&H, 2008), 307–309.

the earth below and which is in the waters under the earth" (Ex. 20:4). As Walton notes, popular prohibition of images has been influenced by four factors: (1) Jewish interpretation, (2) controversies over icons in the Eastern Orthodox tradition, (3) statues of saints in the Roman Catholic tradition, and (4) debate over what constitutes art from a Christian perspective.[10] In the Jewish and Muslim traditions this command led to a prohibition of the representation of any living creature. Christian interpretation up to the nineteenth century was dominated by the idea that, since God was invisible and transcendent, he could not be contained in an image. Others have spiritualized the text, reducing idols to anything to which we devote our energy, money, and worth as deity.

Such misunderstandings of the second command are due to a couple of factors. First is ignorance of the ancient Near Eastern ideas concerning the nature and role of idols. Ancient Near Eastern thinking about idols falls into three categories.

One category is the manufacture of images. In the ancient Near Eastern mind-set, only the god could approve and initiate the manufacturing process. At the end of the process, special ceremonies and rituals, in particular the mouth-opening ritual, allowed the god to inhabit the image and permitted the image to drink, eat food, and smell incense.

A second category concerns the use of the image. As Walton notes, "in the ancient world all formal and public worship revolved around the image."[11] Thus the image involved mediation. It mediated revelation from the deity to the people and also mediated worship by the people to the deity as they brought clothes, drink, and food to honor it.

A third category has to do with ancient Near Eastern perceptions concerning the function and nature of images. After a ceremony to begin the idol's worship, "the material image was animated by the divine essence. Therefore, from now on it did not simply represent the deity but also manifested its presence. However, this does not mean that the image had thereby been deified. The deity was the reality that was embodied in the image."[12]

Misunderstanding of this command is due not only to ignorance of the ancient Near Eastern culture and worldview but also to faulty analysis of the grammar of this text. Let us consider closely the exact text of the second of

---

[10] Walton, "Interpreting the Bible as an Ancient Near Eastern Document," 309–313.
[11] Ibid., 311.
[12] Ibid., 312.

the Ten Words in both Exodus and Deuteronomy. Below, the translations of the KJV and NIV are given:

Exodus 20:4

KJV: Thou shalt not make unto thee any graven image, or any likeness of any thing . . .

NIV: You shall not make for yourself an idol in the form of anything . . .

Deuteronomy 5:8

KJV: Thou shalt not make thee any graven image, or any likeness of any thing . . .

NIV: You shall not make for yourself an idol in the form of anything . . .

The translation of the KJV represents early Jewish rabbinic understanding, no doubt mediated through the Latin Vulgate of Jerome. This is the way orthodox Jews today understand the text and also the way in which Muslims have consistently understood it.

The original text in Hebrew actually joins the objects of the verb with "and." Translation by "or" is completely illegitimate. The text in Exodus 20:4 is difficult, but the early rabbinic understanding does not follow the norms of grammar in Hebrew. Note that the parallel text in Deuteronomy does not have the conjunction "and" but employs instead a bound or construct phrase,[13] "a carved image *of* any form . . ." Certainly the rendering by "or" is contrary to the grammar here. It seems that interpretive traditions have molded Deuteronomy 5:8 to suit their understanding of Exodus 20:4.

If we believe in the analogy of Scripture, however, where we interpret the unclear by the clear, the Jewish understanding cannot be the correct meaning of this text. Consider, for example, the art in the tabernacle and also in Solomon's temple. Artwork in the construction of Solomon's temple had representation of the creation with images of bulls, cherubim, lions, palm trees, and pomegranates (1 Kings 7:18, 25, 36). Since the grammar of the text in Deuteronomy 5:8 is clear, a better approach is to use the clear text there to interpret the unclear in Exodus 20:4. The construction in Exodus 20:4 could be understood as a hendiadys, a common figure of speech in Hebrew literature where one idea is communicated by two nouns or verbs joined by "and." The first notable example in the Bible is

---

[13] A bound or construct phrase in Hebrew indicates a relationship between two words, expressed literally in English by "of."

Genesis 3:16. The Hebrew text has, "I will greatly increase your pain and your pregnancy." This does not mean an increase of pain on the one hand and pregnancy on the other. The next sentence goes on to explain, "In pain you will bring forth children." So the earlier expression must mean "pain in pregnancy"—an example of a hendiadys. In Exodus 20:4, "a carved image and any form" must therefore in the light of Deuteronomy 5:8 mean "a carved image/idol in any form." This is the approach taken by the NIV, and it is one that accurately follows the grammar of the Hebrew language and uses the clear meaning of one text to assist the interpretation of the other rather than impose a faulty interpretation of Exodus on the clear text in Deuteronomy.

Accurate exegesis, then, shows that this text has nothing to do with art or the representation of aspects of the created order with images. Rather, the command has to do with images used as mediators of the presence or revelation of deity from god to human, or mediation of the worship of people to the deity. As Walton observes, the prohibition of images excluded the sort of worship that understood ceremonies and rituals as meeting the needs of the deity through the image.[14]

Second Command: Do Not Bear the Name of God Falsely

Popular misunderstanding also exists concerning the second of the Ten Words: "You shall not lift up the name of Yahweh your God worthlessly (*laššāw'*)" (Ex. 20:7). Several interpretations have been proposed over time. Once again, better knowledge of both cultural setting and linguistic data can improve our understanding of this text.

The basic import of this instruction is not related to the use of God's name idly in blasphemy, minced oaths, or profanity. This is certainly inappropriate, and respect and reverence for the divine name is enjoined in Deuteronomy 28:58.

The traditional view has focused on false oaths, but this does not provide a full picture.

Walton argues that in order to get a valid understanding, the linguistic data must be set within the context of ancient Near Eastern culture. This depends upon a careful definition of magic, the world in which the false or proper use of names occurs. The name of God represents his entire character and person. To use that name brings his person and his power into a particu-

---

[14] Walton, "Interpreting the Bible as an Ancient Near Eastern Document," 313.

lar situation. When we use his name for something that is contrary to who he is or to his character, we lift it up to a lie. The name is equivalent to the identity of God, and the divine identity can be commandeered for illicit use. The problem of identity theft is widely recognized today. Misusing the name of God occurs among Christians today when someone says, "The Lord led me to do such and such a thing," when we know from Scripture that this is not according to the revealed will of God.

D. I. Block proposes a different interpretation for this second command ("You shall not take the name of the LORD your God in vain"; ESV).[15] Traditional interpretations and translations in the English versions may miss the central issue, namely, that of wearing the name of Yahweh as a badge or brand of ownership. The key to this injunction is the verb *nāśa'*, which does not mean "to misuse" or "to pronounce" or "to take" in this text, since all of these translations would require different idioms. Instead, here the normal sense, "to bear, carry," is most suitable. The collocation of this verb with "name" occurs elsewhere only in Exodus 28:12 and 29, where it refers to Aaron, the high priest, bearing the names of the sons of Israel inscribed on two onyx stones on the shoulder pieces of his ephod. As Block explains, to bear the name of God means to have his name branded on one's person as a mark of divine ownership.

Several other passages may be briefly mentioned to support this view. The notion of branding (e.g., cattle) used metaphorically may underlie Isaiah 44:5b:

> This one will say, "I am the LORD's,"
>> another will call on the name of Jacob,
> and another will write on his hand, "The LORD's,"
>> and claim as honorific title the name of Israel.

Further, Deuteronomy 28:9–10 clearly connects belonging to the Lord (i.e., holy to Yahweh) and bearing the name of the Lord:

> [9] The LORD will establish you as a people holy to himself, as he has sworn to you, if you keep the commandments of the LORD your God and walk in his ways. [10] And all the peoples of the earth shall see that you are called by the name of the LORD, and they shall be afraid of you. (ESV)

---

[15] Daniel I. Block, "Bearing the Name of the Lord with Honor," in *How I Love Your Torah, O LORD! Studies in the Book of Deuteronomy* (Eugene, OR: Cascade, 2011), 61–72 (originally published in *Bibliotheca Sacra* 168 [2011]: 20–31).

Finally, observe that when God judged his people in exile, he scattered them among the nations because they had *desecrated his holy name* (Ezek. 36:17–23). Conversely, in Daniel's famous prayer for the end of exile and judgment, he asks God to act for his own sake, *because your city and your people bear your name* (Dan. 9:16–19).

What, then, would the clause "bear the name" mean when modified by the adverbial phrase *laššāw'* ("in vain"; KJV, ESV). Although the noun can mean "empty" or "worthless," it frequently has to do with what is deceitful or false. Isaiah 59:3, "your lips have spoken deceitfully," is a good example (cf. Isa. 5:18). Psalm 139:20 actually alludes to the second of the Ten Words, and the context clarifies the issue:

> They speak against you with malicious intent;
>> your enemies take your name in vain. (ESV)

Here David (according to the title of the Psalm) is confronting men who plan to murder someone and want David to join them in this. This is bearing the name of Yahweh deceitfully, and David identifies them instead as the enemies of God because the act they intend under the umbrella of his name is contrary to who he is and what he represents.

Third, on the basis of the analysis of the second command given by D. I. Block, a further insight is possible concerning commands one and two. According to the numbering scheme of the Catholic-Lutheran tradition, the first command, "no other gods," is identical to the claim "I am your God," and the second command, "no wearing his name deceitfully/worthlessly," is identical to the claim "You are my people," since bearing the name indicated belonging to Yahweh, i.e., wearing his brand mark as a badge of honor. In this way, as shown in table 7.1, the first two of the Ten Words may be seen as an exposition of the Covenant Formula ("I will be your God, and you shall be my people").

Table 7.1: The First Two of the Ten Words as an Exposition of the Covenant Formula

No other gods before me	→	I will be your God
No bearing my name dishonorably	→	You will be my people

The mention of *'el qanna'* ["a jealous God"; KJV, ESV] in the first command adds support for this view, since the Hebrew word *qanna'* refers to acting to protect one's property and the next command indicates that Israel belongs to Yahweh.

Third Command: Keep the Sabbath

The third of the Ten Words is a positive injunction to observe the Sabbath (Ex. 20:8–11). The importance of this injunction is indicated by its length—it is the longest of the Ten Words.

In the twentieth century, scholars attempted to find precursors to the Israelite Sabbath in the nations surrounding ancient Israel. This effort was entirely unsuccessful. The Hebrew *šabbāt* is not connected to the Babylonian *šabbatu*, which is the fifteenth day of the month. Moreover the 7th, 14th, 21st, and 28th days of certain months in the Babylonian calendar were considered unlucky. Nonetheless, the concept of divine rest is well attested in ancient Near Eastern texts, and the cultural context can cast great light on interpretation of the third command.

Six aspects of the notion of divine rest in the ancient Near East, drawn mainly from the great epics such as the Babylonian *Enuma Elish*, are delineated by Walton.[16] These can be briefly summarized as follows: in the ancient epics, (1) the divine rest was disturbed by rebellion; (2) divine rest was achieved after conflict; (3) divine rest was achieved after acts of creation, establishing order; (4) divine rest was achieved in the temple; (5) divine rest was characterized by ongoing rule and stability; and (6) divine rest was achieved by the gods by creating people to do their work.

There are both similarities and differences between the biblical command to observe the Sabbath and the cultural context of the ancient Near East. We need to attend carefully to the linguistic data in the relevant texts. In Exodus 20:8–11, the Israelites are commanded to remember the Sabbath day to consecrate it. In the Old Testament, the notion of remembering is not merely mental recall; it entails acts in space and time based on keeping something at the front of one's mind. Israel is to consecrate the Sabbath; it is a commemorative event that belongs to Yahweh and is to be devoted to him. Both humans—free or slaves, citizens or resident aliens—and animals are to cease from the business and labor ordinarily undertaken to provide for our own life and sustenance. It is an act of faith, acknowledging Yahweh as the creator and giver of life and as the one who rules our lives.

The biblical viewpoint is fundamentally different from the ancient Near

---

[16] Walton, "Interpreting the Bible as an Ancient Near Eastern Document," 319–322.

Eastern perspectives, in spite of many parallels on the surface. Walton says, "in the Old Testament people work for their own benefit and provision, rather than to meet the needs of God or to do his work for him. When commanded to share the rest of God on the Sabbath, it is not to participate in it per se, but to recognize His work of bringing and maintaining order. God's rest symbolizes His control over the cosmos, which His people recognize whenever they yield to Him the day they could have used to provide for themselves."[17]

On the other hand, the parallel between the ancient Near Eastern building of temples for divine rest and the biblical creation narrative culminating in divine rest is valid. The framework of the account of creation in the Bible strongly suggests that the cosmos is constructed as a sanctuary/temple in which God may take up his rest.

Discussion of this command brings us right into the middle of the problem of the relationship between the old covenant and the new, a matter that cannot adequately be discussed in this chapter. Nonetheless, a few comments on the Sabbath are in order.

First, we must note that the Sabbath was the sign between Yahweh and Israel of the old covenant, as is clearly stated in Exodus 31:12–18. Covenants often have a physical sign associated with them. The rainbow was given as a physical sign of God's promise in his covenant with Noah. Circumcision was commanded as a physical sign in the body of every male in Israel as a sign of God's covenant with Abraham. Similarly, the Sabbath is stipulated as a permanent sign between Yahweh and Israel that the God who created the world in six days and then rested has consecrated them to himself.

Second, as we compare the old covenant and the new covenant, we see that the self-identity of the people of the Lord in the old covenant was that of children, while the self-identity of the people of the Lord in the new covenant is that of mature adults (Gal. 3:24–25). The external forms and shadows of the old covenant have been done away with, now that the reality has come in Christ (Col. 2:16–17).

Now, of what does the Sabbath speak? Let us notice at once that, in the two texts in the Old Testament where we have the Ten Words, the reason given for the Sabbath in one text is different from the reason given in the other text. In Exodus, the reason is given in 20:11: God's work of creation was complete; it was finished; they could add nothing to it. They were in-

---

[17] Ibid., 322.

vited to enter his rest and enjoy his work. Hebrews applies this notion to the work of Christ. We cannot do anything to add to the work of Jesus Christ. We are simply to enjoy it.

In Deuteronomy 5:15, a different reason is given for the Sabbath: the people of Israel must remember that they were slaves in Egypt and God brought them out of slavery, so they should give their slaves a chance to rest as they do on the Sabbath. In Colossians 1:12–14, Paul (like many New Testament authors) speaks of the work of the Lord Jesus as a new exodus. Egypt is a picture or symbol of the world; Pharaoh is a symbol of Satan, and the slavery is a symbol of our enslavement to our passion and pride from which Christ has redeemed us in his death on the cross. Jesus is the new Joshua, who will lead those people connected to him by the new covenant to enter and enjoy God's Sabbath rest.

THE JUDGMENTS (EXODUS 20:22–23:33)

Following the "Ten Words" is a section entitled the "Judgments." This section is an expansion on the Ten Words. Although parts of the section are in the form of prescriptive statements (You shall/shall not; e.g., 22:18–23:10), large parts are in the form of conditional sentences, i.e., case decisions or descriptive law or judicial precedents (e.g., 21:2–22:17). Like the Ten Words, provisions for cultic issues (i.e., festivals; e.g., 23:10–19) are mixed together with moral matters and issues of restitution and social justice.

Significant studies comparing and contrasting these materials with counterparts in ancient Near Eastern culture and society have been made in the past thirty years. As noted earlier, citing the work of John Walton, the major legal treatises in the ancient Near East are as follows:

Legal Treatises of the Ancient Near East

The Laws of Ur-Nammu	21st century B.C.
The Laws of Lipit-Ishtar	19th century B.C.
The Laws of Eshnunna	18th century B.C.
The Code of Hammurabi	18th century B.C.
The Old Hittite Laws	17th century B.C.
The Middle Assyrian Laws	12th century B.C.

The consensus from detailed analysis is that these texts are not law codes as we who have a Graeco-Roman heritage think of them, because they are neither *comprehensive* nor *prescriptive*. The ancients loved to compile lists, and these are anthologies of examples that model judicial wisdom. J. Bottéro, an expert in ancient Near Eastern legal material, says:

> In the eyes of its author the "Code" [of Hammurabi] was not at all intended to exercise by itself a univocal normative value in the legislative order. But it did have value as a model; it was instructive and educative in the judicial order. A law applies to details; a model inspires—which is entirely different. In conclusion, we have here not a law code, nor the charter of a legal reform, but above all, in its own way, a treatise, with examples, on the exercise of judicial power.[18]

Bottéro compares legal treatises to treatises for divination and medicine. They are similar in form and function. All three contain conditional statements and are intended to assist practitioners through cases that serve as models or paradigms. As Walton says,

> The medical treatises teach medical practitioners about diagnosis, the divinatory treatises teach the practitioners about prognostication through omens, and the legal treatises teach practitioners (whether future kings or court personnel) about judicial wisdom, all through multiplying examples through patterns.[19]

Again, Bottéro concludes,

> The cuneiform treatises are nothing else but types of paradigms or tables. It was by repetition and the variation of particular cases, of models to be considered in a spirit of analogy, that the substance of the discipline in question was assimilated, that the habit of scientific judgment was formed, that the sense of correct reasoning was acquired at the same time as the capacity to extend these same judgments and reasoning to all the material objects of the science in question, according to their eventual presentation.[20]

Thus the ancient legal treatises were not law codes in the sense in which we think of them in the Western world, but they gave instruction in model justice through model verdicts.

Hammurabi compiled his list of exemplary verdicts as a legitimization of his reign and rule, showing that his skill in administrative justice was

---

[18] J. Bottéro, "The 'Code' of Hammurabi," in *Mesopotamia: Writing, Reasoning, and the Gods* (Chicago: University of Chicago Press, 1992), 156–184.

[19] Walton, *Ancient Near Eastern Thought and the Old Testament* (Grand Rapids, Mich.; Baker, 2006), 289.

[20] Bottéro, "'Code' of Hammurabi," 178.

derived from the sun god Shamash, god of justice. In this sense, there is a similarity between such legal texts and wisdom literature.

It is also important to note that Hammurabi's legal treatise was not considered the "law of the land," and it imposed no obligations on the courts or society. In extensive research and study of court cases from the ancient Near East, never is there any direct reference or appeal to the six major legal treatises that have been frequently listed as "law codes."

The covenant at Sinai (Exodus 19–24) must not only be compared to the culture of the ancient Near East, but contrasted as well. Walton provides a table (table 7.2) that highlights some of the differences:[21]

Table 7.2: Literary Context of the Law in the Pentateuch and Ancient Near East

Exodus 19–24/Deuteronomy	Ancient Near Eastern Treatises
Essentially a self-revelation of deity	Essentially a self-glorification of the king
Covenant charter that synthesizes an entire detailed and organized vision of the "right" exercise of what it means to be a holy nation (Ex. 19:5–6; Deut. 26:19)	Political charter that synthesizes an entire detailed and organized vision of the "right" exercise of justice
Stipulations of the covenant	Treatise on jurisprudence
Portrays the ideal covenant keeper	Portrays the ideal king
The prime purpose of the biblical compilation is sanctification	The prime purpose of the Mesopotamian compilations is justice

Since the covenant in Exodus 20–23 entails covenant stipulations embodying the guidelines and Torah (i.e., instruction) of Yahweh for life in the land, the prescriptive statements were certainly intended to be obeyed. Nonetheless, the case laws illustrate the righteousness of God in an Iron-Age cultural setting and are bound by the psychology of that time. This aspect shows that the "law" is not eternal.

THE CEREMONY OF COVENANT RATIFICATION (EXODUS 24:1–11)

Exodus 24 picks up the narrative after the Ten Words and the Judgments are recounted. The connection is easily seen if one mentally removes the direct

---

[21] Adapted with permission from Walton, *Ancient Near Eastern Thought and the Old Testament*, 293.

discourse or speech in chapters 20–23. Two episodes dominate Exodus 24. The ceremony of covenant ratification is described in verses 1–11. In verses 12–18 Moses ascends Mount Sinai to receive instructions on how Israel is to worship God.

The ceremony of covenant ratification is significant for our understanding of the Sinai covenant. First, Moses reports the Ten Words and the Judgments to the people who, as in Exodus 19:7–8, agree to the covenant. Then Moses commits the Words and Judgments to writing in a document referred to in Exodus 24:7 as "the Book of the Covenant." Early in the morning he builds an altar and erects twelve pillars. Presumably the altar represents Yahweh, for we are clearly told that the twelve stone stelae represent the people, i.e., the twelve tribes of Israel. Moses has assistants from the twelve tribes offer burnt offerings and fellowship/peace offerings. Moses collects the blood from the bulls sacrificed and pours half on the altar. Next he reads the Book of the Covenant, and the people vow to obey and practice the covenant stipulations. Then he scatters/tosses the other half of the blood on the people. In reality he may have actually sprinkled the blood on the pillars that represented the people.

Concerning the blood tossed on the people, Bruce Waltke says, "The latter is called the 'blood of the covenant' because it effects the covenant relationship by cleansing the recipients from sin."[22] This interpretation may appear plausible, but in this instance it is not sustained by the evidence from the text. Fellowship offerings can be for an expression of thanksgiving or can be offered as the result of a vow, according to Leviticus 7:12–18. The latter is appropriate, since covenant making entails vows. The offering in Exodus 24 is not specified as a sin or reparation sacrifice, nor is the verb "sprinkled" used, as is normal for offerings for sin. The blood is applied to the altar representing Yahweh, as well as to the people, and certainly Yahweh does not need to be cleansed from sin. Instead, the ceremony indicates the meaning. Half of the blood is put on Yahweh and half of the blood is put on the people. In between these two symbolic acts is the reading of the Book of the Covenant and the vow of the people to keep its stipulations. The symbolism is that the one blood joins the two parties.[23] What is most similar to the ceremony of Exodus 24 is a wedding. Two people who are not related by blood are now, by virtue of the covenant of marriage, closer than any other

---

[22] Bruce K. Waltke with Charles Yu, *An Old Testament Theology* (Grand Rapids, MI: Zondervan, 2007), 435.
[23] Walther Eichrodt, *Theology of the Old Testament*, trans. J. A. Baker, 2 vols. (Philadelphia: Westminster, 1961), 1:43, 156–157.

kin relation. It is by virtue of the covenant at Sinai that Yahweh becomes the *gō'ēl*, i.e., the nearest relative, and that Israel becomes not just a nation but a "people" (*'am*), i.e., a kinship term specifying relationship to the Lord.

This interpretation is confirmed by the fact that a party representing the people ascends the mountain and eats a meal. Examples of eating a communal meal to conclude a covenant are numerous. This ancient Near Eastern and biblical practice is the basis for banquets at weddings today.

THE COVENANT AT SINAI WITHIN THE LARGER STORY: THE SIGNIFICANCE OF THE FORM

Observing the form of the covenant as given in Exodus and Deuteronomy is important for a proper understanding of the Mosaic covenant and foundational for correlating the old covenant with the new. The form and literary structure in both Exodus and Deuteronomy shows the following points:

(1) The Ten Commandments are foundational to the ordinances and, conversely, the ordinances or case laws apply and extend the Ten Commandments in a practical way to all areas of life. Nonetheless, one cannot take the Ten Commandments as "eternal" and the ordinances as "temporal," for both sections together constitute the agreement or covenant made between God and Israel.

(2) It is common to categorize and classify the laws as (a) moral, (b) civil, and (c) ceremonial, but this classification is foreign to the material and imposed upon it from the outside rather than arising from the material and being clearly marked by the literary structure of the text. In fact, the ceremonial, civil, and moral laws are all mixed together, not only in the Judgments or ordinances but in the Ten Words as well (the Sabbath may be properly classified as ceremonial). Those who claim the distinction between ceremonial, civil, and moral law do so because they want to affirm that the ceremonial (and in some cases, civil) laws no longer apply but the moral laws are eternal. Unfortunately, John Frame in his magisterial work on *The Doctrine of the Christian Life* and Bruce Waltke in his equally magisterial *An Old Testament Theology* perpetuate this tradition.[24] This is an inaccurate representation of Scripture at this point. Exodus 24 clearly indicates that the

---

[24] John M. Frame, *The Doctrine of the Christian Life* (Phillipsburg, NJ: P&R, 2008), 213–217. Frame says, "the distinction [moral, ceremonial and civil law in the Westminster Confession] is a good one, in a rough-and-ready way" (213). Later he admits that "the laws of the Pentateuch are not clearly labeled as moral, civil, or ceremonial" (214). In the end, he struggles to provide clear criteria to show what is and what is not applicable for Christians today from the old covenant. See also Waltke, *Old Testament Theology*, 434, 436.

Book of the Covenant consists of the Ten Words and the Judgments, and this is the covenant (both Ten Words and Judgments) that Jesus, in Matthew 5:17, says he has completely fulfilled, and that Hebrews declares is now made obsolete by the new covenant (Heb. 8:13). What we can say to represent accurately the teaching of Scripture is that the righteousness of God codified, enshrined, and encapsulated in the old covenant has not changed, and that this same righteousness is now codified and enshrined in the new.

(3) When one compares Exodus and Deuteronomy with contemporary documents from the ancient Near East in both content and form, two features are without parallel:

a) in content, the biblical documents are identical to ancient Near Eastern law codes, but they do not have the form of a law code;

b) in form, the biblical documents are identical to ancient Near Eastern covenants or international treaties, but not in content.

This is extremely instructive. God desires to rule in the midst of his people as King. He wants to direct, guide, and instruct their lives and lifestyle. Yet he wants to do this in the context of a relationship of love, loyalty, and trust. This is completely different from Greek and Roman law codes or ancient Near Eastern law codes. They represent an impersonal code of conduct binding on all citizens and enforced by penalties from a controlling authority. We should always remember that Torah, by contrast, means personal "instruction" from God as Father and King of his people rather than just "law"; thus a term like "covenantal instruction" might be more useful.

Our view of the old covenant is enhanced by accurate exegesis that not only attends to the cultural context and language of the text but also allows the text to inform us of its own literary structure and considers the place of the text in the larger story. The biblical-theological framework is especially important, because there we come to see the Ten Commandments not merely as fundamental requirements determining divine-human and human-human relationships as moral principles, but also as the foundation of true social justice and the basis of what it means to be a son or daughter of God, an Adamic figure, i.e., truly and genuinely human.

Chapter 8

THE MOSAIC COVENANT— DEUTERONOMY/MOAB

The book of Deuteronomy brings us to the heart of the matter and also to the matter of the heart in relation to the Mosaic covenant. In particular, Deuteronomy 6:5 is arguably the key text of the Old Testament. This is not stated for rhetorical effect or merely to register an opinion. Our Lord Jesus himself said so in his earthly instruction and teaching (Matt. 22:34–40). We must learn from Jesus and his apostles how to interpret the Old Testament as they did and discover how and why they came to this conclusion.

In John Bunyan's classic *Pilgrim's Progress*, "Christian" is living in the City of Destruction until he is instructed by "Evangelist" to flee the coming wrath and pursue the road to the Celestial City. Away over the bogs and fields he is pointed to a little wicket gate. When he passes through this gate, he will begin his journey to the Celestial City. We can say that Deuteronomy 6:4–9 is the Wicket Gate to the Spiritual High Road (i.e., metanarrative) of the Old Testament.

THE DATE OF DEUTERONOMY

The consensus among scholars of the Old Testament is that the book of Deuteronomy was given its final form in the fifth century B.C. This is unfortunate. The form or structure of the text may be analyzed either as *speeches* or as a *treaty*: these two perspectives are *not* mutually exclusive.

According to key markers in the text, the book can be divided into three speeches given by Moses: (1) 1:1–4:43; (2) 4:44–28:68; (3) 29:1–30:20. Note that narrative in the third person is extremely sparse (1:3–5; 5:1; 27:1, 9, 11; 29:2; 31:1, 7, 9–10, 14–16, 22–25, 30; 32:44–46, 48; 33:2, 7, 8, 12, 13, 18, 20, 22, 23, 24; 34:1–12). This overall structure is confirmed and supported by four key headings in the text arranged in an A, B, A', B' pattern:

A   1:1   These are the words . . .
B   4:44   And this is the Torah
A'   29:1   These are the words . . .
B'   33:1   And this is the Blessing

Alternatively, and not necessarily as a competing structure, the book may be analyzed as having the form of a suzerain-vassal treaty of the type common among the Hittites in the fourteenth century B.C. An example of scholars interpreting the literary structure this way is the work of K. A. Kitchen.[1] My (Peter's) own analysis of the text follows that of Kitchen, but I recognize chapter 27 as corresponding to the Deposition of Text and Public Reading and conclude that the Appeal to Witnesses section of the suzerain-vassal treaty corresponds to chapters 29–30 of Deuteronomy. This analysis can be displayed in table 8.1.

Table 8.1: Deuteronomy as Suzerain-Vassal Treaty

1. Preamble	1:1–5
2. Historical Prologue	1:6–4:44

3. Stipulations
    a. General
    b. Specific
	
	4:45–11:32
	12:1–26:19

4. Document Deposition	27:1–10
5. Public Reading	27:11–26
6. Blessings and Curses	28:1–68
7. Solemn Oath Ceremony	29:1–30:20

As a fundamental point, it must be noted that since no gods exist besides Yahweh, no appeal can be made to them, and the "Witnesses" section of the suzerain-vassal treaty (usually an appeal to a long list of gods) by definition could not be part of a covenant or treaty between Yahweh and Israel. So, in Deuteronomy, the Solemn Oath Ceremony is equivalent to the Witnesses section.

Two major observations are obvious by considering the hard data. First, the form and literary structure of the treaties changes over the centuries, and the form of Deuteronomy best matches only those of the fourteenth century B.C. It does not match the forms of earlier or later treaties.

---

[1] See K. A. Kitchen, *Ancient Orient and Old Testament* (Downers Grove, IL: InterVarsity Press, 1966), 96–98; idem, *The Bible in Its World: The Bible and Archaeology Today* (Downers Grove, IL: InterVarsity Press, 1977), 82; and idem, *On the Reliability of the Old Testament* (Grand Rapids, MI: Eerdmans, 2003), 283–289. Although Kitchen actually dates the exodus to the thirteenth century B.C., he nonetheless argues that the form does not allow a composition date later in time.

Second, while the form of Deuteronomy clearly follows that of the Hittite suzerain-vassal treaties of the fourteenth century, in actuality it represents an amalgam or confluence of the legal treatises and political treaties of its time, since the order of the blessings and curses matches that of the legal treatises, although the fact that there are few blessings and many curses corresponds to the suzerain-vassal treaties. Indeed, the form or structure of the book is that of a covenant or treaty, while the content of the book is similar to a legal treatise.

The evidence from the ancient Near East, then, strongly supports Deuteronomy as coming from the time which the internal evidence of the text claims: the era of Moses.

DEUTERONOMY—THE CENTER OF THE OLD TESTAMENT

The book of Deuteronomy is the center of the entire Old Testament, in terms of both metanarrative and theology.

First, Deuteronomy brings to a climax and conclusion the Pentateuch or first five books of the Bible. According to the book of Genesis, God called Abraham to give him a land from which would emanate his blessing and salvation to the ends of the earth. In Deuteronomy, Abraham's family are now poised at the entrance to that land and they are given instructions on how to live in the land, so that they might be a blessing and bring salvation to the ends of the earth.

The book of Exodus narrates how God redeemed Israel out of Egypt so that they might come to a mountain and worship him and begin to live their lives in conformity with his word as a holy nation and royal priesthood. Further instructions for their worship of God and detailed guidelines on what devotion to the covenant Lord entails are given in the book of Leviticus. The book of Deuteronomy supplements the covenant thus given in Exodus and Leviticus; it completes it (Deut. 29:1). Moreover, the wanderings through the wilderness that are the subject of the book of Numbers bring the people to this very point. Thus, Deuteronomy is the climax of the Pentateuch.

The historical books Joshua, Judges, Samuel, and Kings (known in the Hebrew Canon as the Former Prophets) present a history of Israel based on and evaluated from the point of view of the Israelite covenant, particularly as given in Deuteronomy. For example, Israel and Judah are evaluated on the basis of the command for the centralization of worship in Deuteronomy 12—Israel for the centers established by Jeroboam, and Judah for her high places.

The history of the monarchy is evaluated according to chapter 17 of Deuteronomy. The efficacy of the prophetic word is evaluated on the basis of Deuteronomy 18 (e.g., 2 Kings 24:2). It is commonplace among scholars today to refer to Joshua through Kings as "the Deuteronomistic History" since the perspective of the book of Deuteronomy provides the "historiographic method/philosophy" of the authors. Where scholars are entirely askew, however, is in dating the book of Deuteronomy to the sixth or fifth century B.C. Deuteronomy was written first, and then *afterwards*, the history of Israel was written from the perspective of this central document in the canon of the Old Testament.

The Israelite covenant, especially the expression or form of the covenant as it is constituted in Deuteronomy, is also the basis and foundation for the Latter Prophets Isaiah, Jeremiah, Ezekiel, and the Twelve Prophets. The central concern of the prophets was to call the people back to the covenant. The people constantly violated the covenant by following idols and failing to fulfill the covenant stipulations. As demonstrated so ably by Claus Westermann in his book *Basic Forms of Prophetic Speech*, both their promises and their threats, as well as even their sentences, are all based on the book of Deuteronomy.[2] Just one example is the expression "the stubbornness of their [evil] heart"—an absolute favorite of the prophet Jeremiah. He uses it eight times (Jer. 3:17; 7:24; 9:14; 11:8; 13:10; 16:12; 18:12; 23:17). This expression is derived from Deuteronomy 29:18, and it occurs elsewhere in the Old Testament only in Psalm 81:13 (81:12, English versions).

When Psalms speaks of the Torah of Yahweh—"on his law he meditates day and night" (Ps. 1:2)—the psalmist is referring to the book of Deuteronomy. It is also what is celebrated in the longest Psalm—Psalm 119.

Bruce Waltke has shown that the book most closely connected to the theology of the book of Proverbs is the book of Deuteronomy.[3] Proverbs contains the instruction the king and queen together gave their son to raise him in the way of the Lord. The Torah or instruction of the covenant (Deuteronomy) is presented as a beautiful woman to attract the son to follow this way. Failure to follow this way is not so much sin against the Lord as just plain folly and stupidity, bringing loss in every way in one's life. Similarly, Song of Songs presents the skillful way in marriage. And as far as Job is concerned, without the covenant and the related notion of the *goel* (kinsman redeemer), its instruction on suffering would be emasculated. Precisely be-

---

[2] Claus Westermann, *Basic Forms of Prophetic Speech*, trans. Hugh Clayton White (Louisville: Westminster/John Knox, 1991).

[3] Bruce K. Waltke, "The Book of Proverbs and Old Testament Theology," *Bibliotheca Sacra* 136 (1979): 302–317.

cause Israel is married to Yahweh by virtue of the covenant making at Sinai, thus becoming "his people," he is now their nearest relative who will step in to lift them out of debt and suffering.

The centrality of Deuteronomy to the rest of the Old Testament may perhaps be diagrammed as follows:

Deuteronomy and Genesis (land promised, land entered)
Deuteronomy and Exodus—Leviticus (addition to covenant)
Deuteronomy and Numbers (completes wanderings)
Deuteronomy basis of Joshua—Kings (Deuteronomistic history)
Deuteronomy basis of Prophets
Deuteronomy basis of Wisdom texts

DEUTERONOMY 6:4–5—THE CENTER OF THE BOOK OF DEUTERONOMY

When the book of Deuteronomy is considered from the perspective of the form of the suzerain-vassal treaty, the command in 6:5 ("You shall love the LORD your God with all your heart and with all your soul, and with all your strength") is placed *immediately after* the Preamble and Historical Prologue in the section providing the General Stipulation of the covenant. Within this section, it is, in fact, the *first* command given after material *repeated* from Exodus 19–24, and it is also the *greatest* command among all the covenant stipulations: to be completely devoted and loyal to Yahweh. This command is the foundation to all the requirements and stipulations of the covenant. In the section Deuteronomy 4:45–11:32, Moses is concerned to expound *this one requirement* as fully as possible. Placing Deuteronomy 6:5 within the context of the literary structure demonstrates, as one might expect, that Jesus was right: this is both the first and the greatest command in the covenant—wholehearted devotion to the great King. From what has been said so far, it is therefore the key text of the Old Testament.

WHAT IT MEANS TO LOVE GOD

The central command to love God is modified by three prepositional phrases: (1) with all your heart, (2) with all your soul, and (3) with all your strength. We will consider each of these in turn.

In Hebrew, the word "heart" refers to the core of who you are, the center of each person. It refers, in particular, to the place where we feel, where we think, and where we make decisions and plans, i.e., emotions, mind, and will. This can be easily seen from the following illustrative passages:

A. Feelings:

> A glad heart makes a cheerful face,
> but by sorrow of heart the spirit is crushed. (Prov. 15:13, ESV)

> A joyful heart is good medicine,
> but a crushed spirit dries up the bones. (Prov. 17:22, ESV)

When these proverbs refer to a "glad heart" or a "joyful heart" they are clearly referring to one's emotions and feelings in terms of a healthy psyche.

B. Reasoning:

> But to this day the LORD has not given you a heart to understand or eyes to see or ears to hear. (Deut. 29:4, ESV)

> Make the heart of this people dull,
> and their ears heavy,
> and blind their eyes;
> lest they see with their eyes,
> and hear with their ears,
> and understand with their hearts,
> and turn and be healed. (Isa. 6:10, ESV)

In both Deuteronomy 29:4 and Isaiah 6:10, one *understands* with the heart; surely then what is being referred to is what we normally call the mind. This is the place where we reason and think and understand.

C. Will:

> The heart of man plans his way,
> but the LORD establishes his steps. (Prov. 16:9, ESV)

> May he grant you your heart's desire
> and fulfill all your plans! (Ps. 20:4, ESV)

Proverbs 16:9 and Psalm 20:4 show that the "heart" makes plans and has desires; it is the place where we make decisions. According to H. W. Wolff, the Hebrew word "heart" refers to the mind in approximately 400 out of 814 passages speaking of the human heart. This supports his warning that "we must guard against the false impression that biblical man is determined more by feeling than by reason."[4]

We should note, then, that the biblical language differs markedly from our own in the Western world. For us, the heart is associated with emotions, feelings, love, and Valentine's Day. Conversely, for the Bible, the heart is where we reason and think and make decisions and plans. We can frequently speak of people who cannot bridge the eighteen-inch gap between the head and the heart. The ancient Hebrews knew no such gap. The heart is the center of one's being and the place where emotions, mind, and will operate in harmony and union.

Notice how the text of Deuteronomy 6:5 is quoted in the Gospels:

> [34] Hearing that Jesus had silenced the Sadducees, the Pharisees got together. [35] One of them, an expert in the law, tested him with this question: [36] "Teacher, which is the greatest commandment in the Law?" [37] Jesus replied: "'Love the Lord your God with all your heart and with all your soul and with all your mind.' [38] This is the first and greatest commandment. [39] And the second is like it: 'Love your neighbor as yourself.' [40] All the Law and the Prophets hang on these two commandments." (Matt. 22:34–40, NIV)

Jesus adds the word "mind" in quoting the text to make sure a Greek audience would understand that this is what is conveyed by the Hebrew word for heart.

We should not think that merely intellectual pursuits are equivalent to loving God. According to the context, loving God has to do with fearing him, obeying his commands, and passing on his instructions to another generation.

Second in the command in Deuteronomy 6:5 is to love the Lord "with all your soul." "Soul" renders the Hebrew word *nephesh*. One of the best discussions of this term is, again, by Wolff.[5] The original meaning is "throat," and hence by extension it can refer to our "desire" or "longing." The soul thus designates the organ of "desire" or of "vital needs" which have to be satisfied if man is to go on living. In this way the term comes to mean soul or life. Our entire life in terms of our desires and needs is to be devoted to the Lord.

Third, we are to love the Lord with all our "strength." This renders

---

[4] Hans W. Wolff, *Anthropology of the Old Testament*, trans. Margaret Kohl (Philadelphia: Fortress, 1974), 46–47.
[5] Ibid., 11–25.

the Hebrew word *me'ōd*, normally an adverb meaning "exceedingly" or "greatly." The lexicons give the meaning "power" or "strength" for *me'ōd* as a noun only for Deuteronomy 6:5 and 2 Kings 23:25 in the approximately 300 instances in the Hebrew Bible. Probably the word ought to be construed as functioning as an adverb here as well. The meaning would be, "You shall love the Lord your God with all your heart and with all your soul—and that to the fullest extent."

THE COVENANT FORMULA IN DEUTERONOMY

In our analysis of Genesis 17, we noted the first instance of the Covenant Formula ("I will be their God"; 17:8; cf. v. 7). There are actually three parts to the Covenant Formula: A, "I will be God for you" (occurring 16 times); B, "You shall be a people for him" (occurring 10 times); and C, a combination of the two (occurring 12 times).

The Covenant Formula is found precisely seven times in Deuteronomy as a whole (Deut. 26:17–18 is counted as one instance). Moreover, the Covenant Formula occurs just once in each of the seven sections of the book divided according to the literary structure of Hittite treaties from the fourteenth century B.C. In fact, the Covenant Formula always occurs at a key point in the literary structure of each section (table 8.2).

Table 8.2 Covenant Relationship Formula (CRF)
in the Literary Sections of Deuteronomy

Hittite Treaty Formulary	Represented in Deuteronomy	CRF used (reference)
1) Preamble	1:1–5	None
2) Historical Prologue	1:6–4:44	Formula B (4:20)
3a) General Stipulation	4:45–11:32	Formula B (7:6)
3b) Specific Stipulations	12:1–26:15	Formula B (14:2)
	26:16–19	Formula C (26:17–19)
4) Document Clause	27:1–8	None
	27:9–10	Formula B (27:9)
5) Public Reading	27:11–26	None
6) Blessings and Curses	29:1	Formula B (28:9)
7) Solemn Oath Ceremony	29:2–30:20	Formula C (29:12)

Thus the Covenant Formula is used in a *highly conscious manner*.

THE RELATIONSHIP OF DEUTERONOMY
TO EARLIER COVENANTS

An important question is the relationship between the book of Deuteronomy and Exodus 19–24, designated in Exodus 24:7 as "the Book of the Covenant."

In broad strokes, there are three views of the relation of the book of Deuteronomy to the earlier material: (1) that it is a renewal and expansion of the Sinai covenant, (2) that it is a renewal and expansion of the Abrahamic covenant, or (3) that it is a completely new covenant.

A key passage is Deuteronomy 29:1, which begins a new section, since the curses concluded in 28:68 end the covenant text according to the form and structure of a suzerain-vassal treaty. The text of Deuteronomy 1:1–28:68, the bulk of the book of Deuteronomy, constitutes the actual text of a covenant made (i.e., cut) with the people in the land of Moab before they enter Canaan. The preposition "in addition to" ("besides" in ESV) is crucial in this text. This text clearly states that the book of Deuteronomy is a covenant in its own right, made with the people, in addition to the Book of the Covenant in Exodus 19–24 with expansions in Leviticus and Numbers. Deuteronomy is thus a supplement to—and not a replacement for—the covenant at Sinai. It is a bit like a codicil added to a will (though here the codicil is larger than the will itself).

We know that God made a covenant with Israel at Sinai. We know that the people of Israel violated the covenant in the middle of the proceedings—while it was being inaugurated. We know that the relationship between God and Israel was maintained only by forgiveness on the part of Yahweh. The book of Deuteronomy appears to be a reaffirmation and restating of the covenant instruction (*tôrâ*) just before entering the land of Canaan. Why, then, is the expression "to cut a covenant" used in Deuteronomy 29:1 instead of "to affirm a covenant"?

Before turning to consider the evidence in Deuteronomy, it ought to be noted that the expression *kārat bĕrît*, "cut a covenant," can be used in covenant renewal ceremonies. Quite a number of scholars who have commented on the expressions in Hebrew are confused about how this works. Let us look briefly at Joshua 23–24 as an example.

Covenant Renewal in Joshua 23–24

Chapter 23 reports that, toward the end of his life, Joshua summoned all the tribes of Israel to Shechem. He notes that Yahweh has kept his promises.

Some land remains to be taken, but the Lord will continue to drive out the Canaanites if the Israelites continue to be faithful to the covenant and do not mix with the Canaanites or serve and worship their gods. According to Joshua 23:16, serving and worshiping the gods of Canaan is equivalent to transgressing the covenant of Yahweh. This must be a reference to the covenant made at Sinai and renewed in Deuteronomy.

In chapter 24, Joshua summons Israel to a covenant renewal at Shechem. Verses 1–13 describe the faithfulness and grace of Yahweh toward Israel in bringing them to Canaan and giving them the land. Then in a challenge by Joshua—answered by the people of Israel—that is repeated twice, Joshua stresses that choosing to serve Yahweh means excising all idols and removing all worship of alternative deities. We pick up the thread in verse 24:

> And the people said to Joshua, "Yahweh our God we will serve, and his voice we will obey." So Joshua made a covenant for the people that day, and put in place a decree and a judgment for them at Shechem. And Joshua wrote these words in the book of the Torah of God. And he took a large stone and set it up there under the terebinth that was by the sanctuary of the LORD. And Joshua said to all the people, "Behold, this stone shall be a witness against us, for it has heard all the words of the LORD that he spoke to us. Therefore it shall be a witness against you, lest you deal falsely with your God." So Joshua sent the people away, every man to his inheritance. (Josh. 24:24–28)

What is actually happening here is that the people are making a covenant to keep the covenant at Sinai. Their commitment to Yahweh is divided. They need to put away the idols and give complete commitment and devotion to Yahweh alone. They are renewing their original commitment and solemnizing this renewal as a covenant. So, in fact, *they are making* a covenant *to keep* an earlier covenant. This is different from affirming a covenant verbally (or by acting to fulfill an obligation specified in an earlier agreement) and fully justifies the expression "to cut a covenant." Linguistically, then, "cut a covenant" is always used of making a covenant (for the first time), but can be used of covenant renewals since people make new vows to keep earlier commitments.

This past summer, some close friends in Germany celebrated their silver wedding anniversary. It was a service of worship in the local church with family and friends, exactly as on their wedding day. This was a covenant renewal in the sense that they made an agreement to keep the original agreement. Such is the human condition that we constantly fall away from our position of complete loyalty so that a solemnizing of a renewed commitment is possible.

Scholars have confused the matter by attempting to correlate the expressions *kārat bĕrît* (to cut a covenant) and *hēqîm bĕrît* (to affirm a covenant) with covenant making and covenant renewal. The English word "establish" is, in itself, ambiguous, since one can establish something that is falling apart or establish something for the first time. This is not how these expressions are used. The expression *kārat bĕrît* (to cut a covenant) is normally used for making a covenant and, in a few instances, for renewing a covenant. The reason why *kārat bĕrît* (to cut a covenant) is used for covenant renewals is that humans tend to lag in their loyalty over time. Then they realize that they have lost something of their original commitment and devotion and make a covenant, a promise, a vow, or simply a statement, that they intend to keep the original covenant. This is not the same thing as a person who has never lagged in their commitment and loyalty verbally affirming their continued commitment to the covenant or, more particularly, acting at some time after the original covenant making to uphold their commitment or obligation. The expression *hēqîm bĕrît* (to affirm a covenant) is *never used for a covenant renewal* in Scripture.

Thus, Deuteronomy, rather than Exodus 34, should be viewed and understood as the covenant renewal. Editorial headings in modern English versions frequently label Exodus 34:10–27 as "the Covenant Renewal." There is, however, no real basis for such a description in the text itself. Granted, the chronological sequence of events in Exodus 19–40 is not always abundantly clear. Nonetheless, the rehearsal of these events in Deuteronomy 9:9–29 aids in clarifying the narrative in Exodus. It seems that, after the covenant ratification in Exodus 24, Moses is called to ascend farther up the mountain.

While Moses had written down the Book of the Covenant (Ten Words and Judgments) that God gave him orally, God would now give him the stone tablets and the Instruction (Torah) and the Commandment which he had personally written to instruct them. So when Moses went up the mountain, the cloud, i.e., the glory of Yahweh, covered the mountain for six days, and on the seventh, Moses was summoned and enveloped by the cloud and was on the mountain forty days and forty nights (Ex. 24:15–18). At the end of this time, Moses descended the mountain in anger because the people had broken the first (and second) of the Ten Words and thus violated the covenant (Ex. 32:15–20). No doubt Moses' breaking of the tablets symbolized the broken covenant. Then Moses interceded for the people and was on the mountain another forty days and forty nights (Ex. 34:27–28). During this time God revealed himself to Moses as compassionate and forgiving. Moses appealed immediately to the character of God newly revealed. It is in this context that God makes the following statement:

> And he said, "Behold, I am making a covenant. Before all your people I will do marvels, such as have not been created in all the earth or in any nation. And all the people among whom you are shall see the work of the LORD, for it is an awesome thing that I will do with you. (Ex. 34:10, ESV)

Note particularly in verse 10 the use of the active participle, "I am making a covenant." This is exactly like a present tense in English, and the context indicates that God *is in the midst of* covenant making. First the Ten Words were given verbally; then they were written. The covenant was violated before the stone tablets were given to the people. God forgave Israel at Moses' request and carried on with his covenant making in writing another set of stone tablets to give to the people. There is no indication that Exodus 34 entails a "covenant renewal" apart from the people being given a rewritten set of stone tablets. In the end, the generation entering the covenant at Sinai died in the wilderness and another generation arose. Deuteronomy is a renewal of the covenant with them as well as a covenant made for the first time as a supplement to the covenant at Sinai. There are only three other constructions in the Hebrew Bible where the participle is employed in the standard terminology (*kārat běrît*): Deuteronomy 29:11, 13 and, analogously, Nehemiah 9:38. In each case the participle corresponds to the present tense in English and refers to something in the making that is in the process of being completed.

To sum up the discussion to this point, according to 29:1, the book of Deuteronomy is a covenant in its own right, separate from the covenant at Sinai/Horeb. In essence this covenant is a supplement to the covenant at Sinai. The covenant making on the plains of Moab is also a covenant renewal of the broken Sinai/Horeb-covenant with the subsequent generation.

All instances of "covenant" (*běrît*) in Deuteronomy before 29:1a (aside from a foreign treaty in 7:2) refer to the covenant at Sinai (4:13, 23; 5:2, 3; 7:9; 9:9, 11, 15; 10:8; 17:2; 29:1a; 33:9) or the Abrahamic covenant on which it is based (4:31; 7:12; 8:18). All the instances of covenant after 29:1a in chapters 29–30 refer to the covenant at Moab (29:1b, 9, 12, 14, 21, 25). After chapters 1–30 we find six occurrences of covenant: the instance in 33:9 and in the phrase "the ark of the covenant" refer to the covenant at Sinai

(31:9, 25, 26). Note carefully in 31:25–26 that the book of Deuteronomy (chapters 1–30) is written as a single text and is placed *beside* the ark of the covenant, just as Deuteronomy 29:1 specifies that it is a covenant *in addition to* the covenant at Sinai.

Finally, the two instances in Deuteronomy 31:16, 20 are clearly passages where the covenant at Sinai and the covenant at Moab are fused as one in the author's mind.

Deuteronomy 5:1–6 is an important text. Earlier I (Peter) concluded that the covenant at Sinai and the covenant at Moab may have been fused as one in the author's mind there. Now a better interpretation may be suggested:

> And Moses summoned all Israel and said to them, "Hear, O Israel, the statutes and the rules that I speak in your hearing today, and you shall learn them and be careful to do them. The LORD our God made a covenant with us in Horeb. Not with our fathers did the LORD make this covenant, but with us, who are all of us here alive today. The LORD spoke with you face to face at the mountain, out of the midst of the fire, while I stood between the LORD and you at that time, to declare to you the word of the LORD. For you were afraid because of the fire, and you did not go up into the mountain. He said:
> "'I am the LORD your God, who brought you out of the land of Egypt, out of the house of slavery.'" (Deut. 5:1–6, ESV)

This passage reviews the covenant material from Exodus 19–24 before presenting the main stipulation of the covenant (Deut. 6:5) followed by the detailed stipulations. Verse 2 of Deuteronomy 5 says, "The LORD our God made a covenant with us in Horeb" (ESV) and employs the standard terminology, *kārat berît*, i.e., cut a covenant. This is a clear reference to the Israelite covenant made at Sinai, i.e., Exodus 19–24. Then Moses says, "Not with our fathers did the LORD make this covenant, but with us, who are all of us here alive today" (Deut. 5:3, ESV). The question arises here, what does he mean by "our fathers"? Does this refer to the generation at Sinai that has now passed away, or is it a specific reference to Abraham, Isaac, and Jacob—a normal referent for "fathers" in Deuteronomy? Part of the problem is also the referent of "this covenant" in the same sentence, which has been construed to refer to the book of Deuteronomy, apparently reinforced by the statement at the end of verse 3, "but with us, who are all of us here alive today."

If we bear in mind the general usage of the word "covenant" in the book as a whole and the literary structure, a simple solution may be found: "the fathers" in verse 3 are Abraham, Isaac, and Jacob. The covenant referred to in verse 3 is the covenant at Sinai, which is being distinguished from the Abrahamic covenant. The language at the end of verse 3 is part of the rhetorical device in the book where Moses seeks to connect the people listening to him at Moab with the events in Egypt and at Sinai, even though they were children (under 20) at the time. This cuts the Gordian knot of this verse.

Conclusion

We are now in a position to conclude. The question before us is this: Why was an addition (codicil?) to the covenant at Sinai necessary, and why was the expression "cut a covenant" employed for this?

First, an addition to the covenant at Sinai was necessary because the directions, or instruction (*tôrâ*), encoded in the covenant at Moab cover more adequately the situations of life in Canaan than the directions or instruction (*tôrâ*) encoded in the covenant at Sinai. Thus the instruction in Deuteronomy expands and reshapes the covenant at Sinai for life in the land of Canaan. There is a whole new context and situation even though it is the same covenant. The righteousness of God must be developed and explained for a larger set of circumstances than just life in the desert.

Second, we must put the covenant making at Moab in perspective with what comes before and what comes after. In referring to the covenants that precede it, we do not appeal to terminology imposed from the outside such as covenant obligations versus regulations, conditional versus unconditional, or bilateral versus unilateral covenants. Rather, we can grasp the important points from the metanarrative and from sensitivity to the statements in the biblical text. Creation entails a covenant between God and man on the one hand and between man and the world on the other. Though the humans violate the covenant by failing to show *ḥesed* and *'ĕmet* and disobey the command in the garden, the commitment of the Creator to his creation is reaffirmed and upheld in the covenant with Noah. Second, God makes a covenant with Abraham (Genesis 15). This entails commitments and promises to Abraham and requires Abraham to be an obedient son and servant king. Though Abraham is less than a satisfactory ambassador and agent for Yahweh, God reaffirms and upholds his covenant in Genesis 17. Then at Sinai, Yahweh offers to the nation the role of kingdom of priests and holy nation. They will be bound to Yahweh by covenant and will act as obedient son and servant king in the world. Israel's disloyalty and treachery in worshiping the golden calf violate this covenant. Here there is a *difference* from the earlier covenants: the fulfillment of the covenant rests on the human partner's loyalty. Although God forgave Israel in Exodus 33–34, that entire generation, i.e., that entire Israel, was wiped out in the desert as a judgment for their unbelief in Numbers 14. The covenant needs to be renewed, but the expression *hēqîm bĕrît*, literally, "to affirm a covenant," is entirely inappropriate. God does not need to affirm his continued commitment. And the human partner that made the covenant is dead and gone. It is a brand-new Israel, which has replaced the earlier one, that needs to affirm loyalty to Yahweh in the face of earlier faithlessness and covenant violation. The expression *hēqîm bĕrît* is never used in a situation where a partner fails and now needs to uphold a commitment made previously. No, Israel needs to renew the covenant by making a covenant to keep the earlier one, just as we saw in Joshua 23–24. Then the content or instruction of this covenant can be *added* to the earlier one and can be kept *beside* the ark of the covenant. Earlier we saw that Joshua 23–24 indicates a continuity between the book of Joshua and the Pentateuch. Deuteronomy 29–30 indicates that, in the book of Deuteronomy, Moses is adding something in continuity with the covenant at Sinai. Moses is making a covenant to keep the covenant at Sinai. This is why the expression *kārat bĕrît*, "to cut a covenant," is the only one appropriate for this situation. And this time the covenant is made not only with the people of Israel who are then present, but with all future generations of Israel, so that the children cannot argue that the covenant at Sinai was with their parents and not with them.

Deuteronomy is best seen as a renewal and expansion and shaping of the Sinai covenant focusing particularly on life in the land of Canaan.

It is clear from this analysis that there is no such thing as a Palestinian covenant in Deuteronomy 29–30 as proclaimed by dispensationalists. This is a complete misunderstanding of the literary structure and the function of chapters 29–30 as a Covenant Conclusion Ceremony and of the relationship of the Moab covenant to that of Sinai.

THE SIGNIFICANCE OF THE FORM

Earlier we discussed the significance of the form of the Book of the Covenant and included Deuteronomy in that discussion. Analysis of the book of Deuteronomy requires reinforcement of one or two things.

Just as in Exodus 19–24 the Ten Words are foundational to the Judgments and, conversely, the Judgments applied and extended the Ten Words in a practical way to all areas of life, so in Deuteronomy the Specific Stipulations in chapters 12–26 illustrate application and extension of the basic requirement of loyalty and the review of the Ten Words to various areas of life (in an Iron Age culture).

Once again, the classification of the laws as (a) moral, (b) civil, and (c) ceremonial is foreign to the literary structure of the text. In fact, the ceremonial, civil, and moral laws are all mixed together.

Comparison of Deuteronomy with contemporary documents from the ancient Near East in both content and form reveals that the book belongs to the fourteenth century B.C. in relation to other treaties (see fig. 8.1, where columns 1 and 2 belong to the fourteenth century B.C., while columns 3 and 4 belong to the seventh century B.C.).

Comparison of Ancient Near Eastern Treaty Forms

14TH CENTURY B.C.	14TH CENTURY B.C.	7TH CENTURY B.C.	7TH CENTURY B.C.
LATER HITTITE	EX./DEUT.	SEFIRE	ASSYRIA
TITLE	TITLE	TITLE	TITLE
PROLOGUE	PROLOGUE	WITNESSES	WITNESSES
		CURSES	STIPULATIONS
STIPULATIONS	STIPULATIONS		
		STIPULATIONS	
DEPOSIT	DEPOSIT		
WITNESSES	WITNESSES		
CURSES	BLESSINGS		CURSES
BLESSINGS	CURSES		

Fig. 8.1

The Israelite covenant, as found in the book of Deuteronomy, is without parallel in the ancient Near East in terms of content and form taken together: (1) in content, Deuteronomy is most similar to ancient Near Eastern legal treatises, but it does not have the form of a law treatise; (2) in form, Deuteronomy is most similar to ancient Near Eastern treaties, but not in content. This is obvious from fig. 8.2.

Comparison of Ancient Near Eastern Laws/Treaties and Deuteronomy

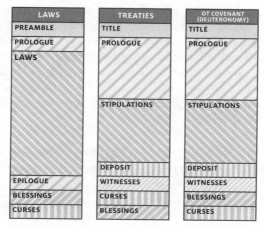

LAWS	TREATIES	OT COVENANT (DEUTERONOMY)
PREAMBLE	TITLE	TITLE
PROLOGUE	PROLOGUE	PROLOGUE
LAWS		
	STIPULATIONS	STIPULATIONS
	DEPOSIT	DEPOSIT
EPILOGUE	WITNESSES	WITNESSES
BLESSINGS	CURSES	BLESSINGS
CURSES	BLESSINGS	CURSES

Fig. 8.2

God desires to direct and instruct the lives/lifestyle of his people; yet he wants to do this in the context of a family relationship characterized by love, loyalty, and trust. This is completely different from Greek and Roman law codes or ancient Near Eastern legal treaties. We should always remember that Torah means "instruction" rather than "law." It might be better for Christians to simply speak of the "instruction" in the covenant.

THE RELATIONSHIP OF THE ISRAELITE COVENANT TO THE ABRAHAMIC COVENANT

In order to construct a metanarrative that is true to the biblical text, we must not only accurately determine the meaning of the foundational texts; we must also listen to what the text says about interrelationships between two or more covenants.

Two main points are made in the text concerning the relationship of the Israelite covenant to the Abrahamic covenant. First, the exodus from Egypt is a fulfillment of the covenant with Abraham (Ex. 2:24; Deut. 7:7–9; 9:5; Jer. 11:2–4). In Genesis 15, when God made the covenant with Abraham, he predicted that Abraham's descendants would be enslaved and mistreated in a country not their own for four hundred years, but afterwards would come out with great possessions. Among the several texts that refer to this, we can cite Deuteronomy 7:7–9 as an example:

> [7] The LORD did not set his affection on you and choose you because you were more numerous than other peoples, for you were the fewest of all peoples. [8] But it was because the LORD loved you and kept the oath he swore to your forefathers that he brought you out with a mighty hand and redeemed you from the land of slavery, from the power of Pharaoh king of Egypt. [9] Know therefore that the LORD your God is God; he is the faithful God, keeping his covenant of love to a thousand generations of those who love him and keep his commands. (NIV)

Here, deliverance from enslavement in Egypt is attributed to the Lord keeping his covenant of love. This is a clear reference to his promise to Abraham in Genesis 15.

Second, Exodus 19:5–6 shows that, by means of the Israelite covenant, God intends for the nation to fulfill the Adamic role reassigned to Abraham. Through covenant, God will bring his blessing and establish his rule in the lives of his people and, through them, to the rest of the world.

Chapter 9

THE DAVIDIC COVENANT

Another key point in the narrative plot structure of Scripture is the agreement or covenant that God initiated with David, king of Israel. We shall call this agreement the Davidic covenant, following the language of the biblical text.

As we shall see, the Davidic covenant functions in the larger story in a number of significant ways. In the history of the people of Israel, it inaugurates a divinely designed model of kingship for the nation. Furthermore, it implements the kingship of Yahweh among his people at a deeper and higher level. In addition to addressing concerns and problems of the developing nation of Israel, the Davidic covenant carries forward in specific ways the intentions and purposes of God expressed in the Sinai covenant and, even further back, in the covenant with Abraham.

First we shall look at the context and historical situation in which kingship was inaugurated. Then we shall examine the main passages on the covenant with David and also look at how this was appropriated and understood by later texts of the Old Testament, particularly Isaiah 55. Finally, we shall briefly describe the connections and relations between the Davidic covenant and the Sinai covenant and the covenant with Abraham.

JOSHUA

Joshua was a leader like Moses. He led the people into the land of Canaan, the land promised to the patriarchs in the covenant with Abraham. The book of Joshua is divided into two parts: the first half describes the conquest of the land; the second half describes the division of the land among the twelve tribes of Israel according to their *clans*. This result was a clear fulfillment of the Israelite covenant, but also led Israel to a higher level of commitment, as we see when the book ends with a ceremony of covenant renewal (Josh. 24:25). The expression employed there is *kārat běrît*, i.e., to cut a covenant. Some scholars have falsely assumed from such texts that the expression *kārat běrît* does not always refer to covenant initiation, but can be used for covenant renewal. This is an erroneous conclusion. What in fact happened is that Joshua *made a covenant* with the people *to keep the covenant*—the Israelite covenant inaugurated through Moses at Sinai and Moab. So technically, from a linguistic point of view, *kārat běrît* refers only to covenant initiation. Another example, precisely similar to Joshua 24, is 2 Kings 23:2–3, where King Josiah makes a covenant (*kārat běrît*) to keep or uphold the Sinai covenant, i.e., "to perform the words of this covenant" (*hēqîm-eth dibrê habběrît hazzō't*).

JUDGES

The next period is dark in every way. The nation of Israel is constantly breaking the covenant at this time. The writer of the book of Judges portrays recurring cycles in which (1) the people break the covenant and sin against Yahweh, (2) Yahweh disciplines them by allowing aggression against Israel by foreign nations, (3) there is a call to repentance and a cry for help, and (4) Yahweh raises up a hero or deliverer, called a judge, who rescues the people from their enemies and rules them for a time. At the end of this book, the author comments, "In those days there was no king in Israel; everyone did what was right in his own eyes" (Judg. 21:25). Here the author is really referring to the condition of the people and how the covenant would be preserved. He is saying that, despite the lack of human support that might have preserved a political or religious ideal, in spite of the fact that there was no king and each person followed his own standard, Yahweh, by direct intervention through the judge or savior figures, preserved the covenant with Israel at this time. The book of Judges, then, suggests that, in any age, the people of Israel would not owe their existence to political constitutions devised by themselves, such as the monarchy; they would owe it to the faithfulness of their covenant partner, who would never defect from his obligations to which he was bound by oath and promise.

SAMUEL AND THE BEGINNING OF THE MONARCHY

When the book of Samuel opens, the worship of God is debased among the people of Israel. Eli, the high priest, was primarily responsible for this because he was not able to discipline his sons, Hophni and Phineas. God prepared Samuel as the man to rescue his people from this crisis.

In 1 Samuel 8, the elders of Israel ask Samuel to appoint a king to lead them, like the nations surrounding them. This request reveals a number of issues confused in the minds of the people. First, Samuel was a judge. Normally Yahweh appointed the judges by his Spirit. It was not an office that was passed to one's natural sons as in a dynasty. Second, the people wanted a king like the nations surrounding them. Here the problem was not in wanting a king per se. God had planned for this from the start. Man was created as the divine image in order to "rule over the fish of the sea and the birds of the air and over every living creature that moves on the ground" (Gen. 1:26–28). He was placed in the garden of Eden to exercise sovereignty over it and over all things. Later, when God made his last new start, he told Abraham and Sarah that kings would come from them (Gen. 17:6, 16), and this promise was reaffirmed to Jacob (Gen. 35:11). Jacob's blessing on the tribes, given at the time of his death, announced that "the sceptre will not depart from Judah, / nor the ruler's staff from between his feet, / until he comes to whom it belongs / and the obedience of the nations is his" (Gen. 49:10). Even Balaam, in his second oracle, says, "the shout of a king is among them," (Num. 23:21), and in his fourth oracle, "a star shall come out of Jacob and a sceptre shall rise out of Israel" (24:17). Finally, Moses in Deuteronomy 17:14–20 lays down provisions and regulations for a monarchy brought about according to God's choice and God's timing. The king must be the man of Yahweh's choice (v. 15) and must govern the people according to the principles of the Israelite covenant (vv. 18–20). The problem was not, then, in wanting a king. It was in wanting one like the nations had. Kingship in Canaan at this time was centralized, absolute, and contained the potential abuse of power. In addition, there was a danger that through alliances and treaties the Israelites would depend on others and not on the Lord. Moreover, since kings would come to the throne by dynasty and not by direct intervention from the Lord, God's direct rule of the people could be thwarted.

SAUL: 2 SAMUEL 6

The book of Samuel relates that, because of the degeneration of worship and the disobedience of the people, God allowed the Philistines to capture the ark. Symbolically, this indicated that Yahweh had departed from his people and gone into a self-imposed exile. The return of the ark in 2 Samuel 6 and the choosing of a site for the temple indicate that Yahweh is returning to live in the midst of his people as King. The fact that 2 Samuel 6 precedes 7 shows that only when the kingship of Yahweh is firmly established can the issue of kingship in Israel be discussed. A sanctuary for the Lord comes before the monarchy.

Another significant factor is the emergence of the office of prophet in Israel at this time. Samuel is the beginning of the prophets. The office of prophet also comes directly from the Israelite covenant (Num. 12:6–9; Deut. 18:15–22), and it arises at this time because it provides a check against the absolute rule of the king and makes sure that Yahweh—that God—is ruling the people through the king of Israel. For every David there must also be a Nathan who can come directly into the king's presence and confront his decisions and actions by the authority of the word of God.

DAVID: 2 SAMUEL 7

The main passages in the Old Testament dealing with the Davidic covenant are 2 Samuel 7 with its parallel text in 1 Chronicles 17, and Psalm 89 (esp. vv. 3–4 and 19–37). While 2 Samuel 7 does not specifically call the arrangement a covenant, the term *běrît* is in fact used in 2 Samuel 23:5; Psalm 89:3, 28, 34, 39; 132:11; and 2 Chronicles 13:5. Moreover, *ḥesed*, the term used of the Davidic covenant in Isaiah 55:3, *is used* in 2 Samuel 7:15.

Let us begin by carefully determining the literary structure of the text so that we can observe how this communication is shaped:

2 Samuel 7—Outline

I. God's promise to David 1–17
   A. David's plan 1–3
     (David proposes to build a house for Yahweh)
   B. God's promise 4–17
     1. Will you build a house for me? 4–7
     2. I will build a house for you! 8–16
       a. Promises to be realized during David's lifetime . . 8–11a
       b. Promises to be realized after David's death 11b–16
         i. The covenant promises–Yahweh's part 11b–13
           seed
           kingdom
           throne (eternal)
        ii. The covenant relationship—the king's part . . 14–15
          (Obedience in a father-son relationship)
        iii. Summary of the covenant promises 16
          an eternal seed
          an eternal kingdom
          an eternal throne
II. David's prayer to God 18–29
   A. David's praise and worship 18–24

The passage is divided in half, with the first half narrating the revelation of divine promises given to David and the second half recording David's response in worship. When it says in verse 18 that "King David went in and sat before the Lord," it means that he entered the sanctuary to reflect, worship, and pray.

Again, the first half is divided into two parts: in the first part David proposes to build a grander sanctuary of cedar paneling than the present temporary tent. In response, God promises to build a house for David. There is a play on the word "house." The "house" that David wants to build for Yahweh is a sanctuary or temple. The "house" that Yahweh will build for David is a dynasty or royal family line. This play on words is taken up again and again in later Scripture. For example, in Amos 9 the prophet predicts a future time when the sorry state of the Davidic dynasty, a "fallen hut" (v. 11), will be rebuilt. Since the context also refers to bringing down the temple, which had become devoted to corrupt worship, both dynasty and temple are involved in the reference to the "fallen hut" of David.

David's initial plan is approved by the prophet Nathan and then revoked when Nathan is given a divine revelation by dream or vision in the night. This is significant because it is part of a theme in 2 Samuel, that kingship in Israel must be subservient to Yahweh, the Great King.

In 2 Samuel 7:8–16, the section detailing the divine gift and promises to David, several key markers of the literary structure need to be observed. First, the shift from past verb forms in verses 8 and 9a to forms marking future time in the middle of verse 9 clearly marks the break between past blessings and future promises. Second, the messenger formula that opens verse 8 ("thus says the Lord of Armies") is repeated in verse 11b, albeit in a different form ("and Yahweh announces to you"). This is a clear marker in the text, along with the temporal clause beginning verse 12 and referring to a time after David's death, to separate the promises to be fulfilled during David's life from the promises to be fulfilled after David's death.

The covenant clearly demarcates both divine and human obligations.

The divine obligations or promises are divided by the literary structure into promises to be fulfilled during David's lifetime and promises to be fulfilled after David's death. The former are listed in verses 8–11a: (1) a great name, (2) a firm place for Israel as the people of God, and (3) rest for David from his enemies. The latter are listed in verses 11b–13 and 16. What Yahweh promises David here is a lasting dynasty, kingdom, and throne. The promises are given initially in verses 11b–13 and are repeated in verse 16. At the center of this A-B-A' chiastic structure is the covenant between Yahweh and David, defined as a father-son relationship. This stresses the need for obedience to Yahweh on the part of the king.

Traditionally, theologians have viewed the Davidic covenant as unconditional. It is true that the content of the covenant consists in the mighty promises made by Yahweh. Nonetheless, as verses 14–15 show, faithfulness is expected of the king, and these verses foreshadow the possibility of disloyalty on the part of the king, which will require discipline by Yahweh. In effect, verses 14–15 are saying that the covenant will be fulfilled not only by a faithful father alone (i.e., Yahweh keeping his promises), but also by a faithful son (i.e., the obedience of the king to Yahweh's Torah). The chiastic literary structure actually portrays in a visual manner the nature of the covenant: faithfulness and obedience in the father-son relationship is crucial, but it is supported on both sides by the faithfulness and sure promises of Yahweh to David of descendants, kingdom, and throne (the order is the same before and after the chiastic center). This same chiastic literary structure is observed in Psalm 132:11b–12, a later commentary on the Davidic covenant. Verses 11a and 12b emphasize the promises of God, and verse 12a speaks of the need for an obedient son. Thus, once more, the promises of God undergird and support on both sides the need for a faithful, obedient son.

The consideration given by later texts to both divine and human obligations in the covenant will be noted shortly. First, however, the reason for describing the relationship between Yahweh and the Davidic king as "father" and "son" must be fully explained. Factors involved in this include the use of the word *bēn* (son) in Hebrew, the cultural context of kingship in Canaan and in the ancient Near East, the use of familial language in treaties, and the canonical context of the passage.

A literal, physical family relationship is clearly contrary to the context. Nonetheless, *bēn*, the term for "son" in Hebrew, has a much broader field of meaning than "son" in English. In an agrarian, preindustrial economy and society, trades were normally transmitted within a family setting. In this way, sons customarily did what their fathers did, in addition to displaying common characteristics passed on from family setting, upbringing, and genetics. Thus the term "son" can be used to mean "possessing the characteristics" of something. In the parable of the vineyard in Isaiah 5:1, the beloved has a vineyard "on a horn, a son of fatness." The horn, i.e., a hillside or terrace on a mountain spur or slope, is "a son of fatness," i.e., characterized by abundant produce. An idiomatic English translation would be "a fertile hillside."

The ancient Near Eastern and Canaanite cultural context is significant. In Egypt, from at least 1650 B.C. onward, people perceived the king as the image of god because he was the son of god. The emphasis was not on physical appearance. For example, a male king could be the image of a female goddess. What is stressed is that the behavior of the king reflects the behavior of the god. The king as the image of god reflects the characteristics and essential notions of the god.

From Ugarit we have the story of King Keret, who is described as the son of El. His excellent health must indicate his divine origin.

The Old Testament records an Aramean king of Damascus known as Ben-Hadad (1 Kings 15:18, 20). By his name, he is the son of his god. Documents from both Amarna and Ugarit show a number of people from various levels of society whose names are of the format "son of [Divine Name]." Thus we do not know if the name Ben-Hadad proves that he considered himself as the representative of Hadad (Ba'al) to his people. It might depend on whether the name was a birth name from his parents or a name he took upon coming to the throne.

The Canaanite and ancient Near Eastern culture shows that the notion of the king as a son of god was well established. The meaning may have differed in Egypt, Canaan, and Mesopotamia, but the common denominator is the idea that the king represents the character of the god in some way to the people.

Also in the ancient Near East, those bound by suzerain-vassal treaties may refer to each other as father and son. This has a significant bearing on 2 Samuel 7. Earlier theologians discussed covenants in terms of unconditional or conditional promises. More recently, covenants have been evaluated according to suzerain-vassal models on the one hand or royal grant models on the other. The former emphasizes the obligations of the vassal king to the suzerain, the latter the obligations of the great king to his noble or vassal. The Davidic covenant has frequently been classified as a royal grant, yet it does not fit neatly either the unconditional-conditional categories or the more recent suzerain-vassal versus royal grant models. Second Samuel 7:14–15 clearly emphasizes the need for obedience on the part of the son, yet the literary structure shows that this is undergirded primarily by the promises of the father.

Second Samuel 7 must also be read according to the arrangement of the books in the Hebrew Canon. A canonical reading indicates that the Davidic king is inheriting the role of both Adam as son of God and Israel as son of God, according to the instructions of Deuteronomy 17. This can be briefly reviewed and summarized at this point.

First to be considered is the fact that humans are created as the divine image, according to Genesis 1:26–28. The divine image defines human ontology in terms of a covenant relationship with the creator God on the one hand and with the creation on the other hand. The former may be captured by the term "sonship" and is implied by Genesis 5:1–3.

The latter relationship, i.e., between humans and the creation, may be reflected in the terms "kingship" and "servanthood." Earlier we noted that in the ninth century B.C. Tell Fekheriyeh Inscription, "image" refers to the king's majestic self and power in relation to his subjects, while "likeness" refers to the king's petitionary role and relation to the deity. The ancient Near Eastern data confirm and correspond exactly to this exegesis of the biblical text.

As Genesis 2:4–25 shows, the Adamic son is like a priest in a garden sanctuary. He must first learn the ways of God in order to exercise the rule of God as God himself would.

Second, Israel inherited this Adamic role. Yahweh refers to the nation as his son in Exodus 4:22–23. The divine purpose in the covenant established between God and Israel at Sinai is unfolded in Exodus 19:3–6. As a kingdom of priests, they will function to make the ways of God known to the nations and also to bring the nations into a right relationship to God. Since Israel is located geographically on the one and only communications link between the great superpowers of the ancient world, in this position she will show the nations how to have a right relationship to God, how to treat each other in a truly human way, and how to be faithful stewards of the earth's resources. This is the meaning of Israel's sonship.

Third, Deuteronomy 17 intimates that the king will be the leader in this role. Verses 16–20 describe the manner in which the future king is to exercise his responsibilities. After three negative commands in verses 16–17, verses 18–20 specify three positive commands, all relating to Torah: (1) the king shall copy the Torah; (2) the king shall have the Torah with him; and (3) the king shall read the Torah. In other words, the only positive requirement is that the king embody Torah as a model citizen. This is exactly the point of the father-son relationship set out in 2 Samuel 7.

The response of David (2 Sam. 7:18–29) to this revelation through the prophet Nathan reveals David's own understanding of the covenant. In this regard, the problematic verse 19 is critical. In verse 18 David expresses the fact that he and his house have been highly exalted. Now in verse 19, however, he says that this honor is dwarfed by the promises concerning the distant future: *zôʾt tôrat hāʾādām* ("This is the instruction for humanity"). This clause has been enigmatic for scholars.

The 1984 NIV rendering, "Is this your usual way of dealing with man?" represents a standard interpretation. However this interpretation is problematic. First, reading the clause as an affirmative, declarative statement is far more normal when no contextual or grammatical signals exist to indicate a question. Second, although "manner" is suggested as the possible meaning of *tôrâ* by the Oxford Lexicon, "instruction" or "law" is by far the first meaning that comes to mind. In the bound phrase, the free member may be subject or object. When the free member is a person, it is frequently a subjective genitive, but construing it as object gives good sense here. Thus we should translate, "This is the instruction for humanity."

The 2011 NIV rendering, "and this decree is for a mere human," is no improvement. What could David mean when he says that the covenant revealed through Nathan is Yahweh's instruction for humanity? In verses 14–15 the human obligations in the relationship between Yahweh and the Davidic king are indicated by establishing a father-son relationship. We saw that, in the ancient Near East, a country or region was thought to be ruled by the god of that territory, and the king was considered the representative of the local god. This explains how the king could be called "the son of God." Therefore, as the divine son, the Davidic king was to effect the divine instruction, or *tôrâ*, in the nation as a whole and was, as a result, a mediator of the Mosaic Torah. However, since the god whom the Davidic king represented was not limited to a local region or territory, but was the creator God and Sovereign of the whole world, the rule of the Davidic king would have repercussions for *all* the nations, not just for Israel. This is developed in Psalm 2 and many other psalms, but is *already* suggested in 2 Samuel 7. Thus, faithfulness on the part of the Davidic son would effect the divine rule in the entire world, much as God intended for humanity in the covenant of creation as indicated by the divine image in Genesis 1:26ff. This, we submit, is the logic behind David's response in 2 Samuel 7:19, and this is why he claims that a covenant that makes the Davidic king son of God is the instrument of bringing Yahweh's Torah to all the nations. David's own understanding of divine sonship is clearly indicated by his statement in verse 19 that the covenant is God's charter or instruction for humankind.

The parallel text in 1 Chronicles 17:17 is problematic textually, but instructive. The clause in verse 17 corresponding to *zôʾt tôrat hāʾādām* in 2 Samuel 7:19 is *ûreʾîtanî ketôr hāʾādām hammaʿălāh*. The best proposal for the meaning of the noun *tôr* (= form; not an error for *tôrâ*) in 1 Chronicles 17:17 is in the translation "you see me according to the rank of the man placed high." This is equivalent to the last words of David in 2 Samuel 23:1, where he refers to Nathan's oracle as a *běrît* and calls himself "the man set on high." The statement in Psalm 89:27 (v. 28, Hebrew version) is similar:

> I will also appoint him my firstborn,
>> the most exalted of the kings of the earth. (NIV)

The second line explicates the meaning of the Davidic sonship as being "the most exalted of the kings of the earth."

All of these texts represent interpretations of verse 19 of 2 Samuel 7, and show that since the god who is represented by the Davidic king is both supreme and universal, the Davidic king has the highest rank among human kings. Despite critical textual problems, 2 Samuel 7:19 is the key to the universalization of the messianic vision in the Psalms and Prophets.

In the response section, 2 Samuel 7:18–29, note how the word "good" (v. 28) can be used to refer to the covenant. This demonstrates that the term *běrît* need not occur in a text for the author to be speaking about a covenant.

LATER INTERPRETATIONS OF 2 SAMUEL 7

Brief observations are now in order on the consideration given by later texts to both divine and human obligations in the covenant between Yahweh and David. These texts are also crucial in a correct interpretation of Isaiah 55:3, and frequently scholars have depended heavily on links particularly with Psalm 89.

What has not been noted sufficiently in recent scholarship is that, while later writers do adapt and apply Nathan's oracle to their present context and theological tensions, their exegesis is more firmly rooted in the original oracle than is frequently allowed. This is because the oracle itself has elements that are both conditional and unconditional. Later writers may focus more on the unconditional aspects of 2 Samuel 7:11b–13 and 16 (e.g., 2 Sam. 22:51 = Ps. 18:50), or on the conditional aspects of verses 14–15 (1 Kings 2:3–4; 6:12; 8:25; 2 Chron. 6:16; 7:17–18; Ps. 132:12; Jer. 22:1–5, 24). Indeed in Psalm 89, which is so focused on the unconditional aspect, the conditional side does surface. Two verses in particular should be highlighted:

Psalm 89:30–33

[30] If his sons abandon my Torah
   and do not walk in my ordinances
[31] if they profane my statues
   and do not keep my commands
[32] I will punish their transgression with a rod
   and their offense with strokes
[33] but my covenant loyalty I will not cancel from him
   and I will not prove false in my faithfulness

Verse 30 relates directly to Deuteronomy 17 and emphasizes that the Davidic king must know and keep Torah in order for this to be the basis of his rule of the nation (as in Isaiah 11:3a). While the emphasis is on the faithfulness of Yahweh, the need for Torah-keeping on the part of the king is duly noted.

Psalm 89:49

Where are your former *ḥăsādîm*, O Lord,
   which you swore to David in faithfulness?

This text appeals to the acts of *ḥesed* promised by Yahweh in the Davidic covenant and performed by the Lord for at least some of the descendants of David, although apparently not in the life situation of the psalmist.

First Kings 3:6 and parallel 2 Chronicles 1:8 are illuminating in revealing Solomon's understanding of the role of David's faithfulness in the fulfillment of Yahweh's promise:

Solomon answered, "You have shown great kindness to your servant, my father David, because he was faithful to you and righteous and upright in heart. You have continued this great kindness to him and have given him a son to sit on his throne this very day." (NIV)

Here Yahweh performs his covenant obligation, but David performs his as well, and thus the promise is fulfilled.

Lastly, before considering Isaiah 55, 2 Chronicles 6:42 must be treated as the only other place where the bound phrase *ḥasdê dāwīd* occurs. Here we may note that the emphasis is not only on Yahweh fulfilling his covenant obligations, but also on the Davidic son fulfilling his.

The first section of 2 Chronicles 6 (vv. 1–11) entails the blessing of Solomon. Verse 4 contains references to Yahweh's promises to David. Two promises are mentioned in verse 5: (1) choosing a city for the temple, and (2) choosing a leader over Israel. Then verse 6 observes the fulfillment of these two promises: (1) Yahweh chose Jerusalem for the temple, and (2) he chose David to rule his people Israel. Verses 7–11 go on to explain why it would be David's son and not David who would build the temple that stores the documents of the Mosaic Torah, or Israelite covenant. The explanation appeals directly to Nathan's oracle. The two themes established in verses 1–11, choice of Jerusalem for temple and choice of David for leader, are important for understanding the Chronicler at the end of the prayer.

The second section (vv. 12–42) records the prayer of Solomon. In verse 14 Solomon begins by praising Yahweh as the God who keeps covenant and *ḥesed* to those who walk before him in complete devotion. This is central. Certainly the covenant with David entails promises that Yahweh must keep to be faithful. But the oracle through Nathan makes clear that Yahweh will keep them only to and through a faithful son. Therefore, from the Chronicler's point of view, the promises of Yahweh will be fulfilled only when the throne is occupied by an obedient son. What the subsequent course of history shows is that Yahweh not only must keep the promises but also must provide the obedient son, if the covenant is to be maintained.

Verse 15 of 2 Chronicles 6 emphasizes that Yahweh spoke with his mouth and fulfilled with his hands the commitments he made to Solomon in regard to David, his father.

In verse 16 Solomon asks Yahweh to fulfill his promises to David concerning David's sons only if the sons faithfully follow Torah, *as David did*. Verse 17 repeats the request for Yahweh to fulfill his promise.

To this point Solomon is calling upon Yahweh to be faithful to his promises to David, but he has underscored (1) the obedience of David and (2) the necessity of the obedience of the sons for the promises to work.

Verses 18–40 constitute a request that God hear prayers made in and toward this temple. The various situations are all based on the Mosaic covenant (Exodus and Deuteronomy).

At the end of the prayer something interesting happens in the Chronicler's account, which is different from the prayer in 1 Kings 8. First, 2 Chronicles 6:39b and 40 quickly summarize verses 50–53 of 1 Kings 8. Then in 2 Chronicles 6:41–42, the Chronicler quotes, almost verbatim, Psalm 132:8–10. When we recall that the book of Psalms was Israel's Hymnal, the reader of Chronicles immediately picks up Psalm 132 as part of the context in 2 Chronicles 6. This is because Psalm 132 addresses the concerns raised at the beginning of 2 Chronicles 6: (1) the choice of Zion for the temple, and (2) the choice of David and his sons as leaders of Israel. From the historical point of view of the Chronicler, both of these have been in grave jeopardy. Yet Psalm 132 is a *prayer* for Yahweh to keep his oath to David based upon a faithful David. This is the clear meaning of verse 12 and especially of the phrase in verse 10, "on account of David your servant." The Hebrew for "on account of" is the preposition *ba'ăbûr*, employed in 49 instances in the Hebrew Bible: in 18 of those instances *ba'ăbûr* is bound to an infinitive or prefixed verb form and means "in order that." In the 31 remaining instances the preposition is bound to a proper noun/pronoun or suffixed verb form and means "on account of" or "for the sake of." In every case where the preposition is bound to a proper noun, the prepositional phrase means "on account of what a person did" and not "on account of doing something on behalf of a person." In 2 Chronicles 6:42 the phrase *ḥasdê dāwîd* substitutes for *ba'ăbûr dāwîd* in the citation of Psalm 132:10 and therefore probably means the same thing. In this way the Chronicler has Solomon praying for Yahweh to keep his promises on account of the faithfulness of David. It would work well in the context to understand it to mean that Solomon is appealing to Yahweh to be faithful because of the obedience of his father, David. However, in the context of Chronicles, with its messianic focus, this is more likely a hope in a future king who will at last be an obedient son, so that the promises may be fulfilled by Yahweh.

In sum, some of the later texts emphasize the part of the son (1 Kings 2:2–4; 6:12; 8:25; 9:4–9; 2 Chron. 6:42; 7:17; Ps. 132:11–12) while others stress the faithfulness of the father (2 Sam. 22:51; 1 Kings 3:6; 8:15, 24–26; 1 Chron. 17:13; 2 Chron. 1:8; 2 Chron. 6:4, 10, 14–15, 16; 7:10; Ps. 89:28–37; Jer. 33:19–26) in the covenant relationship.

INTERPRETATION OF ISAIAH 55:3

[3] Incline your ear, and come to me;
    hear, that your soul may live;
and I will make with you an everlasting covenant,
    my steadfast, sure love for David.
[4] Behold, I made him a witness to the peoples,
    a leader and commander for the peoples.
[5] Behold, you shall call a nation that you do not know,
    and a nation that did not know you shall run to you,
because of the LORD your God, and of the Holy One of Israel,
    for he has glorified you. (Isa. 55:3–5, ESV)

Isaiah 55:3–5 is an extremely important text in relation to understanding both the Davidic covenant and the new covenant. Scholars have debated the interpretation of the phrase *ḥasdê dāwīd* in verse 3, a phrase rendered in the King James Version by "the sure mercies of David."

Extended discussion and treatment in our larger work (*Kingdom through Covenant*) demonstrated two things: (1) the most natural interpretation of the phrase in Hebrew is not "acts of mercy/loyal love" shown to David, but "acts of mercy/loyal love" performed by David; and (2) the name David is not a reference to the historical figure who was a great king of Israel, but a way of referring to the coming king or Messiah. The figurative language in which the Davidic king and kingdom are portrayed as a majestic tree cut down (Isa. 6:13) and the reference to the shoot and root in Isaiah 53:2 clearly connect this text to the vision of the future king who is the shoot and root of Jesse in Isaiah 11:1, 10. As Motyer notes, "the reference to *Jesse* indicates that the *shoot* is not just another king in David's line but rather another David."[1] This kind of use of the name David occurs in the chronologically earlier prophecy, Hosea 3:5, and is a usage similar to those in Jeremiah (30:8–9) and Ezekiel (34:23, 24; 37:24, 25).

With the above exposition of "sonship" in the Davidic covenant of 2 Samuel 7 and the understanding that Isaiah 55:3 refers to a future David,

---

[1] Alec Motyer, *The Prophecy of Isaiah: An Introduction and Commentary* (Downers Grove, IL: InterVarsity Press, 1993), 121 (emphasis his).

the pieces of the text can now be put together. This approach best suits the flow of thought in Isaiah and best explains what the phrases "witness of the peoples" and "leader and commander of the peoples" mean in context; it best explains the apposition of "faithful acts of loyal love by David" to "eternal covenant" and why "faithful" is used as a modifier. These arguments can be set forth as follows.

The first vision of a future restored Zion is found in Isaiah 2, where Mount Zion becomes the highest mountain in the new world and all the nations stream to it to receive instruction (*tôrâ*) and the word of the Lord. This vision, along with the one in chapter 4, shows that the future Mount Zion has inherited the role of both Eden and Sinai and that the city, once a whore (1:21), is now characterized by social justice (1:26), as the term "holy" (4:3) indicates.

The vision in 9:6–7 and 11:1–10 brings a new twist. A future king, a new David, will arise. He will delight in the fear of the Lord, here a synonym for Torah as in Psalm 19. Thus he will fulfill the command of Deuteronomy 17:18–20 and as a result will implement the social justice of the Torah (Isa. 11:3b–5). According to verse 10, the King himself will become a banner for the nations. Here we see that the nations who stream to Zion in 2:1–4 will receive the Torah of Yahweh *through* the Davidic King. The servant of Yahweh—already connected to this future king—will bring justice to the nations (42:1, 3–4; 49:1, 6). Also, in the context of a Servant Song, the fact that a banner is raised to the nations is repeated in 49:22. In short, as the Son of God, a future David, will bring God's instruction and rule to all the nations, as indicated in 2 Samuel 7.

What acts of *hesed* on the part of the future David can constitute an eternal covenant? The arm of Yahweh is part of the new exodus theme that permeates all of Isaiah. The occurrence in 50:2 initiates a focus on the arm that reaches a climax in the Fourth Servant Song, 53:1 (cf. 51:5, 9; 52:10). Nevertheless, when Yahweh rolls up his sleeves and bares his arm, no one would have believed it. The future king does not crush his enemies and rid the land of evil (11:3–5) by military force, prowess, and strategies, but simply by his word (11:4; 49:2; 50:4) and by offering himself as a reparation offering (*'āšām* 53:10). Thus the means and manner in which Yahweh's Torah is brought to the nations and in which his kingship is effected among them (a commander and leader of the peoples) is detailed by the four Servant Songs, and in particular by the Fourth Song (52:13–53:12). It is the acts of *ḥesed* on the part of the servant that establish and initiate the discussion on the eternal covenant in chapter 54, of which 55:3 continues the thread. It is because the servant is the "covenant of the people" in himself (42:6; 49:8) that the apposition of *mercies of David* and *eternal covenant* in verse 3 makes sense.

Isaiah 55:4–5 speaks of the future David being a witness to the nations and a leader and commander of the peoples. This speaks far more of fulfilling the human obligations in the Davidic covenant than of a specific focus on fulfilling the divine obligations. The central function of the king is to effect the instruction of Yahweh in the lives of the people and even to the nations: "this is the instruction for humankind" (2 Sam. 7:19). This is what is prominent in Isaiah. The servant of Yahweh brings Yahweh's Torah to the distant islands.

A lexical study of *'ēd*, the word for "witness," shows that a witness functions in *covenant* relationships, especially with a view to restoring broken relationships. Moreover, the background of Isaiah 19 is significant. *David* is to the *nations* what the *altar* is to *Egypt* in Isaiah 19:20. He speaks to the nations of their covenant disloyalty, of their broken obligations to the creator God, and he brings about the restoration of the covenant relationship between Yahweh and the nations. As stated earlier, the means and manner in which Yahweh's Torah is brought to the nations and in which his kingship is effected among them is detailed by the four Servant Songs, and in particular by the Fourth Song (52:13–53:12). And this is why a nation that does not know Israel, and also one that Israel does not know, comes running to her (55:5) through the work of her king as witness.

The king is also a "leader and commander of peoples." These words emphasize the king as a person under divine authority who acts strictly under the orders of Yahweh for the benefit of Yahweh's people, and not someone who uses absolute power for his own aggrandizement. In other words, these terms show that the coming king will implement the rule of God in the lives of his people. Isaiah employs *leader* because the future David fulfills the role of obedient son in the framework of the Davidic covenant.

CONCLUSION

In conclusion, "the faithful kindnesses of David" mentioned in Isaiah 55:3 are kindnesses performed by David—a rubric for the future king in this text. The faithful or obedient acts of loyal love are those of the servant king in

Isaiah 53, whose offering of himself as an *'āšām* and whose resurrection enables him to bring to fulfillment the promises of Yahweh in the Davidic covenant, and who is at the same time the basis for the new or everlasting covenant. This future king then fulfills the roles required for the king in Deuteronomy 17 and 2 Samuel 7 by bringing the divine instruction or Torah to Israel (Deuteronomy 17) and, indeed, to all the nations (2 Sam. 7:19). He is therefore a leader and commander of the peoples and becomes a covenant witness in himself to the nations. This is exactly how Acts 13:34 interprets Isaiah 55.

THE FULFILLMENT OF PROMISES TO DAVID

The promises entailed in the covenant with David are divided by the text into two: (1) those to be fulfilled during his lifetime, and (2) those to be fulfilled after his death. Second Samuel 7:8–11a gives the promises to be fulfilled during David's lifetime: (1) a great name, (2) a firm place for Israel as the people of God, and (3) rest for David from his enemies. Second Samuel 8 gives a list of David's victories and is placed by the author strategically after chapter 7 to show the fulfillment of these three promises. According to 8:13, "David made a name for himself when he returned from striking down 18,000 Edomites in the Valley of Salt." The defeat of the enemies listed in chapter 8 shows that God made a firm place for his people Israel through these victories. In 1 Kings 5:4 Solomon attests to the fact that he has rest on every side—a legacy received from his father David.

The promises to be fulfilled after the death of David are also three: (1) an eternal house, (2) a kingdom, and (3) a throne. There are two ways in which God could give David an eternal house. It could be that every descendant would be successful in producing a male heir—something that has always created problems for every human royal house. Or it could be that someday, a descendant would be born who would never die. According to the New Testament, this is what happened: the promise of an eternal house/seed is fulfilled in Jesus Christ, descendant of David, who because of his resurrection is an eternal person. And through the coming, person, and work of Jesus Christ, an eternal kingdom has already begun (2 Pet. 1:11). The authors of the New Testament make plain that, having risen from the dead and having ascended to the right hand of the Father, Jesus is ruling from an eternal heavenly throne (Acts 2:29–36; Heb. 12:22–24).

RELATIONSHIP OF THE DAVIDIC COVENANT TO THE MOSAIC/ISRAELITE COVENANT

As we have seen in the exposition of 2 Samuel 7, the king of Israel was to be the administrator of the Israelite covenant. By depending on Yahweh for military victories, the king would point the people to the kingship of Yahweh. In his rule of the people, the king would represent God's social justice and would also embody in his person the obedience of the people. Thus kingship in Israel was to be a means of accomplishing Exodus 19:3b–6: the king would be a devoted servant and son of God and would also function as a priest, instructing the nations in the righteousness of God and inviting them to come under the rule of Yahweh.

We see the priestly role of David in that he wears an ephod. The description of David in 2 Samuel 6:14 is identical in the Hebrew text to that of Samuel in 1 Samuel 2:18. We further see the priestly role of the Davidic king in Psalm 110:4. All of this indicates that the king will accomplish in his person the purpose that God had for the nation of Israel as a whole, to be a kingdom of priests. The king will embody the nation in himself.

In the Fourth Servant Song (Isa. 52:12–53:12), we see that there is a sense in which the king *is the nation in himself* and yet can also be the deliverer of the nation. Genesis 20:4 is an excellent illustration of the corporate solidarity between king and people that was part and parcel of the culture of the ancient Near East:

> [1] Now Abraham moved on from there into the region of the Negev and lived between Kadesh and Shur. For a while he stayed in Gerar, [2] and there Abraham said of his wife Sarah, "She is my sister." Then Abimelech king of Gerar sent for Sarah and took her. [3] But God came to Abimelech in a dream one night and said to him, "You are as good as dead because of the woman you have taken; she is a married woman." [4] Now Abimelech had not gone near her, so he said, "Lord, will you destroy an innocent nation? [5] Did he not say to me, 'She is my sister,' and didn't she also say, 'He is my brother'? I have done this with a clear conscience and clean hands." (Gen. 20:1–5, NIV)

Notice in this text that God communicates to Abimelech that he is a dead man because he has taken a married woman. Abimelech responds, "Lord, will you destroy an innocent nation?" The culture assumes that to kill the *king* is to destroy the *nation* (*gôy*). This is a clear illustration of federal headship: the king *is* the nation *in himself*. Thus it is natural in the plan of God for the king of Israel, as Israel, to accomplish for the nation as a whole what the group of individuals have failed to do.[2]

RELATIONSHIP OF THE DAVIDIC COVENANT TO THE ABRAHAMIC COVENANT

The relationship between the Davidic covenant and the Abrahamic covenant is described by various texts in two ways. First, God will use David to bring rest to his people and give them a place. Compare for a moment Genesis 15:18–21, Deuteronomy 11:24, and 1 Kings 4:20–21:

> [18] On that day the LORD made a covenant with Abram, saying, "To your offspring I give this land, from the river of Egypt to the great river, the river Euphrates, [19] the land of the Kenites, the Kenizzites, the Kadmonites, [20] the Hittites, the Perizzites, the Rephaim, [21] the Amorites, the Canaanites, the Girgashites and the Jebusites." (Gen. 15:18–21, ESV)

> Every place on which the sole of your foot treads shall be yours. Your territory shall be from the wilderness to the Lebanon and from the River, the river Euphrates, to the western sea. (Deut. 11:24, ESV)

> [20] Judah and Israel were as many as the sand by the sea. They ate and drank and were happy. [21] Solomon ruled over all the kingdoms from the Euphrates to the land of the Philistines and to the border of Egypt. They brought tribute and served Solomon all the days of his life. (1 Kings 4:20–21, ESV)

The borders of the land as envisioned in Genesis 15:18–21 are defined in Deuteronomy 11:24 as Israel's "place." First Kings 4:20–21 indicates that this geographical "place" belonged to Israel during the time of Solomon, David's son. So the covenant with David was a means to fulfill the promises in the Abrahamic covenant.

Second, God will use David to bring blessing to the nations as promised in the covenant with Abraham. The covenant with David is the charter, or instruction, for mankind. Isaiah 55 shows how the future king will, by his acts of lovingkindness, be a witness and a commander and leader of the peoples as he brings the divine instruction, or Torah, to all the nations.

---

[2] For a detailed discussion of the corporate solidarity between king and people in the Fourth Servant Song see Gentry, "Atonement in Isaiah's Fourth Servant Song (Isaiah 52:13–53:12)," *The Southern Baptist Journal of Theology* 11/2 (2007): 20–47.

The relation of the Davidic king to the Abrahamic covenant is described precisely by Psalm 72:17. We could render the verse thus:

> May his name endure forever,
> his name make shoots as long as the sun!
> May they consider themselves blessed by him,
> all nations call him happy!

The flow of thought in the psalm is simple. Either "by" or "for" Solomon, it begins in verse 1 as a prayer to God to give his judgments and righteousness to the king. In verse 2 the result is that the king will judge with social justice. In such a kingdom the cause of the needy and weak are given justice. His rule is extended to universal space and time. In verse 10, kings from the ends of the world pay tribute, and in verse 11, all nations serve him. So far we have an excellent exposition of 2 Samuel 7:19. In Psalm 72:12–17, the same theme is developed in another "round of discourse" on the same topic. The needy and weak receive help. The psalmist prays that many will offer prayer all day long for this king so that his name and the prosperity of his rule continue. Verse 17 fits appropriately into this flow of thought, praying that his fame will endure and that individuals of all nations will declare themselves blessed by him and will call him happy. The Davidic covenant narrows the mediator of blessing to the nations from the nation of Israel as a whole to the king, who represents and stands for the nation.

These considerations of Psalm 72 are strengthened by the arrangement in the final redaction of the Hebrew Psalter. Note the placement of Psalms 2 and 72 at the beginning of the First Book and the ending of the Second Book in the Psalter respectively. The former announces a victory for Yahweh's king and the latter speaks of the kingdom established. These connections indicate that the blessing to the nations promised to Abraham is coming through the Davidic King/kingdom.

Chapter 10

THE NEW COVENANT

WHO WERE THE PROPHETS, AND WHY DID THEY SPEAK OF A NEW COVENANT?

The metanarrative of Scripture begins with a creator God who made our world, our universe. As Creator, he is committed to caring for and sustaining all of his creation. He governs and rules wisely over all his creatures and works. The apex and crown of his creative work is humankind. He has entrusted to the human race the administration and stewardship of his world. This *covenantal arrangement* was violated by human disloyalty and rebellion. The first man decided to act and manage things independently of the Creator. Everything is now riddled with chaos and evil.

God responds to human rebellion in various ways as the story unfolds. At the center of the plan to restore his ruined world and bring it to serve his original intention are a series of agreements called covenants. First, the covenant with Noah upholds the commitment of the Creator to his creation as a whole. Then God begins to work through one individual, Abraham, and through his family, Israel, to model a new humanity in right relationship with the creator God and with one another. The Israelite covenant at Sinai (supplemented by Deuteronomy) forges the nation into the people of God and governs life in the land. The covenant with David institutes a kingship where the rule of God is established among his people, with the king functioning as covenant administrator. What God planned for the nation as a whole will now be implemented through the king and his leadership.

Later on, between 750 and 550 B.C, a group of men who functioned as spokesmen for God were raised up to call attention to the failure of the people to be covenant keepers. These were the prophets, servants of God who spoke for him. Confronting the people of God, they exposed the clever and devious ways by which the people had gradually slipped away from a proper relationship with God and with one another as defined by the Israelite covenant. The prophets were given visions from God and announced coming events. Some events would happen fairly soon, others would not happen for some time. They announced various ways in which God would act to deal with his faithless people and bring his overall plan of restoring his broken creation to fulfillment. Because the people had broken and violated the Israelite covenant, the prophets announced that God would put in place a new covenant in which not only would *he* be faithful, but his people would be faithful too.

REFERENCES TO THE NEW COVENANT

The prophets spoke of the new covenant in different places at different times in a variety of ways. Five times they refer to the everlasting covenant, three times to a covenant of peace, three times to a promise that God will give his people a new heart and a new spirit, and only once is the phrase "new covenant" actually used. But they are all referring to the same thing:

> *Major Texts Dealing with the New Covenant*
> 1. Everlasting covenant: Jeremiah 32:36–41; 50:2–5; Ezekiel 37:15–28 (esp. v. 26); Isaiah 55:1–5; 61:8–9.
> 2. Covenant of peace: Isaiah 54:1–10 (esp. vv. 9–10); Ezekiel 34:20–31 (esp. v. 25); 37:15–28 (esp. v. 26).
> 3. Promise of a new heart and a new spirit: Ezekiel 11:18–21; 18:30–32; 36:24–32 (esp. v. 26) [cf. Isa. 59:21].
> 4. New covenant: Jeremiah 31:31–34.

In the New Testament, this same covenant is referred to as the new covenant five times (Luke 22:20; 1 Cor. 11:25; 2 Cor. 3:6; Heb. 8:8; 9:15) and only once as the everlasting covenant (Heb. 13:20). Thus the title for this covenant most used in the Old Testament is employed only once in the New Testament, and the title employed only once in the Old Testament is the most used in the New Testament.

THE NEW COVENANT IN ISAIAH

Our larger work (*Kingdom through Covenant*) deals extensively with the various treatments of the new covenant by all of the prophets. Here, only Isaiah 54, Ezekiel 16, and Jeremiah 31 will be discussed.

Isaiah 54:1–55:13

Isaiah 54:1–55:13 is a major text dealing with the new covenant. We see the term "covenant of peace" in 54:10 and "everlasting covenant" in 55:3. The following outline shows how this text fits into the larger section of Isaiah 38–55:

First, the outline of the literary structure of Isaiah 38–55 shows that the return from exile involves two distinct issues and stages. As already noted, Isaiah 38–55 looks farther into the future, beyond the judgment of exile, to the comfort and consolation of Israel, i.e., bringing them back from exile. Then the Lord will establish Zion as the people/place where all nations will seek his instruction for social justice. This is described in the language of the exodus, so that the return from the Babylonian exile will be nothing less than a new exodus—indeed a greater exodus! This new exodus is also described by the term "redeem" (*gā'al*), which refers to the duties of the nearest relative. Since by virtue of the Israelite covenant Yahweh is Israel's nearest relative, he will "buy back" his people from exile as he once delivered them from bondage and slavery in Egypt. The return from exile, however, is not a single task. The promises of redemption are divided into two distinct events: release (42:18–43:21) and forgiveness (43:22–44:23). Release refers to bringing the people physically out of exile in Babylon and back to their own land; forgiveness entails dealing fully and finally with their sin and the broken covenant. It has been neatly expressed that you can take the people out of Babylon, but how do you get Babylon out of the people?

The books of Ezra and Nehemiah show that the people have returned from exile but have not changed at all in terms of their relationship to God: the failure to practice social justice remains a central problem. That is why, for a postexilic prophet like Zechariah, the return from exile is both a present reality and a future hope. The exile will be over only when God deals with the people's sin and renews the covenant, the temple is rebuilt, and the Lord returns to dwell in their midst as King.

Zechariah 3:9 and 5:5–11 show that the forgiveness/removal of sins is still future. Indeed, the major point of Daniel's vision of seventy weeks is that the exile will not be over in seventy years, but rather in seventy weeks of years: "Seventy sevens are decreed for your people and your holy city to finish transgression, to put an end to sin, to atone for wickedness, to bring in everlasting righteousness, to seal up vision and prophecy and to anoint the Holy of Holies" (Dan. 9:24). So there are two issues in the return from exile: physical return from Babylon, and spiritual deliverance from bondage and slavery to sin. And corresponding to these two issues there are two distinct agents of redemption: Cyrus and the servant. The former will bring about the first task: physical return to the land of Israel (Isa. 44:24–48:22); the latter will bring about the second task: the forgiveness of sins (49:1–53:12).

The Abrahamic covenant undergirds the introductory section (40:1–42:17) of Isaiah 40–55. At the heart of the covenant with Abraham is the promise that blessing will come to the entire world through Abraham and his family, Israel. The arrangement in this section is important. The consolation of Israel comes first because at this time Israel is under a curse; she is part of the problem and not part of the solution. First, God must console and restore Israel, and only then can he use Israel to be an instrument of consolation and restoration for all the nations. After consolation is defined in terms of redemption (1) from exile and (2) from sin (42:18–44:23), Isaiah describes in 44:24–53:12 the work of Cyrus to accomplish the former before proceeding to develop the work of the servant of the Lord to accomplish the latter.

The literary structure sheds light on the identity of the servant. Debate over the identity of the servant has raged for centuries and continues to the present time. One good reason for this debate is in the text itself: it is characteristic of Isaiah's style to begin discussing a topic in an ambiguous and mysterious manner and to add critical information bit by bit until the matter is plain. For example, in the oracle against Babylon in 21:1–9, Isaiah begins by talking about the Wilderness by the Sea. Only at the end, in verse 9, does one realize that the prophet is speaking about Babylon. Isaiah's presentation of the servant of Yahweh is similar. At the start, in 41:8, the servant is Israel, who in the biblical-theological scheme of the larger story has inherited the Adamic roles of son of God and servant king, and who in the covenant at Sinai in Exodus 19:5–6 was called to be a holy nation and a kingdom of priests. The servant, however, seems to be deaf and disobedient in Isaiah 42:18–19. This contradicts the picture of the servant in 42:1–9 and especially in 50:4–11. Israel as a servant is in dire need herself, not just of rescue from exile and all that entails, but also of a full resolution of the problem of a broken covenant relationship (e.g., 43:22–28). Idolatry and social injustice are endemic in Israel. This is the dilemma: how can God keep his promises to Abraham when Israel has completely failed as the servant of the Lord? Israel was to model three things to the rest of the nations: (1) faithfulness and loyalty in their relationship to God, (2) social justice in their human relationships, and (3) responsible stewardship of the creation/environment.

The answer to this question is addressed immediately in the Second Servant Song, which begins the detailed response to this question (49:1–13). At the beginning of this Second Song we hear again in 49:3 the affirmation that Israel is the servant (cf. 41:8). So the servant is the nation. Yet in verses 5–6, the servant's task is to bring the nation back. This is a return from exile, both physically and spiritually, as described earlier. How can the servant be both the nation and the deliverer of the nation? There is only one possible solution that resolves this conundrum fairly, and Isaiah has prepared us for this in the first part of his work: the servant must be the future king described earlier (e.g., 11:1–10). As an individual, the king can say, "I am Israel." The king can represent the nation as a whole, yet he also can be distinguished from Israel. This is difficult for Americans to grasp because we have no monarchy. In monarchies, both ancient and modern, there is a sense in which the king *is* the nation. At the same time, the king is the deliverer of the nation and fights her battles for her. Many Christians move too quickly to identify Jesus of Nazareth as the servant of Yahweh without following carefully the progression in the text; the main problem with the standard Jewish interpretation of identifying the servant as the nation is that the nation of Israel is, neither in the text nor in history, able to rescue itself, let alone atone for its own sins.

The theme of chapter 54 is bringing back the exiles, bringing about reconciliation between God and his people, restoring the covenant relationship, and rebuilding Zion, since the city of God in terms of people has been so decimated. What ties together the diverse paragraphs and sections is a metaphor in which the people of God are represented as a woman. In verses 1–3, the people of God are pictured as a barren woman who now has more children than the married woman. In verses 4–10, the people of God are portrayed as a forsaken wife (i.e., divorced woman), someone who has long borne the reproach of widowhood, but who is now reconciled and married to her creator God. Included in this section is a comparison of the promise of the new covenant to the promise of the Noahic covenant; just as God promised that never again would he judge by a flood, so now he promises never again to be angry with his people. Finally, in verses 11–17, the woman is the city of Zion, lashed by storms but now fortified by redoubtable foundations and battlements and rebuilt with stunning precious jewels and stones. Thus, in the brief span of 17 verses, the new covenant is in some way either compared or correlated and linked to all of the previous major covenants in the Bible.

Chapter 54, then, discusses the new covenant, which is based on the death and resurrection of the servant king in chapter 53. Certain key words join the Servant Song in chapter 53 to this chapter. The "many" in 53:11–12 are the many in the miracle family in 54:1—the exact same word in Hebrew. The seed or offspring of the servant, seemingly cut off in 53:8, but appearing after his resurrection, are now the descendants who possess the nations in 54:3. The Just One justifies the many in 53:11. He makes them righteous. The city is established in righteousness in 54:14, which is almost equivalent to vindication from accusing opponents in 54:17. And the servant in the singular becomes the servants of the Lord in the plural in 54:17.

Outline of Isaiah 54:1–17
A. Sarah: the barren woman 54:1–3
B. Israel: the deserted wife 54:4–10
C. Zion: the afflicted woman 54:11–17
    1. The city rebuilt 11–14a
    2. The city secure 14b–17

THE MIRACLE FAMILY (54:1–3)

God's people are called to burst out in ringing shouts of joy. They need to prepare for a massive expansion in the family. Why? Isaiah 54:3 says that their descendants will inherit/occupy/possess the nations. This statement is somewhat vague in itself. It might be interpreted to mean that Israel will at last conquer the nations surrounding and troubling them. But verse 1 will not permit this interpretation. It talks about the children of the desolate woman far surpassing those of the married woman. What does this mean? The married woman is Israel during the days of the old covenant. The desolate woman is the decimated Israel who comes back from the destruction of exile. The family restored after the exile is far more numerous than before. From the point of view of the New Testament, it becomes clear: Israel inherits the nations because they become part of the family.

The barren woman in the history of Israel is Sarah. The allusion to the times of Abraham and Sarah is also clear from the allusion to the tent (v. 2) and the mention of seed/descendants. Thus the reference to the barren woman is a way of referring to the Abrahamic covenant and so recalls the promise to Abraham of descendants as numerous as the sand on the seashore and as the stars of the sky. But the covenant with Abraham also promised blessing to the nations through Israel. Thus Israel dispossesses the nations, not as a destructive military conquest but as instruments of "blessing" (Gen. 12:2), bringing them into the family. Simply bringing the exiles back to the land to grow and prosper as a nation does not explain sufficiently the need for a massive enlargement of the family tent.

THE RECONSTITUTED MARRIAGE (54:4–10)

The next section, verses 4–10, speaks of God as husband, maker, and redeemer. This is a clear reference to the Israelite/Mosaic covenant, the covenant made between God and Israel at Sinai. This marriage relationship was broken by Israel's unfaithfulness, and God brought the curse of exile upon Israel, and so he forsook (i.e., divorced) his unfaithful wife. But this display of wrath was only for a moment, so to speak. The marriage relationship was broken, the wife forsaken/widowed, but now reconciliation brings about renewing of the marriage.

Verse 4 begins by commands that call the woman out of disgrace, humiliation, and shame. She must forget the shame of her youth. This represents the four hundred years of bondage and slavery in Egypt, when Israel was at the beginning of her life as a nation. She must no longer remember the reproach of her widowhood. This represents the seventy years of exile in Babylon. She had been married to the Lord, but she was an unfaithful wife and ended up deserted and alone like a widow; all her lovers (i.e., idols/alliances with foreign nations), and even her husband, turned their backs upon her.

Verse 5 speaks of the Lord as Israel's husband and maker. God is not only the creator God, the God of all the earth, but he is the creator and maker of Israel as a nation. Through the covenant at Sinai he married Israel and so is her husband, and now he is the redeemer, i.e., the nearest relative, who has the duty to buy her back from exile and slavery.

According to verse 6, Israel may feel like a woman who was married as a high school sweetheart and was then rejected. This, however, is only a momentary turning away. God will now show her compassion, mercy, and covenant loyal love forever. The marriage relationship will be restored. There will be a new covenant, called a covenant of peace in verse 10 to emphasize the fact of reconciliation. God's anger has been appeased and finished. Israel may now benefit from the healing of a broken relationship in a new covenant. The new covenant renews and restores the broken old covenant. But it is more than that. It is a new covenant, different from the old one and superior to it, because it depends not upon God's people but instead upon the everlasting kindness of God himself. Momentary wrath is contrasted with everlasting love and mercy.

This is illustrated by a comparison between the new covenant and the covenant God made with Noah. Just as he promised there that never again would he judge the entire world by a flood, so now he is promising never again to be angry with his people. The mountains will give way and the hills will totter, but his *ḥesed*, his covenant faithfulness and love, will never be taken away in the new covenant. That is why it is called a covenant of peace.

THE CITY OF RIGHTEOUSNESS (54:11–17)

1. The City Reestablished/Rebuilt (vv. 11–14a)

Verses 11–17 speak of the woman as a city, the city of Zion. She has been afflicted and lashed by storms but will be rebuilt and reestablished. Her new foundation will have a solid construction of mortar and stone. She will be adorned by precious jewels and fiery, sparkling stones. This construction represents the fact that all will know the Lord.

The city of Zion brings to mind the Davidic covenant and the place where Yahweh rules in the midst of his people as King, and where his Son, always a descendant of David, represents his rule to the people and to the nations beyond.

In verse 13 we read that "all your sons will be taught by the LORD." This correlates perfectly with Jeremiah 31:33–34. What is new about the new covenant is that in the covenant community all are believers. In the Israelite/

Mosaic covenant—indeed in the Abrahamic covenant that the Israelite covenant seeks to implement in Iron Age Israel for the nation as a whole—one is born into the covenant community. This results in a situation where one may be a member of the covenant community but not a believer. In the new covenant community, the believing community and the covenant community will be perfectly coextensive. This is what Isaiah means when he says, "all your sons will be taught by the LORD," and this is the explanation of the statement that the restored city will be built with beautiful and lasting materials. It is comparable to Peter's picture of believers in the new covenant as living stones in the new temple (1 Pet. 2:5). Since every covenant member knows the Lord, every member or "piece" of the city will constitute beautiful and lasting materials, i.e., jewels. The proof that this is the correct interpretation lies in the fact that the Hebrew word translated as "taught" means "disciple." The same word is used of the servant of Yahweh in Isaiah 50:4 and applies to the people of the Lord here because, according to 54:17, they too are servants of the Lord.

2. The City Secure (vv. 14b–17)

The city is established in righteousness. This is part of her foundation and will characterize this community. This righteousness will also protect and save her in the end. The same word is used in verse 17 almost in the sense of vindication against those who accuse her in court.

The Lord does not promise that the renewed city will have no enemies, will experience no attacks. But she is not to be afraid. There is no need for terror. In terms of destroying weapons, Yahweh is in charge of the manufacturer, the product, and the intent of the user. Nothing will harm the city of God. No weapon forged against her will prosper or succeed. Any accusing tongue will in fact be pronounced guilty by the city of God, and God's people will triumph in court. Peace between God and his people results in peace and wholeness for them.

This city is the final resting place of the servants of the Lord, the reward and vindication for all that they have suffered because of their faithfulness to God (54:17). Subtly and quietly, but also unmistakably, Isaiah links them to the greatest servant of all. As he was a disciple, taught by the Lord (50:4), so are they (54:13). They have suffered affliction (54:11), as did he (53:4). And as he will surely be vindicated (50:8), so will they (54:17). They are called servants of the Lord because they follow in the footsteps of the perfect servant. They share his sufferings and will also share in his glory. They are "his offspring," the fruit of his sacrifice (53:10), and the city of God will be their home.

The new covenant therefore brings to fruition God's promises and purposes in all the other covenants: (1) it brings the numerous seed promised in the Abrahamic covenant, (2) it brings the righteousness between God and humans and among humans aimed at in the Israelite covenant, and (3) it establishes the city of God ruled by the Davidic King. All of this is as certain as the promises to Noah.

Isaiah 55:1–5

In Isaiah 55:3 God announces that he is initiating an everlasting covenant. This covenant is described as the acts of loyal love performed by David, i.e., the atoning death of the servant king in chapter 53. Here Isaiah is connecting the Davidic covenant and the new. The new covenant will accomplish what was promised in God's covenant with David. Second Samuel 7:19 reveals that the covenant with David is God's instruction for all mankind. Isaiah follows this up by speaking of the Gentiles being called by Israel, who then look to Israel's king as their commander and leader who, as witness, brings the instruction (Torah) of the Lord to them. This is exactly what happened when Peter and Paul began proclaiming the good news to the nations in the book of Acts.

THE NEW COVENANT IN EZEKIEL

The new covenant is described in a number of passages in Ezekiel (11:16–21; 16:59–63; 18:1–4, 30–32; 34:17–31; 36:22–36; 37:15–28). Only one passage will be discussed here.

At the heart of establishing God's kingship in the world is worship. We saw this indicated by Genesis 2, which depicts Adam and Eve placed in a garden sanctuary. Only as they spend time in the presence of God will they be equipped to implement his rule in the world in the way in which God himself would relate to his creation. Israel inherited the Adamic role of son of God at the exodus (Ex. 4:22), and the priority of worship becomes evident right away with the instructions to build the tabernacle. When the construction of this portable tent for worship was complete, a bright cloud symbolic of the divine presence settled on the tent to show that the creator God was dwelling in the midst of his people as King (Ex. 25:8; 40:34).

This is where prophets like Isaiah, Jeremiah, and Ezekiel fit into the story. The people of God had repeatedly violated the terms of the Israelite covenant. Love of God and love of one's neighbor had been replaced by idolatry and the corruption of social justice in every way. As a result, Israel's worship had become hollow and hypocritical. Jeremiah is the first of the latter prophets in the Hebrew Canon. In Jeremiah 7–10 we have his famous "Temple Sermon": "Do not trust in deceptive words and say, 'This is the temple of the LORD, the temple of the LORD, the temple of the LORD!'" (Jer. 7:4, NIV). The threefold repetition is the strongest form of emphasis possible. Jeremiah is saying, "You can't live as you please and then treat the temple like a good luck charm or a rabbit's foot." The people thought they would always be protected as long as God was dwelling among them. Jeremiah's message was that covenant violation meant that God would be true to his threats and bring upon his people the curse of exile (Deuteronomy 28). Most importantly, he could no longer live among them, since their behavior and lifestyle contradicted his own character as expressed in the Torah.

Ezekiel carries the "Temple Sermon" of Jeremiah one step further. The opening vision shows the bright cloud, the glory of the Lord, in motion, and the divine throne has wheels. *Why?* Because God is getting ready to move out! God is surrounded by social injustice and idolatry, and the temple has lost its five-star hotel status—he can no longer live there. This message must have come as an awful shock to the people of Judah. In Ezekiel 8–11 the opening vision is developed further and the bright cloud—the glory of the Lord—actually begins to move from the temple to the Eastern Gate. Finally, the glory of the Lord departs from the city of God. We express it in these terms to show that the city of God can no longer be the city of God when God is no longer there.

In response to our larger work, *Kingdom through Covenant*, a review by Doug Moo for the Gospel Coalition noted a flaw in the treatment of Ezekiel 16. Further research led to a better interpretation—one where the Abrahamic covenant provides the basis for Gentile and Jew in one new covenant community.[1]

Ezekiel 16:59–63

[59] This is what the Sovereign LORD says: "I will deal with you as you deserve, because you have despised my oath by breaking the covenant.

---

[1] See http://www.thegospelcoalition.org/article/kingdom-through-covenant-a-review-by-douglas-moo.

[60] Yet I will remember the covenant I made with you in the days of your youth, and I will establish an everlasting covenant with you. [61] Then you will remember your ways and be ashamed when you receive your sisters, both those who are older than you and those who are younger. I will give them to you as daughters, but not on the basis of my covenant with you. [62] So I will establish my covenant with you, and you will know that I am the LORD. [63] Then, when I make atonement for you for all you have done, you will remember and be ashamed and never again open your mouth because of your humiliation," declares the Sovereign LORD. (NIV)

This passage concludes an extremely long parable (63 verses) in which Jerusalem is depicted as a bride cheating on her husband on many occasions with a long litany of lovers. Her feckless loyalty and constant and incorrigible covenant violation are compared to the sins of Samaria to the north and of Sodom to the south. This comparison turns out to be rather unfavorable for Jerusalem.

The plot of the parable can be briefly summarized. Jerusalem is depicted as a child born to Canaanite ancestors who is cast away by her parents, i.e., the ancient Near Eastern equivalent of abortion/infanticide. Yahweh sees this baby abandoned in the field to die, "kicking about in its blood," and commands it to live. Much later, after puberty, Yahweh passes by a second time and sees a young woman ready for adornment and marriage, and he marries her. His gifts to his bride of costly garments and expensive jewelry bring her far-flung fame for her beauty and even royalty. Although historical points of reference cannot always be pinpointed in the parable, the baby appears to correspond to the Abrahamic covenant, while the mature young woman getting married would correspond to the Mosaic covenant, with royalty perhaps keeping the Davidic covenant in view.

Next the parable details the downward spiral of the bride into adultery and harlotry. In the ancient Near East, harlots were frequently married women, so this is why the repeated term "fornication" is associated with adultery in this parable. Her sexual unfaithfulness corresponds to various forms of idolatry and alliances with foreign nations in pursuit of military support. The downward spiral reaches its nadir in child sacrifice and in the fact that this harlot has to pay her lovers to have sex with her instead of their paying her for sex.

Jerusalem's sins are so terrible in this R-rated depiction of her crimes that she completely *embarrasses* her pagan neighbors, designated as Samaria and Sodom and portrayed as her sisters. Since Ezekiel is writing after

722 B.C., when the northern kingdom of Israel fell to Assyria and the people of Israel were deported and foreign peoples were imported to live there, the northern neighbors of Jerusalem constitute the mixed race of Samaritans that resulted from these events. The behavior, lifestyle, and rejection of Yahweh's Torah by the Samaritans is described and deplored in 2 Kings 17:24–41. The people of Sodom are condemned because their abundance of life's necessities had resulted in arrogant independence from God and led to many social injustices. Nonetheless, Jerusalem's acts of covenant violations were so bad by comparison that her sins actually *justified* the conduct of her "sisters," Sodom and Samaria!

As a result, Yahweh promised to gather Jerusalem's neighbors to attack and destroy her. Finally, God would restore the fortunes of all three: Samaria, Sodom, and Jerusalem (this is the order in the text). At the end of Ezekiel 16, the verses we have quoted explain the basis for this restoration.

According to verse 59, Jerusalem will experience the curses of the covenant because of her many acts of unfaithfulness. Verse 60 speaks of Israel breaking the covenant, and then it speaks of God affirming (*hēqîm běrît*) an everlasting covenant with them. The first part is clear: breaking the covenant means that Israel violated the covenant made at Sinai and reaffirmed in Deuteronomy. But what does the text mean by affirming or perhaps upholding an everlasting covenant? Two problems are entailed in this question: (1) does the expression *hēqîm běrît* follow the normal meaning here as elsewhere, and (2) what is the everlasting covenant of which Ezekiel speaks?

Everywhere else, the expression *kārat běrît* (to cut a covenant) is used to describe covenant making. The expression *kārat běrît* indicates a covenant that did not exist previously and is now being initiated between partners for the first time. Excellent examples are Isaiah 55:3, Jeremiah 31:31, and Ezekiel 17:13, 34:25, and 37:26. Conversely, *heqîm běrît* usually indicates affirming a covenant or promise already in place. Yet Ezekiel 16:60, 62 employs *heqîm běrît* for an everlasting covenant. How are we to interpret and understand the language of Ezekiel at this point? Is there a development in the language so that "cut a covenant" and "establish/affirm a covenant" are now synonyms? A change for these expressions is unlikely, since Ezekiel uses both *kārat běrît* (3x) and *heqîm běrît* (2x), and a clear distinction between *kārat běrît* and *heqîm běrît* can be seen in Jeremiah 34, a writing close in time to that of Ezekiel, as well as in the much later Qumran Scrolls (e.g., CD 15.8, 4Q381 69.1.8; CD 3.13, 1QS 5.21–22, 8.10). We should assume, then, that the distinction established between the two expressions also works in Ezekiel. God is saying he will uphold a covenant that is already initiated. The problem is in understanding "eternal covenant" in Ezekiel 16:60.

The parable storyline suggests that the everlasting covenant is the Abrahamic covenant. God will give Samaria and Sodom to Jerusalem, not on the basis of the covenant with Israel at Sinai (i.e., his marriage to the young woman), but rather on the basis of the covenant with Abraham (the aborted baby rescued). A connection between Ezekiel 16 and Leviticus 26:40–42 supports interpreting the everlasting covenant as the Abrahamic covenant. True, Ezekiel is describing here what will happen when God makes a new covenant with Israel. But in the text itself, he is saying that the future restoration for Israel and the gift of other peoples to Jerusalem will come about not on the basis of the Israelite covenant at Sinai but instead on the basis of the Abrahamic covenant. The Israelite covenant was broken, but the Abrahamic covenant still stands. Ezekiel may be describing what will happen in the new covenant, but the term "covenant" in this text refers to the Israelite and Abrahamic covenants respectively. This interpretation better explains Ezekiel 16:60–62, since it is the nations (Samaria and Sodom) who receive blessing with Israel in this text, and it is the Abrahamic covenant that specifies salvation for the nations through Israel.

It is interesting that the term "everlasting covenant" occurs sixteen times in the Old Testament: two times of the covenant with Noah (Gen. 9:16; Isa. 24:5), five times of the covenant with Abraham (Gen. 17:7, 19; Ps. 105:10; Ezek. 16:60; 1 Chron. 16:17), once of the covenant with David (2 Sam. 23:5; cf. 2 Chron. 13:5), five times of the new covenant (Isa. 55:3; 61:8; Jer. 32:40; 50:5; Ezek. 37:26), and three times of covenant signs (Gen. 17:13; Ex. 31:16; Lev. 24:8). Nowhere in the Old Testament is the Israelite/Mosaic covenant at Sinai called an everlasting or permanent covenant.

Thus the following interpretation of Ezekiel 16 is proposed: *běrît* in verse 59 is the Mosaic covenant. In verse 60, *běrît*, first use, is the Mosaic covenant and *běrît*, second use, is the Abrahamic covenant. Likewise in verse 61 *běrît* is the Mosaic covenant while in verse 62 *běrît* is the Abrahamic covenant. Yahweh is saying to Israel that both Samaria and Sodom will be given to Jerusalem as daughters, not on the basis of the Mosaic covenant but rather on the basis of the Abrahamic covenant. "Being given as daughters" means that the neighboring nations (Samaritans and Sodomites) are now *family*. God will uphold his promises to Abraham that through him the nations will be blessed even though the nations were not blessed through the Mosaic covenant, since Israel as a nation failed as a light to the nations.

Thus Jerusalem will be given both Samaria and Sodom, but not on the basis of the Israelite covenant. This statement shows that, in the new covenant, the old divisions in Israel are healed and the Gentiles are included.

THE NEW COVENANT: JEREMIAH

Jeremiah's basic message can be summarized in a very few words: "the Babylonians are coming." Jeremiah ministered from 627 B.C. to just a few years after the destruction of Jerusalem in 587 B.C. During this time he witnessed the fall of the Neo-Assyrian empire and the rapid rise of the Babylonian empire led by Nabopolassar and his famous son, Nebuchadnezzar. Jeremiah knew that the attempts of kings like Josiah to reform the nation were inadequate, and in his famous "Temple Sermon" he warned the people about hypocritical worship, just as Isaiah before him and Ezekiel after him.

Early in Jeremiah, in 4:2, the prophet clearly states that if and when Israel returns to a right relationship with God, the blessings will flow to the nations as the Abrahamic covenant promises. This interpretation of Jeremiah 4:1–2 is confirmed and strengthened by the oracle of Jeremiah 12:14–17, which reads as follows:

> [14] This is what the LORD says: "As for all my wicked neighbors who seize the inheritance I gave my people Israel, I will uproot them from their lands and I will uproot the house of Judah from among them. [15] But after I uproot them, I will again have compassion and will bring each of them back to their own inheritance and their own country. [16] And if they learn well the ways of my people and swear by my name, saying, 'As surely as the LORD lives'—even as they once taught my people to swear by Baal—then they will be established among my people. [17] But if any nation does not listen, I will completely uproot and destroy it," declares the LORD. (NIV)

Yahweh speaks of "all my wicked neighbors who harm the inheritance which I gave to my people Israel." Historically speaking, this would refer to the lands and peoples surrounding Israel who have brought harm to its land and people down through the years: the Arameans, the Edomites, the Moabites, the Philistines, and, wider afield, the Assyrians, Babylonians, and Egyptians, to name just a few of them.

Verse 14 speaks of an exile, not just for Judah but also for each of these lands and peoples. The verb "uproot" may have a double meaning: uprooting a land would mean sending the people into exile; uprooting Judah from among them would mean bringing Judah back from exile. What is astonishing, however, is that according to verse 15, *each land* and *people* will have a return from exile. And when all the exiles are brought home, if the nations learn from Israel to swear by the God of Israel, then they will be "built up" or established in the midst of the restored Israel. If they do not, each will be permanently eradicated as a nation.

What is precisely parallel in this text to Jeremiah 4:1–2 is the idea that, through a renewed and restored Israel (who is faithful and loyal to the Lord and practices social justice), the nations may become worshipers of this same Lord and will be established *in the midst* of the renewed people of God.

What is additional and new in 12:14–17 is that the notion of a return from exile applies to the nations as well as to Judah and Israel. This idea is developed further in 16:14–18, where the metaphor of fishing for men is used as a way of describing the work of God in bringing the exiles, whether Jews or Gentiles, home. The fact that Jesus refers to Jeremiah 16 in Matthew 4:18–19 proves that he has come to bring the exiles home in his ministry: this would include both Jews and Gentiles.

Jeremiah 31:27–40

We come now to Jeremiah 31:27–40—not only the main passage in Jeremiah on the new covenant but the only place in the Old Testament where the term "new covenant" is actually employed. The full text is cited here without apology; the author of Hebrews does the same thing, making it the longest citation of the Old Testament in the New (vv. 31–34, cf. Heb. 8:8–12). This again reveals the importance of this text:

> [26] At this I awoke and looked, and my sleep was pleasant to me.
> [27] "Behold, the days are coming, declares the LORD, when I will sow the house of Israel and the house of Judah with the seed of man and the seed of beast. [28] And it shall come to pass that as I have watched over them to pluck up and break down, to overthrow, destroy, and bring harm, so I will watch over them to build and to plant, declares the LORD. [29] In those days they shall no longer say:

"'The fathers have eaten sour grapes,
    and the children's teeth are set on edge.'

[30] But everyone shall die for his own iniquity. Each man who eats sour grapes, his teeth shall be set on edge.

[The New Covenant]

[31] "Behold, the days are coming, declares the LORD, when I will make a new covenant with the house of Israel and the house of Judah, [32] not like the covenant that I made with their fathers on the day when I took them by the hand to bring them out of the land of Egypt, my covenant that they broke, though I was their husband, declares the LORD. [33] For this is the covenant that I will make with the house of Israel after those days, declares the LORD: I will put my law within them, and I will write it on their hearts. And I will be their God, and they shall be my people. [34] And no longer shall each one teach his neighbor and each his brother, saying, 'Know the LORD,' for they shall all know me, from the least of them to the greatest, declares the LORD. For I will forgive their iniquity, and I will remember their sin no more."

[35] Thus says the LORD,
who gives the sun for light by day
    and the fixed order of the moon and the stars for light by night,
who stirs up the sea so that its waves roar—
    the LORD of hosts is his name:
[36] "If this fixed order departs
    from before me, declares the LORD,
then shall the offspring of Israel cease
    from being a nation before me forever."

[37] Thus says the LORD:
"If the heavens above can be measured,
    and the foundations of the earth below can be explored,
then I will cast off all the offspring of Israel
    for all that they have done,
        declares the LORD."

[38] "Behold, the days are coming, declares the LORD, when the city shall be rebuilt for the LORD from the Tower of Hananel to the Corner Gate. [39] And the measuring line shall go out farther, straight to the hill Gareb, and shall then turn to Goah. [40] The whole valley of the dead bodies and the ashes, and all the fields as far as the brook Kidron, to the corner of the

Horse Gate toward the east, shall be sacred to the LORD. It shall not be plucked up or overthrown anymore forever." (ESV)

Many discussions of this passage delimit the text as verses 31–34. Note, e.g., the editorial heading "The New Covenant" in the ESV, setting off verses 31ff. Certainly the phrase "Behold the days are coming" probably marks the beginning of an oracle or unit; verses 27 and 38 begin with the same phrase. Note, however, that verse 26 says that Jeremiah awoke and his sleep was pleasant to him. This indicates that the normal means of communicating to the prophet was in dreams and visions (see Num. 12:6) and that as the content represented good news rather than the usual bad news, Jeremiah found his sleep sweet to him this time. At the same time, the statement that Jeremiah awoke is a clear indication of the end of the divine communication at verse 25, so that what we have attached at the end of the Book of Consolation (chs. 30–31) are several smaller sections appended to it. As we will see, verses 27–30 are integral to verses 31–34 and important for the interpretation of the new covenant. It is for this reason that we have delimited the unit as verses 27–40, subdivided by the recurring introductory phrase into three sections. The messenger formula at the onset of verse 35 also marks a new paragraph. In all, then, the section contains four paragraphs. Discussions of the new covenant do not, in general, consider the flow of thought integral to these four paragraphs, but instead, they isolate verses 31–34 unnecessarily and focus attention on only that paragraph.

Explanation of this text will be focused around four questions: (1) When did Jeremiah predict the new covenant would be initiated? (2) With whom would God make this covenant? One of the parties is obviously God, but how should we define and delimit the other (human) party? (3) How is this covenant like the old (Israelite) covenant, and how is it unlike it? In other words, precisely what is *new* about the new covenant? and (4) What is the power or promise of the new covenant? I.e., is this renewed covenant any better than the former one made at Sinai and supplemented by Deuteronomy on the plains of Moab?

TIME

Verses 27, 31, and 38 of chapter 31 all begin with the phrase "Behold, days are coming." This phrase also occurs at 30:3, the general introduction to the Book of Consolation:

[1] The word that came to Jeremiah from the LORD: [2] "Thus says the LORD, the God of Israel: Write in a book all the words that I have spoken to you. [3] For behold, days are coming, declares the LORD, when I will restore the fortunes of my people, Israel and Judah, says the LORD, and I will bring them back to the land that I gave to their fathers, and they shall take possession of it." (ESV)

The general introduction to the Book of Consolation announces, "Behold, days are coming." The next occurrence(s) of this phrase are the three instances in verses 27–40. Indeed, this is a familiar phrase in Jeremiah (occurring some fourteen or fifteen times), but is found only rarely elsewhere in the Old Testament. Note carefully that the word "days" has no article. The translation "*the* days are coming" is not accurate. The text simply says, "days are coming." The days are indefinite. We must not take this as a technical term in the eschatology of the Old Testament or in the writings of the prophets. It simply refers to an *indefinite* future. Whether this indefinite time in the future is near or remote is left entirely unspecified in the prophecy.

PARTIES

According to the text, Yahweh makes the new covenant "with the house of Israel and the house of Judah" (Jer. 31:31). The human partner is specified in this way because, in Jeremiah 5:11 and elsewhere, this is the party that has broken the covenant made at Sinai and prevented the blessings from flowing to the nations. We have already seen, however, from earlier passages in Jeremiah, that the Gentiles or non-Jewish nations will be established in the midst of Israel in this restored people of God. They too are the exiles who will be brought home by the fishers of men.

Let us now follow this through and see how it is interpreted in the New Testament by Jesus and the apostles.

First, note the clear reference to Jeremiah's new covenant by Jesus during his last Passover meal—which was also his institution of the Lord's Supper. In Matthew 26:26–29 Jesus redefines the Jewish Passover meal as a drama portraying his atoning death on the cross. This drama then interprets his crucifixion in precisely those terms: a new exodus that brings about forgiveness and reconciliation on the basis of the sacrifice of himself as a "Passover lamb." In this drama, the cup represents "my blood of the covenant which is poured out for many for the forgiveness of sins." Although the exact phrase "new covenant" is not recorded in Matthew's account, it is included in Luke 22:20.

The reference in Matthew to blood "poured out for many" is a clear allusion to Isaiah 53:10–12, where the servant of the Lord is a "Passover lamb" whose atoning death brings about forgiveness for "the many." The reference to Jeremiah's new covenant is explicit, at least in Luke, and the allusion is also clear in Matthew. Jesus' last Passover meal, then, is converted into a new ceremonial tradition in which the cup represents his life (as Passover lamb) sacrificed to bring about the forgiveness of sins in the new exodus defined by Isaiah and Jeremiah.

Once the connection between the institution of the Lord's Supper in the Gospels and Isaiah 53 and Jeremiah 31 is established, it is interesting to note that Jesus gives this meal to *his disciples*. That is to say, he does not view it as a covenant with the house of Israel and the house of Judah interpreted as all of Judaism indiscriminately in the first century, but rather as a covenant with those *who are his followers*, regardless of ethnicity—Jew first, and later on, also non-Jew.

Another key passage that addresses the question of "how do we define the human party in the new covenant" is Romans 11:13–24:

[13] Now I am speaking to you Gentiles. Inasmuch then as I am an apostle to the Gentiles, I magnify my ministry [14] in order somehow to make my fellow Jews jealous, and thus save some of them. [15] For if their rejection means the reconciliation of the world, what will their acceptance mean but life from the dead? [16] If the dough offered as firstfruits is holy, so is the whole lump, and if the root is holy, so are the branches.

[17] But if some of the branches were broken off, and you, although a wild olive shoot, were grafted in among the others and now share in the nourishing root of the olive tree, [18] do not be arrogant toward the branches. If you are, remember it is not you who support the root, but the root that supports you. [19] Then you will say, "Branches were broken off so that I might be grafted in." [20] That is true. They were broken off because of their unbelief, but you stand fast through faith. So do not become proud, but fear. [21] For if God did not spare the natural branches, neither will he spare you. [22] Note then the kindness and the severity of God: severity toward those who have fallen, but God's kindness to you, provided you continue in his kindness. Otherwise you too will be cut off. [23] And even they, if they do not continue in their unbelief, will be grafted in, for God has the power to graft them in again. [24] For if you were cut from what is by nature a wild olive tree, and grafted, contrary to nature, into a

cultivated olive tree, how much more will these, the natural branches, be grafted back into their own olive tree. (ESV)

Paul is explaining in this passage the benefits of the new covenant and, in particular, how this covenant relates to those who are genetically Israelites, since for the most part during Paul's ministry they rejected Jesus as Messiah. Paul's main mission has been to take the good news to the Gentiles, and this has met with great success. What are we to make of the fact that, during and since Paul's ministry, few Jews but many Gentiles are believing in Jesus and being added to the church? This is the painful problem addressed in Romans 9–11. Paul explains that the acceptance of the person and work of Jesus by the Gentiles, the nations, will arouse jealousy among those of the historical race of Israel and will motivate them to come to faith in Jesus Christ.

As is well known, Paul employs the metaphor of an olive tree to represent Israel. This is derived from Jeremiah (Jer. 11:16; cf. Hos. 14:6). It is common in the Old Testament to represent kings and kingdoms by tall, stately trees and fruitful plants. So the olive tree for Paul represents Israel, and the Jeremiah passage is fundamental for his comments in Romans 11. Unbelieving and rebellious Israelites have been removed, and individuals from other nations have been joined to this one people of God, the new and transformed Zion. As we saw earlier, this theme was already adumbrated in Jeremiah, though it was not stated there as clearly as in the New Testament.

For description of precisely what human parties are entailed in the new covenant, the passages in Ephesians 2 and 3 are among the clearest in the New Testament:

[11] Therefore remember that at one time you Gentiles in the flesh, called "the uncircumcision" by what is called the circumcision, which is made in the flesh by hands—[12] remember that you were at that time separated from Christ, alienated from the commonwealth of Israel and strangers to the covenants of promise, having no hope and without God in the world. [13] But now in Christ Jesus you who once were far off have been brought near by the blood of Christ. [14] For he himself is our peace, who has made us both one and has broken down in his flesh the dividing wall of hostility [15] by abolishing the law of commandments expressed in ordinances, that he might create in himself one new man in place of the two, so making peace, [16] and might reconcile us both to God in one body through the cross, thereby killing the hostility. [17] And he came and preached peace to you who were far off and peace to those who were near. [18] For through

> him we both have access in one Spirit to the Father. [19] So then you are
> no longer strangers and aliens, but you are fellow citizens with the saints
> and members of the household of God, [20] built on the foundation of the
> apostles and prophets, Christ Jesus himself being the cornerstone, [21] in
> whom the whole structure, being joined together, grows into a holy temple
> in the Lord. [22] In him you also are being built together into a dwelling
> place for God by the Spirit. (Eph. 2:11–22, ESV)

> [1] For this reason I, Paul, a prisoner for Christ Jesus on behalf of you
> Gentiles—[2] assuming that you have heard of the stewardship of God's
> grace that was given to me for you, [3] how the mystery was made known
> to me by revelation, as I have written briefly. [4] When you read this, you
> can perceive my insight into the mystery of Christ, [5] which was not made
> known to the sons of men in other generations as it has now been revealed
> to his holy apostles and prophets by the Spirit. [6] This mystery is that the
> Gentiles are fellow heirs, members of the same body, and partakers of the
> promise in Christ Jesus through the gospel. (Eph. 3:1–6, ESV)

When Paul speaks in Ephesians 2:15 of "one new *man*," he is obviously
thinking of a new *Adam* and is saying that the *church*—by virtue of the new
creation resulting from the resurrection of Jesus Christ, and by virtue of the
union of head (Christ) and body (church)—constitutes this new Adam, a
renewal of the Adamic role initiated with Abraham and his family.

The Gentiles—members of nations and peoples in the earth apart from
or outside of the nation of Israel, who were alienated from the commonwealth of Israel—have been forged together with believers from Israel into
one new humanity. Verse 14 says that "he made both groups/the two groups
one." And again verse 15 says that "he created in him the two (groups)
into one new man/humanity." There is no future for either Israelite or non-
Israelite apart from the church, and there is no separate future for either Israelite or non-Israelite—both will be part of the church. This is the body of
humans who will survive the destruction of this creation and will be placed
within the creation of a new heavens and a new earth.

Ephesians 3:5 says that this truth was not made known earlier *as it has
now been revealed* to the apostles and prophets of the church of Jesus Christ.
The truth that the nations would be included in Israel is taught in the Old
Testament, but what is new is that this would happen *in Christ Jesus*:

> [25] I do not want you to be ignorant of this mystery, brothers, so that
> you may not be conceited: Israel has experienced a hardening in part until

the full number of the Gentiles has come in. [26] And so all Israel will be saved, as it is written:

> "The deliverer will come from Zion;
>   he will turn godlessness away from Jacob.
> [27] And this is my covenant with them
>   when I take away their sins." (Rom. 11:25–27, NIV)

Romans 11:25–27 is a debated passage among Christians, especially in the polemics of covenant theology versus dispensationalism. Some have taught that the "fullness of the Gentiles" refers to the so-called "church age," and that when it is over, then the geopolitical kingdom will be restored to Israel and physical Israel will be saved. They may also appeal to the book of Daniel, which describes four Gentile kingdoms followed by the kingdom of God. Unfortunately, everyone may be blinded by the assumptions they have and the way they put the metanarrative of Scripture together. We all bring such assumptions to the reading of any particular text.

In Romans 11, Paul has just portrayed Israel in terms of an olive tree, some of whose natural branches have been removed and some of whose branches are now non-Jewish branches grafted into the one root and tree. This means that the new humanity and restored Israel is based on faith and covenant relationship to the Lord rather than on ethnicity. During the period in which the exiles are brought home, a large number of "Gentile exiles" (to use Jeremiah's own imagery) will be brought home first, and this will motivate a large number of Jewish exiles to be brought home toward the end. But the Jewish exiles will be *brought back* to the one olive tree. We must interpret "all Israel" within the context of Paul's teaching in Romans 11. There is no separate future for physical Israel outside of the church—the only humanity to inhabit the new creation. And this is not so-called replacement theology. It is what the prophets teach about the renovated and restored Zion.

THE NEW COVENANT AND THE OLD: CONTINUITY AND DISCONTINUITY

How is this new covenant like the old (Israelite) covenant, and how is it unlike it? In other words, precisely what is *new* about the new covenant? Jeremiah 31:31–34 describes the new covenant. Scholars have debated extensively the meaning of the word "new" in Hebrew. Does it mean a renewed covenant, or a covenant that did not exist previously? Is it a new development, or is it a renewing of something earlier? We should let the statements in Jeremiah 31:31–34 define what is meant by a new covenant. Hebrews 8 also tells us that, by speaking of a "new" covenant, Jeremiah makes the Mosaic covenant "old," obsolete, and passing away.

It is important to pay attention to the grammatical and literary structures in the text. Scott J. Hafemann has helpfully diagrammed the text to aid in clarifying the flow of thought.[2] The argument of Jeremiah 31:31–34, according to its constituent propositions, is as follows:

v. 31   "Behold, days are coming," declares the LORD, "when I will make a new covenant with the house of Israel and with the house of Judah.

v. 32a   *Specifically–negatively*: I will not make it like the covenant which I made with their fathers . . .

v. 32b   because they broke my covenant (at Sinai)

v. 32c   although I was a husband to them," declares the LORD.

v. 33a   *Specifically–positively*: "But this is the covenant which I will make with the house of Israel after those days," declares the LORD. "I will put my law within them and I will write it upon their heart.

v. 33b   *Immediate Result*: "I will be their God and they will be my people."

v. 34a   *Ultimate Result*: "They will no longer teach each other saying, 'Know the LORD,'

v. 34b   because they will all know me, from the least of them to the greatest of them," declares the LORD.

v. 34c   *Basis for this Result*: "I shall forgive their iniquity, and I shall remember their sin no more."

Several points in Jeremiah's announcement of the new covenant must be noted.

First, the new covenant is the divinely promised answer to the perennial problem of Israel's hard-hearted rebellion against the Lord. The Hebrew expression "the stubbornness of his/their heart" (Deut. 29:18; Jer. 3:17; 7:24; 9:14; 11:8; 13:10; 16:12; 18:12; 23:17; Ps. 81:12) occurs ten times in the Old Testament: the one instance in Deuteronomy is picked up by Jeremiah, who uses the phrase a total of eight times. Thus nearly all the occurrences are in Jeremiah. This, along with other phrases used by Jeremiah, such as "the incurable wound" in chapter 30, demonstrates his emphasis on the fact that

---

[2] Adapted from Scott J. Hafemann, "The Covenant Relationship," in *Central Themes in Biblical Theology: Mapping Unity in Diversity*, ed. Scott J. Hafemann and Paul R. House (Grand Rapids, MI: Baker, 2007), 49.

Israel's rebellion is intractable: she cannot avert the coming anger and wrath of God. Judgment is absolutely certain. The new covenant looks beyond judgment to a future in which God will provide a solution to the stubbornness of his partner in the old covenant. The direction and instruction of God for righteous relationships will be internalized and written upon the heart. Since the heart of the people will be "circumcised" (Deut. 10:16; 30:6), that is, transformed, they will be a faithful covenant partner. The new covenant will not be like the Israelite covenant, because the people broke that covenant. Now the people of the Lord will be completely faithful and loyal; they will be covenant keepers. Thus the new covenant in Jeremiah must be interpreted against the background of the faithless and stubborn heart of Israel in the old covenant.

The writing of the divine instruction upon the heart corresponds to the promise made earlier in Jeremiah that the ark of the covenant would become obsolete:

> [16] And when you have multiplied and been fruitful in the land, in those days, declares the LORD, they shall no more say, "The ark of the covenant of the LORD." It shall not come to mind or be remembered or missed; it shall not be made again. [17] At that time Jerusalem shall be called the throne of the LORD, and all nations shall gather to it, to the presence of the LORD in Jerusalem, and they shall no more stubbornly follow their own evil heart. [18] In those days the house of Judah shall join the house of Israel, and together they shall come from the land of the north to the land that I gave your fathers for a heritage. (Jer. 3:16–18, ESV)

In the new covenant, there will be no ark because God's instruction will be written on the hearts of human beings. Christians, then, are the ark in the new covenant, because the church is the temple. The people of God will faithfully keep the new covenant. God's instruction will be internalized; it will be ingrained in their thinking, feeling, and planning. Paul picks this up in 2 Corinthians 3:3 when he speaks of the evidence for the new covenant in the Corinthian Christians:

> You show that you are a letter from Christ, the result of our ministry, written not with ink but with the Spirit of the living God, not on tablets of stone but on tablets of human hearts. (NIV)

Second, the covenant relationship with God is the immediate result of God "writing" the divine direction for living and the instruction of the new

covenant upon the hearts of believers. This is clear from the Covenant Formula, "I will be their God and they shall be my people." Notice, again, how
Paul applies the Covenant Formula to the Corinthian Christians in 2 Corinthians 6:14–18:

> [14] Do not be yoked together with unbelievers. For what do righteousness
> and wickedness have in common? Or what fellowship can light have with
> darkness? [15] What harmony is there between Christ and Belial? What
> does a believer have in common with an unbeliever? [16] What agreement
> is there between the temple of God and idols? For we are the temple of the
> living God. As God has said: "I will live with them and walk among them,
> *and I will be their God, and they will be my people."*
>
>   [17] "Therefore come out from them
>   and be separate,
>   says the Lord.
>
>   Touch no unclean thing,
>   and I will receive you."
>   [18] "I will be a Father to you,
>   and you will be my sons and daughters,
>   says the Lord Almighty." (NIV)

Paul backs up his command not to be "yoked together with unbelievers" by a
pastiche of citations from the Old Testament. First, from Leviticus 26:11–12
comes the Covenant Formula. Then, from Isaiah 52:11 is a call to the exiles
to leave Babylon and join the community of the new exodus with the promise "I will receive you" added from Ezekiel 20:41, where another paragraph
on the same topic can be found. Finally, 2 Corinthians 6:18 seems to apply
the father-son relationship of the covenant with David (2 Sam. 7:14) to all
the members of the new covenant community.

Third, the result of inaugurating the new covenant will be that a community will be created in which "they will no longer teach each other,
saying, 'Know the LORD,' because they will all know me, from the least
of them to the greatest of them, declares the LORD" (Jer. 31:34). This is a
most significant statement, whose import has not been well understood.
To begin to grasp the meaning, it must be understood that this verse is a
statement that stands in contrast to verses 29–30 and answers the problem
posed by these words:

[29] In those days people will no longer say,

> "The fathers have eaten sour grapes,
>   and the children's teeth are set on edge."

[30] Instead, everyone will die for his own sin; whoever eats sour grapes—his own teeth will be set on edge. (NIV)

Verse 29 recites a proverb going around among the exiles in Babylon. Normally when a person eats sour grapes, their own lips pucker up. To claim that the parents ate sour grapes and the lips of the children puckered up is a way of saying that the children have been judged (i.e., exiled) for their parents' sins. In the Abrahamic and Mosaic covenants, the structure of the community was profoundly racial and tribal, and the human mediators were sinful. The new covenant will have a human covenant mediator, namely Jesus Christ, who is prophet, priest, and king in one person. In the old covenant community, these covenant mediators sinned and the community suffered because of *faulty mediators*. In the new covenant, however, our covenant mediator is without sin and, as a result, the community will never suffer because of a faulty mediator.

What verse 34 is saying, however, in contrast to verses 29–30, is that, in the old covenant, people became members of the covenant community simply by being born into that community. As they grew up, some became believers in Yahweh and others did not. This resulted in a situation within the covenant community where some *members* could urge other *members* to know the Lord. In the new covenant community, however, one does not become a member by physical birth but rather by the new birth, which requires faith on the part of each person. Thus only believers are members of the new community: all *members* are *believers*, and *only* believers are members. Therefore, in the new covenant community, there will no longer be a situation where some members urge other members to know the Lord. There will be no such thing as an unregenerate member of the new covenant community. All are believers, all know the Lord, because all have experienced the forgiveness of sins. Paedo-baptists have argued that there is an already and not yet to the fulfillment of verse 34. They do so to bolster their view of paedo-baptism and their view of the church as a mixed community. But the new covenant is different from the Abrahamic covenant in *structure*, right from the start. Membership in the Abrahamic covenant community is defined by physical birth, with circumcision as the sign; membership in the new covenant community is defined by the new birth, by regeneration by faith in Jesus Christ, with baptism as the sign of this faith. How can an infant baptism be a sign of the child's faith?

What Jeremiah is teaching in 31:33–34 is identical to what Isaiah is teaching in Isaiah 54:13: "All your children shall be taught by the LORD, and great shall be the peace of your children" (ESV). Everyone in the covenant community will experience reconciliation (peace) with God, and so everyone will have a living relationship with the Lord, and so the divine instruction for living will be written upon the heart.

As the last part of verse 34 indicates, the basis for these characteristics of the new covenant community is the divine forgiveness of sins brought about by the establishment of the new covenant.

Jeremiah 31:34 is important since it shows that the Presbyterian understanding is flawed. There are no covenant members who are not believers. This challenge to the Presbyterians must be given in humility since, by and large, they have had a much better grasp of the meaning and role of the covenants than Baptists.

The metanarrative of the system of covenant theology is not true to the Bible because it does not pay adequate attention to what the biblical texts say in defining the relationship(s) of one covenant to another. First, we cannot speak of "the covenant" in the way the theologians of classic covenant theology do, because this language is never found in the Bible. Instead, we can speak only of the covenants (plural), i.e., the covenant with creation, the covenant with Abraham, the Israelite covenant, the Davidic covenant, and the new covenant. Furthermore, we must let the biblical texts define the relationships between them.

In the Abrahamic covenant, God promises blessing for Israel and for the nations through Israel. The Israelite covenant is inaugurated to implement the promises to Abraham. The Davidic covenant reveals that the blessing will come through the king of Israel (rather than through the nation as a whole) as he administers justice to Israel and to the nations. Israel's idolatry and sin is covenant violation, and thus the plan of salvation for the world appears doomed. The new covenant restores the broken relationship between God and Israel by bringing about the forgiveness of sins. Redemption is the achievement and victory of a Davidic king who then administers righteousness to a restored Israel in which Jew and Gentile are created to be the new humanity. The community of the new covenant is the only humanity to inherit a new creation—a new heavens and earth.

In the present time, when there is overlap between the old creation and the new, God rescues believers in Jesus Christ from "the authority of darkness" and "transfers them to the kingdom of his beloved son," according to Colossians 1:13. In the church, believers experience the blessings of the new covenant. In what way, however, does the new covenant "administer" the unregenerate? The only blessings the unregenerate receive are the blessings given, in the covenant with creation, to all humans alike.

Fourth, the expression "I will cut a new covenant" (*kārat běrît*) shows that God is not simply affirming the Sinai covenant or renewing the Sinai covenant; he is initiating or inaugurating a new covenant. Therefore the new covenant is not the old covenant. It is a *new covenant*. This automatically renders the Israelite covenant obsolete as a code or formalized agreement. Recall that the Israelite covenant is both a law treatise and a covenant or vassal treaty. A new arrangement or code will be put into place between God and his people, but the instruction in that code will be the same. As a result, when we compare and contrast the old and new covenant, we can say that we are not bound to the old covenant as a code, but that the righteousness of God demonstrated in the old covenant has been enshrined and incorporated into the new.

This is something that in general is poorly grasped in many discussions of the Christian life. As a Christian, I am not bound by the Ten Commandments, because they are part of an agreement between God and Israel that does not apply to me. My relationship to God is based upon and defined by the new covenant. Those like the theonomists who want to put the Christian under the old covenant are false teachers. Nonetheless, within the new covenant the divine instruction calls me to love my neighbor so that adultery, murder, stealing, etc., are still covenant violations. The righteousness of God has not changed.

Some of the similarities and differences between the old and new covenants can be diagrammed simply:

Similarity of the New Covenant to the Old Covenant
1. Basis is the same (the grace of God)
2. Purpose is the same (cf. 1 Pet. 2:9–10)
3. Initiated by blood (Heb. 9:6–10:18)
4. Character of divine instruction is the same (Rom. 13:8; Gal. 5:14)

Dissimilarity of the New Covenant to the Old Covenant
1. Better mediator (without sin) (Heb. 8:6; 9:15; 12:24)
2. Better sacrifice (Heb. 9:6–10:18; Isa. 42:6; 52:13–53:12)
3. Better provision (the Spirit of God; Ezek. 36:24–28)
4. Better promise (impartation of a new heart) (Ezek. 36:24–28)

THE POWER OF THE NEW COVENANT: DARING TO DRAW NEAR

Hidden and tucked away in the Book of Consolation, separate from the paragraphs on the new covenant, are some amazing statements concerning the power and promise of the coming new situation. Let us consider the amazing prediction of Jeremiah 30:21–22:

> [21] Their prince shall be one of their own,
>   their ruler shall come from their midst;
> I will bring him near, and he shall approach me,
>   for who would otherwise dare to approach me?
>   says the LORD.
> [22] And you shall be my people,
>   and I will be your God. (NRSV)

The import of these words for the new covenant can be developed under three headings.

1. No One Can Approach God on His or Her Own Initiative

Jeremiah employs a bold figure of speech in this text. This figure of speech is usually not translated in most of the English versions. Verse 21c might be rendered, "For who would mortgage his heart to draw near to me?" This metaphor draws a comparison between a person using property as collateral for a loan and a person giving away his life for something. Just as mortgaging a house or property due to one's desperate financial straits is an extreme and radical step, even more so is it an act of desperation to give away one's heart, i.e., one's life. The inner person is one's most precious possession. Jeremiah portrays a man selling his soul, as it were, to have an audience with God. Could one's most valuable possession be used as collateral to gain an audience with God? Absolutely *no*! There is no initiative on the part of a human that can bring him close to God; the initiative must come from God and God alone.

2. God Has Brought the King-Priest of His People Near

Although no human initiative can bring a person into the awesome presence of the divine King of kings and Lord of lords, God has brought the King of his people near. This is of greater moment than that of Esther coming before the great king of the Persian empire. J. A. Thompson comments,

> To enter the divine presence unbidden was to risk death. The ruler thus appears to be undertaking a sacral or priestly function rather than one that is specifically political. The picture is of a ruler-priest performing both political and priestly duties. Such a concept was well known in the Middle East.[3]

We should carefully note the language used in verse 21. The text speaks of a prince (*addîr*) or ruler (*mōšēl*). The first word is literally a "mighty one" and the second is a participle from a generic verb "to rule." John Bright is right to note that the normal term for "king" (*melek*) is avoided for the same reasons that the author of Samuel prefers "leader" (*nāgîd*): to avoid the Canaanite idea of kingship in terms of self-serving absolute power. Furthermore, the verb "to draw near" (*nāgaš*) and the verb "to bring near" (*qārab*) belong primarily to the description of priestly service and work. The language of this text, then, portrays a coming figure who is both priest and king. The combination of priest and king is extremely rare in the messianic texts of the Old Testament (cf. Psalm 110) but indicates that the coming figure fulfills an Adamic role planned by God from the beginning for a man over his creation. The text also speaks of the coming ruler coming from the midst of Israel. This is exactly the language used in Deuteronomy 18:15 for God raising up a prophet, and perhaps also in Deuteronomy 17:15 of God choosing a king for Israel.

3. We Can Draw Near through Him

The implication is that those who are joined to this ruler—his people—can draw near to God through him. This is made explicit in Hebrews 10:19–22:

> [19] Therefore, brothers, since we have confidence to enter the Most Holy Place by the blood of Jesus, [20] by a new and living way opened for us

---

[3] See J. A. Thompson, *The Book of Jeremiah*, New International Commentary on the Old Testament (Grand Rapids, MI: Eerdmans, 1980), 562. John Bright notes that "the ruler here (the word "king" is avoided) discharges a sacral or priestly function, rather than one that is specifically political" (John Bright, *Jeremiah: A New Translation with Introduction and Commentary*, Anchor Bible 21 [New York: Doubleday, 1984], 280). Cf. also *The Hebrew and Aramaic Lexicon of the Old Testament*, ed. L. Koehler and W. Baumgartner, et al., trans. M. E. J. Richardson, study edition, 2 vols. (Leiden: Brill, 2001), s.v. נגשׁ.

through the curtain, that is, his body, [21] and since we have a great priest over the house of God, [22] let us draw near to God with a sincere heart in full assurance of faith, having our hearts sprinkled to cleanse us from a guilty conscience and having our bodies washed with pure water. (NIV)

Verses 35–36 of Jeremiah 31 speak of the new covenant as enduring, as lasting, as permanent, by affirming that it is as enduring as the divine arrangement that gave the sun to light up the day and the moon and stars to light up the night. Although some argue that this is a reference to the covenant with Noah rather than to creation, the text of verses 35–36 mentions specifically the sun as a light for the day and the stars as a light for the night. This is more obviously a reference to Genesis 1:14–16 than to Genesis 8:22. If one allows for a covenant with creation that is reaffirmed and upheld in Genesis 6–9, then one can have it both ways.

Finally, Jeremiah 31:38–40 describes the dimensions of the renovated and restored Jerusalem and claims that even the areas formerly used for refuse will be devoted to the Lord. Not all of the locations mentioned in the text are known, but Jeremiah appears to move from the northeast to northwest, then to southwest and around to southeast. It seems that the geography of the new Jerusalem will be different, and that the Valley of Hinnom, defiled by corpses and garbage, will become holy to the Lord. The new Jerusalem will be both different and expanded from the old.

THE NEW COVENANT AND THE COVENANT WITH DAVID

Israel's story throughout the Old Testament is not one of success. Israel was called through the Mosaic covenant to be a devoted son in relationship to God and to provide a priestly service, bringing divine blessing to the nations, showing them how to treat one another in genuinely human ways and how to be good stewards of the earth. Yet instead of displaying faithful, loyal love (*ḥesed* and *'ĕmet*) to God and others and dealing in social justice (justice and righteousness), she is completely riddled by corruption and social violence. Jeremiah notes that the hearts of the people are like an incurable wound: they do not have a circumcised heart—one of complete devotion to the covenant Lord (Jer. 17:9). Like an incurable wound, their hearts are constantly unfaithful.

The covenant with David appears to be a way out of the problem. The king of Israel represents the nation and will do for the nation as a whole what they have completely failed to do in bringing blessing to the nations. Isaiah 7 is a critical moment in the history of the Davidic monarchy. The king should go out and fight the battles for the nation, but the real enemy is within—the incurable wound of the uncircumcised heart. In the end, the Davidic house as represented by Ahaz completely fails to administer the Mosaic covenant and refuses to trust Yahweh. So the kingdom of David, compared to a stately tree like all the ancient kingdoms, becomes a tree cut down. Isaiah sees a shoot coming out of the stump in Isaiah 11. Jeremiah 23:5 affirms that only God can bring new growth out of the dead stump. We must wait until the New Testament, where we have a king from the line of David who is pictured as a new David. In his atoning death he meets the real enemies—sin, death, and Satan—and clobbers them. This not only allows Israel to be rescued from her self-destructive path; it opens a fountain of blessings for all the nations. In this way the new covenant brings to fulfillment the divine intentions in the Abrahamic, Mosaic, and Davidic covenants.

PART THREE

THEOLOGICAL INTEGRATION

Chapter 11

"KINGDOM THROUGH COVENANT"

A Biblical-Theological Summary

A lot of territory has been covered in the previous chapters. In this final chapter, we will "tie together" the biblical data into an overall biblical-theological synthesis. "Kingdom through covenant" nicely captures our understanding of the progression of the biblical covenants, which in turn is the glue that unites the Bible's entire metanarrative. We will unpack this expression in two steps. First, we will describe our understanding of the term *kingdom* and how the idea of the *kingdom of God* is developed across the Canon. Second, we will summarize our understanding of the relationship between kingdom and covenant and how it is *through the progression of the covenants* that God's kingdom comes to this world centered in our Lord Jesus Christ.

KINGDOM THROUGH COVENANT

The idea of the *kingdom* has already been discussed in previous chapters, but now we want to summarize it biblically and theologically. Thomas Schreiner is correct when he insists that the *kingdom of God* "is of prime importance in New Testament theology,"[1] and, we would add, for the entire Bible. Graeme Goldsworthy is also correct to note that, "The idea of the rule of God over creation, over all creatures, over the kingdoms of the world, and in a unique and special way, over his chosen and redeemed people, is the very heart of the message of the Hebrew scriptures."[2] Five points succinctly capture our understanding of *kingdom*.

1. Scripture begins with the declaration that God, as Creator and triune Lord, is the sovereign ruler and King of the universe. In this important sense, the entire universe is God's kingdom since he is presently Lord and King. From the opening verses of Genesis, God is introduced and identified as

---

[1] Thomas R. Schreiner, *New Testament Theology: Magnifying God in Christ* (Grand Rapids, MI: Baker, 2008), 41.
[2] Graeme Goldsworthy, "Kingdom of God," in *NDBT*, 618.

the Lord who created the universe by his word, while he himself is uncreated, self-existent, self-sufficient, and in need of nothing outside himself (Ps. 50:12–14; 93:2; Acts 17:24–25). That is why the God of the Bible is the only true God, utterly unique, and unwilling to share his glory with any created thing (Isa. 42:8). This is also why God alone is to be worshiped, trusted, and obeyed; he is the King, and the entire universe is his kingdom. This truth is illustrated by Psalm 103:19: "The LORD has established his throne in the heavens, and his kingdom rules over all" (cf. Ps. 47:8; Dan. 4:34–35).

In addition, God's kingly work in creation is never presented as an end in itself; rather, it is the beginning of God's eternal plan (Eph. 1:11; Rev. 4:11) in time, which he now directs and governs toward a specific *telos*. Creation leads to providence, and both creation and providence establish the eschatological direction of God's plan worked out in terms of his specific covenantal relationships with his creation, which, in the end, all leads to a specific goal centered in Christ (cf. Col. 1:15–20). Even though the specific *wording*, "kingdom of God," is not found until much later in Scripture, the *idea* is taught in the opening pages of the Bible.

2. Although the triune God is universal King, given the Fall, everything changes. Before the Fall, God as Creator and King creates a world that is beautifully summarized by the phrase, "it was very good" (Gen. 1:4, 10, 12, 18, 21, 25, 31). Even though the nature of this goodness is disputed, in light of Genesis 3, it must minimally convey moral goodness and purity. Yet now, in light of human rebellion, God's rightful rule over the entire creation is rejected by his creatures. Sin is essentially rebellion against the claims of the King—moral autonomy—and so, as a result of our sin, we now stand under God's judicial sentence of condemnation, guilt, and death (Gen. 2:16–17; Rom. 3:23; 6:23). It is in light of the Fall that the Old Testament makes an important distinction between the sovereignty and rule of God over the entire creation, and the coming of his *saving reign* in the context of a rebellious creation, to make all things right. The creation, which was originally created good, has now gone wrong because of sin. If God chooses to make things right, he as the Lord and King must act savingly, which sets the stage for the development of the redemptive storyline of Scripture, for the coming of a Redeemer to set creation right—to usher in the *saving reign* of God in this world. As D. A. Carson reminds us, "Ultimately that plot-line anticipates the restoration of goodness, even the transformation to a greater glory, of the universe gone wrong (Rom. 8:21), and arrives finally at the dawning of a

new heaven and a new earth (Revelation 21–22; cf. Isa. 65:17), the home of righteousness (2 Peter 3:13)."[3] On the one hand, then, the kingdom of God will exclude all sin and rebellion. On the other hand, it will include all that is redeemed according to God's gracious will and action. Eventually, when all sin and evil is put down, we will see the fullness of God's kingdom, which Scripture describes in new creation categories, in contrast to that which was lost in the old creation due to Adam's sin and rebellion, acting as our representative head.

3. How does God's kingdom come, in this *saving* sense? As the Old Testament unfolds, God's kingdom is revealed and comes *through* the biblical covenants in a twofold way. First, it comes *through* the covenant relationship God has established with his creatures. Amazingly, our triune God has graciously chosen to create humans as his image-bearers, literally his priest-kings, to be in covenant relationship with him. Our covenant Lord has given us the supreme privilege of knowing him, and as we fulfill the purpose of our existence as his servant-kings, God's rule is extended throughout the life of the covenant community *and* to the entire creation. Even though God does not need us in order to achieve his purposes, incredibly he has chosen us to fulfill his sovereign rule in this world in the context of a covenant relationship of loyal love (*ḥesed*) and faithfulness (*'ĕmet*). Thus, it is *through* this covenant relationship that we are to fulfill the purpose of our existence in relationship to our covenant God. Yet, sadly, we have failed in our calling.

Second, God's kingdom also comes *through* the biblical covenants diachronically. In other words, it is *through* the biblical covenants, across time, that God chooses to reverse the disastrous effects of sin and usher in his saving reign over this world. Following the loss of Eden, redemption is linked to the election of a people—Noah and his family, the descendants of Abraham, and uniquely through the Davidic king. These people, uniquely tied to the nation of Israel, are promised a land to dwell in; they will be the means of blessing to the nations. *Through* the biblical covenants these covenant promises, which ultimately stretch back to God's initial promise in Genesis 3:15, are realized. In the exodus, which becomes a pattern of redemption, God reveals his redemptive plan. At Sinai, the people of God are constituted as a theocratic nation—a *kingdom* of priests called to serve the Lord, reveal God to the nations, and *through* Israel as a nation to usher in God's saving reign to this world. Though rebellion leads to delay, the nation is eventually given

---

[3] D. A. Carson, *The Gagging of God: Christianity Confronts Pluralism* (Grand Rapids, MI: Zondervan, 1996), 202.

possession of the land. Here the structures of government develop toward kingship under the dynasty of David in Jerusalem. Solomon builds the temple as the place where reconciliation and fellowship with God are established, a temple that stretches back to the garden-sanctuary of Eden itself. The rule of the Davidic kings is representative of the rule of God over his kingdom. But Israel *and* the kings fail; the kingdom divides and judgment falls. God's saving reign is not realized through these people and covenant mediators; it is only typified and foreshadowed. Ultimately it awaits the coming of the great antitype of Adam, Noah, Abraham, Moses, Israel, and David and his sons: Jesus Christ our Lord. It is only through this obedient Son that God's long-awaited kingdom is inaugurated in this world *through* the new covenant.

4. In the Old Testament, these promises, hopes, and expectations are proclaimed and announced by the prophets. Through the prophets, God announces hope for the nation of Israel and for this poor, lost world. The prophets who proclaim an overall pattern of renewal do so by recapitulating the past history of redemption and projecting it into the future, when the Lord comes to save his people through a new exodus, a new Jerusalem, a new Davidic king to rule in a glorious and eternal kingdom—all of which is tied to the dawning of the new covenant age. In this way, the prophets anticipate the coming of the LORD and Messiah, specifically associated with the Davidic king, who will usher in God's kingdom, making all things right and reversing the effects of sin and death. But what is crucial to note is that this coming of God's *kingdom* will occur only *through* the inauguration of the new covenant by the work of the Messiah, thus bringing to fulfillment all the previous covenants.

5. As the New Testament begins, this Old Testament background serves as the basis for its teaching on the kingdom. In the Gospels, and the entire New Testament, the *kingdom* refers primarily to *God's kingly* and *sovereign rule*, and it is especially tied to God's *saving reign* that has broken into this world in the life, death, and resurrection of Christ Jesus. It does *not* primarily refer to a certain geographical location; the phrase tells us more about *God* (the fact that he reigns) than about anything else. In Jesus, the Bible announces that the long-awaited kingdom has come and that the rule of sin and death has been destroyed. Through Jesus' obedient life and death, he has *inaugurated* God's kingdom over which he now rules and reigns—it is *already* here. And as the resurrected and ascended King, he commands all people to repent and to enter that kingdom of life.

The New Testament also stresses that even though, in Jesus, the kingdom is here, it is still *not yet* since it awaits its consummation in Christ's return. This "already–not yet" tension, which characterizes New Testament eschatology, is famously known as "inaugurated eschatology," i.e., the "last days" that the Old Testament anticipated and predicted have actually arrived in the coming of the Lord Jesus, yet they still await their full consummation.[4] Even though in principle the promised new age is here, there is still more to come.

This tension is presented in a number of ways. For example, in regard to the kingdom, the New Testament teaches that the covenant Lord who rules over all (e.g., Ps. 93:1; 97:1; 99:1; 103:19; Dan. 4:34–35) has now brought his saving reign and rule to this fallen world in Jesus Christ as evidenced, for example, by the coming of the Spirit (Matt. 12:28; Luke 11:20) and the miraculous signs and preaching (Luke 4:16–30; cf. Isa. 61:1–2; 58:6; 29:18). Truly in Jesus, God's sovereign saving rule has broken into this world (Matt. 4:17; Mark 1:14–15). However, even though the kingdom is *now* here, Jesus still teaches us to pray, "Your kingdom come" (Matt. 6:10), and he speaks to his disciples of a future day when he will come "in his kingdom" (Matt. 16:28; Luke 23:51), "which clearly refers to the future fulfillment of the kingdom promise."[5] The same is true of the coming of the Spirit. Because Jesus has come and has won victory in his cross, resurrection, and ascension, he has poured out the *promised* Spirit (Acts 2; cf. John 14–16; Eph. 1:13–14). However, the gift of the Spirit is the deposit and guarantee of our promised inheritance awaiting us in the future. Thus, the reception of the Spirit means that we have become participants in Christ and now partake of the powers of the "age to come." Yet, the New Testament insists that what the Spirit gives is only a foretaste of far greater blessings to come. As Anthony Hoekema summarizes, ". . . we may say that in the possession of the Spirit we who are in Christ have a foretaste of the blessings of the age to come, and a pledge and guarantee of the resurrection of the body. Yet we have only the firstfruits. We look forward to the final consummation of the kingdom of God, when we shall enjoy these blessings to the full."[6] In these ways and many more, the New Testament teaches that in Christ the "last days" have arrived, but they are not yet consummated in all of their fullness.

---

[4] See Schreiner, *New Testament Theology*, 41–116, for a more in-depth treatment of inaugurated eschatology.
[5] Schreiner, *New Testament Theology*, 51. The "not yet" reality of the kingdom is also seen in such texts as Matthew 5:3–12; 8:11–12; 13:24–30, 36–43; 22:1–14; 25:1–13, 31–46; 26:29, etc.
[6] Anthony A. Hoekema, *The Bible and the Future* (Grand Rapids, MI: Eerdmans, 1994), 67.

It is for this reason that the New Testament stresses that, in Christ's coming, the *fulfillment* of all of the hopes and expectations of God's promised plan of redemption has now taken place. Moreover, precisely because Jesus has fulfilled the Old Testament, there is massive change or discontinuity from what has preceded, which entails that in Christ an incredible epochal shift in redemptive-history has occurred, unlike any other time in history. This is why, even though the New Testament continues the basic storyline of the Old Testament, now that Christ has inaugurated the entire new covenant age, many of the themes that were basic to the Old Testament are now transformed. D. A. Carson notes a few examples of the kind of transformation that has taken place in light of the epochal shift Jesus inaugurated:

> "Kingdom" no longer primarily conjures up a theocratic state in which God rules by his human vassal in the Davidic dynasty. It conjures up the immediate transforming reign of God, dawning now in the ministry, death, resurrection, ascension, and session of Jesus, the promised Messiah, and consummated at his return. Eschatology is thereby transformed. The locus of the people of God is no longer national and tribal; it is international, transracial, transcultural. If the Old Testament prophets constantly look forward to the day when God will act decisively, the New Testament writers announce that God has acted decisively, and that this is "good news," gospel, of universal, eternal significance and stellar importance. Thus kingdom, Christology, eschatology, church, gospel, become dominant terms or themes. Temple, priest, sacrifice, law, and much more are transposed; national and tribal outlooks gradually fade from view.[7]

In addition to various Old Testament themes being transformed due to Christ's coming, the structure of the redemptive-historical timeline has also changed. From an Old Testament perspective there is a distinction between "this present age"—an age characterized by sin, death, and opposition to God as represented by earthly *kingdoms*—and "the age to come"—an age in which the covenant Lord will come to rescue his people through his Messiah and to usher in his *kingdom*, i.e., his saving rule and reign. But how are these two ages related to each other? They are related to one another in a chronological sequence. "This present age" ends with the coming of the Messiah, and with his arrival dawns the "age to come." Thus, from an Old Testament viewpoint, there is only *one* coming of Lord and Messiah in power and might (see fig. 11.1). And when the Lord and Messiah will finally come and

---

[7] Carson, *Gagging of God*, 254.

usher in the "last days" and the "age to come," it will be an age characterized by the eschatological hope and expectation spoken of by the prophets. For example, when the "age to come" arrives, it will bring with it the coming of God's saving rule and reign—his kingdom—evidenced by the arrival of the new covenant, the dawning of the new creation, judgment upon all of God's enemies, and salvation for the people of God associated with the Day of the Lord. All of these great realities will come at once.

Old Testament

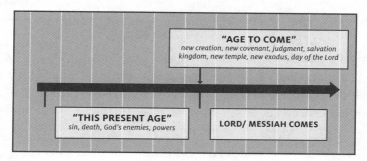

Fig. 11.1

The New Testament, however, modifies this basic timeline. It now speaks of Messiah's *two* comings, not just one, as well as an overlap of the ages. In the first coming—all that is associated with the Son's incarnation, life and ministry, death, resurrection, ascension, and Pentecost—the "age to come" is now here, just as the prophets said. But even though the future age is here in principle, it is not fully here until Christ returns in glory and power. As such, "this present age" continues until the second coming even though the "age to come" has been inaugurated in Christ. In this sense, there is an overlap of the ages.

Sometimes this overlap is illustrated by a World War II analogy between D-day and V-day. In World War II, D-day brought about an incredible victory for the allied troops. As a result of that day, the enemy was decisively defeated and it was only a matter of time before final victory would be achieved, even though the war was not yet over. D-day is then compared to the first coming of Christ, which, in principle, has ushered in the "age to come," but not yet in its fullness. Thus, in Christ's first coming, God's promise of redemption has now been realized. God's saving reign—his kingdom—has broken into this world, and along with it the new covenant and the new creation. Sin, death, and the power of the Evil One have been destroyed. It is only a matter of time before final victory is won; in principle, the victory has been won and is now guaranteed. Yet, our D-day still awaits our V-day, i.e., our final victory when Christ comes again and consummates what he began. Thus, in this overlap of the ages, this in-between-the-times, even though we as the people of God are no longer associated with "this present age" since we are no longer "in Adam" but are now "in Christ"; even though we are participants in the future age and now have eternal life, justification before God, and the Spirit who indwells us (all realities associated with the "age to come"); we still await the fullness of Christ's victory and the arrival of his kingdom in consummated glory. But what Christ has won in his first advent is now our guarantee and pledge that the future age is not a vain hope, but a certainty. In light of this, the New Testament restructures the Old Testament timeline as follows (see fig. 11.2).

New Testament

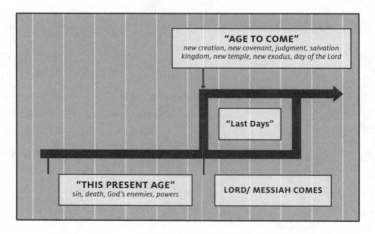

Fig. 11.2

It is within this overall teaching that the New Testament announces the arrival and inauguration of the *kingdom* in Christ Jesus. It is not an overstatement to say that the New Testament's teaching of inaugurated eschatology and its relation to consummated eschatology, whether in the Gospels, Paul, or other New Testament books, forms the entire context within which the New Testament expounds the kingdom, eternal life, the gift of the Spirit, the church, salvation, eschatology, and, most importantly, Christology. To say that Christ has *fulfilled* all of God's plans and purposes, that he has inaugurated *God's kingdom* and has ushered in the "age to come" and all that is associated with that "age," is a staggering affirmation, pregnant with Christological import. But it is also important to note that the New Testament's teaching on the *kingdom* cannot be understood apart from the biblical covenants, a point to which we now turn.

KINGDOM *THROUGH COVENANT*

From what has been stated, it should be evident how we think *kingdom* and *covenant* are related. It is primarily *through* the biblical covenants viewed across time that we learn how God's *kingdom* arrives. This is why grasping the *progression* of the covenants is at the heart of grasping how God's kingdom dawns in Jesus; how God's redemptive promise is realized; and how the entire metanarrative of the Bible hangs together, since the biblical covenants constitute the framework and backbone for the entire storyline of Scripture.

The relationship between the covenants has been and is today disputed in theology, especially between the theological camps of covenant and dispensational theology and their varieties. Minimally, however, Christians have affirmed that God has *one* plan of salvation and that history is the working out of that plan centered in Christ. In addition, most Christians also agree that the storyline of Scripture moves clearly from creation to Fall, from Abraham to David, and finally to Christ. Yet, contrary to "covenant theology," which has the tendency to speak of God's one plan of salvation in terms of *the* "covenant of grace," and contrary to "dispensational theology," which tends to partition history in terms of dispensations, it is more biblical to think in terms of a *plurality* of covenants (e.g., Gal. 4:24; Eph. 2:12; Heb. 8:7–13), which are part of the progressive revelation of the *one* plan of God, and *all* of which reach their *telos*, terminus, and fulfillment in Christ. This allows us to speak properly of the *continuity* of God's plan across time, now fulfilled in the new covenant, and it also helps us avoid flattening the relationships between the covenants and downplaying the *discontinuity* or significant progression between them. Before we summarize our understanding of how the covenants fit together, let us briefly highlight five important hermeneutical points that are crucial in "putting together" the biblical covenants.

Crucial Hermeneutical Points to Remember

1. *Progressive revelation and its significance for grasping the unfolding of the covenants.* Everyone agrees that Scripture comes to us over time. God's self-disclosure, alongside his redemptive work, unfolds in a progressive manner by unique twists and turns, largely demarcated by the biblical covenants. In this way, God's *one* eternal plan unfolds step-by-step, ultimately finding its culmination in Christ, and the covenants are the primary means by which God's plan is unveiled to us. Given this fact, it is best to view *all* of the covenants as interrelated and dependent upon one another. As God acts to redeem, the covenants disclose God's eternal plan and reveal many truths, such as: who God is, the purpose of our creation, and how we are to live in relationship with God and each other. Most importantly, in light of the tragedy of human sin, the covenants not only teach us how God chooses to redeem a fallen people for himself and set everything right, but they also reveal a tension in the covenant relationship between God and his image-bearers. We discover how God is always faithful and true to his promises while we are not, even though he demands our perfect obedience as his responsible creatures. As the covenants unfold, we discover how God's promises to restore his elect to covenant relationship with him from every tribe, nation, people, and tongue is ultimately achieved through the obedient work of God the Son incarnate, which was God's plan from all eternity (see, e.g., Eph. 1:4, 9–10).

    2. *The three horizons of biblical interpretation and their importance for the covenants.* Intimately related to a diachronic reading of the biblical covenants are the three horizons of interpretation, as discussed in chapter 1. In chapters 2–10, each covenant was placed within three expanding contexts. First, the covenant in question was interpreted within its own immediate redemptive-historical context (i.e., textual horizon). Second, to understand properly how that covenant fit in God's unfolding plan, it was placed in relation to what preceded it (i.e., epochal horizon), and *intertextual* connections were developed so that we could understand better the interrelations between earlier and later revelation. Third, the covenant was then placed in relation to later covenants and, ultimately, in relation to the coming of Jesus and the inauguration of the new covenant. By tracing out the bibli-

cal covenants in this fashion we are able to see how the entire plan of God is *organically* related and how it reaches its culmination and fulfillment in Christ. Also, it is only when we do this that we rightly see how the *parts* of God's plan ultimately fit with the *whole*, and that the theological conclusions we then draw are truly *biblical* and thus warranted.

3. *The typological patterns of Scripture are developed through the covenants.* In chapter 1 we noted the importance of the "promise-fulfillment" theme and the typological patterns of Scripture for understanding Scripture. We also noted how central the biblical covenants are to both of these areas. By grasping the unfolding nature of the covenants, we better understand how all of God's promises are yes and amen in Christ (2 Cor. 1:20), and how *all* of the typological patterns, first and foremost, find their fulfillment in Christ. Thus, starting in creation and then developed *through* the covenants, we discover how specific God-intended patterns, centered in specific persons, events, and institutions, reach their *telos* in Christ and the new covenant age.

For example, Adam, as the covenant head of the old creation, anticipates and looks forward to the coming of the "last Adam," our Lord Jesus, who is the head of the new covenant. In the meantime, as the biblical covenants are introduced and then progressively develop, "little Adams" show up on the stage of human history that take on the role of the first Adam (e.g., Noah, Abraham, Israel, David). Yet none of these "little Adams" are the ultimate fulfillment, although they point beyond themselves in prophetic expectation of the "last Adam" to come. In this way, through the diachronic and inter-textual unfolding of the covenants, these typological patterns take on greater definition and clarity until that to which they point finally arrives. What is true of Adam is also true of other typological patterns, whether they be various persons (e.g., Moses, Israel, David, prophets, priests, and kings), events (e.g., the exodus), or institutions (e.g., sacrificial system, tabernacle/temple). It is by this means that Scripture moves from lesser to greater, and grounds the newness of the new covenant fulfilled in Christ.

4. *The new covenant is the* telos, *terminus, and fulfillment of the biblical covenants.* Since *all* of the biblical covenants are part of the one plan of God, no covenant is unrelated to what preceded it, and no covenant can be understood apart from its fulfillment in Christ, it is right to say that *all* of the biblical covenants reach their *telos* in Christ and the new covenant. Obviously, we are not minimizing the truth that what Jesus has inaugurated must still be consummated, or that we still live in an overlap of the ages

and it is not until Christ returns that this "present age" will end (and thus the creation realities of the Noahic covenant continue). Instead, what we are arguing is that, now that Christ has come, all of the previous covenants find their *telos* in him. What the previous covenants revealed, anticipated, and predicted through various patterns, types, and instruction, is now here, albeit in inaugurated form. That is why our Lord is presented as the new covenant head, who in his person and work is greater than Adam by undoing what Adam did and thus winning for us the new creation; the true seed and offspring of Abraham, who brings blessings to the nations by his cross work; the true Israel, fulfilling all that she failed to be; and David's greater son, who rules the nations and the entire creation as King of kings and Lord of lords.

However, the fact that Christ has *fulfilled* the previous covenants does not entail that the earlier covenants have no value for us today or that we can jettison the Old Testament from our Bibles. After all, the previous covenants serve their role in God's redemptive plan and revelation of himself; they are forever part of Scripture, which is for our instruction, growth, and ministry (2 Tim. 3:16–17). Yet, now that Christ has come, Christians are no longer under these previous covenants *as covenants*. A crucial implication of this point is that we, as new covenant believers, must view and apply the previous biblical covenants to ourselves in light of Christ, to whom each of the previous covenants pointed and who fulfills every aspect of them completely. This observation is crucial in discerning how the previous covenants "carry over" to Christians in regard to our lives.

5. *Categorizing the biblical covenants as either unconditional or conditional is inadequate.* A common way to distinguish the biblical covenants is to employ the unconditional-unilateral (royal grant) versus conditional-bilateral (suzerain-vassal) distinction.[8] It is on this basis that the Abrahamic, Davidic, and new covenants are often characterized as royal grant covenants (unconditional), while the covenants with creation and Israel are described as suzerain-vassal covenants (conditional). From here a variety of theological conclusions are drawn, such as the larger law-gospel contrast so that the covenant with creation and Israel's covenant are viewed as "law," while the Abrahamic, Davidic, and new covenants are viewed as "gospel." As

---

[8] See, e.g., Craig A. Blaising and Darrell L. Bock, *Progressive Dispensationalism* (Wheaton, IL: BridgePoint, 1993), 128–211; Paul R. Williamson, *Sealed with an Oath: Covenant in God's Unfolding Plan*, New Studies in Biblical Theology 23 (Downers Grove, IL: InterVarsity Press, 2007), 17–43; Michael S. Horton, *God of Promise: Introducing Covenant Theology* (Grand Rapids, MI: Baker, 2006), 23–110.

discussed in the previous chapters, however, we dissent from this common way of distinguishing the biblical covenants. As the exposition has demonstrated, this way of viewing the covenants is reductionistic. Instead, the covenants consist of unconditional (unilateral) and conditional (bilateral) elements blended together. In fact, it is precisely due to this blend that there is a deliberate *tension* within the covenants—a tension that is heightened as the storyline of Scripture and the biblical covenants progress toward their fulfillment in Christ.

On the one hand, the covenants gloriously unveil the sovereign promise making and covenant keeping God who never fails. As Creator and Lord, he chooses to enter into relationships with his creatures, and in those relationships he always shows himself to be the faithful partner—true to himself, his own character, and his promises—and as such, he calls us to trust him completely. The author of Hebrews captures this point well. As he reflects on the certainty of God's covenant promises in Christ, he writes, "So when God desired to show more convincingly to the heirs of the promise the unchangeable character of his purpose, he guaranteed it with an oath, so that by two unchangeable things, in which it is impossible for God to lie, we who have fled for refuge might have strong encouragement to hold fast to the hope set before us" (Heb. 6:17–18, ESV). The covenants, then, reveal first and foremost our gracious triune God who is the promise maker and keeper and who unilaterally guarantees that his promises will never fail. Whether it is with Adam or with other covenant heads, God's commitment to his image-bearers and creation, tied to his promise in Genesis 3:15, will never fail. That same promise runs across the entire Canon, and it is *through* the biblical covenants that it takes on greater clarity and expansion until it reaches its crescendo in the person and work of Christ.

On the other hand, *all* the biblical covenants also demand an obedient partner. God as our Creator and Lord demands from his image-bearers, who were made to know him, complete devotion and obedience. In this sense, there is a conditional or bilateral element to the covenants. This is certainly evident with Adam as he is given commands and responsibilities to fulfill, with the expectation that he will do so perfectly. Furthermore, in the Noahic covenant, obedience is also demanded, which is also true of Abraham, the nation of Israel, David and his sons, and in the greatest way imaginable in the coming of the Son, who obeys perfectly and completely in his entire life and supremely in his death on a cross (Phil. 2:6–11).

Yet, as the biblical covenants progress through redemptive-history, this *tension* grows, since it becomes evident that it is only the Lord himself who remains the faithful covenant partner. From his initial promise in Genesis 3:15 to reverse the effects of sin and death; from his increasingly greater promises made through the covenants; from the beautiful picture of covenant initiation in Genesis 15, which demonstrates that he takes the covenant obligations solely upon himself; from the provision of a sacrificial system to atone for sin (Lev. 17:11); from repeatedly keeping his promises to a rebellious and hard-hearted people, God shows himself, time and time again, to be the faithful covenant partner. By contrast, all the human covenant mediators—Adam, Noah, Abraham, Israel, David and his sons—show themselves to be unfaithful, disobedient covenant breakers—some to a greater extent than others. As a result, there is no faithful, obedient son who fully obeys the demands of the covenant. Obedience *must* be rendered, but there is no obedient image-bearer/son to do so. How, then, can God remain the holy and just God that he is and continue to be present with us in covenant relationship? How can he remain in relationship with us unless our disobedience is removed and our sin is paid for in full? It is *through* the covenants that this *tension* increases, and it is *through* the covenants that only one answer is given: it is only if God himself, as the covenant maker and keeper, unilaterally acts to keep his own promise through the provision of a faithful covenant partner that a new and better covenant can be established. It is only in the giving of his Son, and through the Son's obedient life and death for us, that our redemption is secured, our sin is paid for, and the inauguration of an unshakable new covenant is established.

It is only by maintaining the dual emphasis of unconditional/conditional in the biblical covenants, leading us to their fulfillment in the unbreakable new covenant grounded in God's obedient Son, that we appreciate Scripture's incredible Christological focus. The storyline of Scripture as told by the covenants leads us to him. He is the one, as our great prophet, priest, and king, who accomplishes our salvation. It is in Christ alone, God the Son incarnate, that the covenants find their fulfillment and this built-in *tension* finds its resolution.

With these five summary hermeneutical points in place, let us now sketch out a biblical-theological summary of how we understand the relationship between the covenants and their fulfillment in Christ and the inauguration of the new covenant age.

A Summary of the Biblical Covenants

ADAM AND THE COVENANT WITH CREATION

Covenant theology has primarily spoken of the covenant in Genesis 1–2 as the "covenant of works," and dispensational theology rarely speaks of a covenant with creation. For covenant theology, the "covenant of works" was made with Adam as the head and representative of the entire human race. To him and his entire posterity, eternal life was promised upon the condition of perfect obedience to God's law. However, due to his disobedience, Adam, along with all humanity, was plunged into a state of sin, death, and condemnation. But God, by his own sovereign grace and initiative, did not leave the human race in this condition but instead gave a saving promise, wherein God graciously offered to sinners life and salvation through the last Adam, the covenantal head of his people, the Lord Jesus Christ.

Even though this formulation is standard for covenant theology, numerous people have questioned the validity of a "covenant of works" or of any covenant in Genesis 1–2 due to the absence of the word "covenant" (*běrît*) in the text, and also out of discomfort with the idea of Adam *working* to gain favor or merit with God. One must demonstrate caution regarding the notion of *works* in this context, as if Adam is attempting to earn his salvation given that he already stands in right relationship with God, yet there is ample reason to contend for a "covenant of creation," with Adam serving as the covenant mediator, for at least three reasons. First, the absence of the word "covenant" in Genesis 1–2 does *not* entail that there is no covenant. Exegetically, as argued in chapters 2–3 of this book, the distinction between the words "cut" and "establish" regarding the covenant is important. In Genesis 6:17–18 and 9:8–17, the covenant with Noah is "established" and not "cut." The word "cut" refers to the initiation or origination of a covenant, while "established" assumes that a covenant relationship is already in place, or it refers to a covenant partner verbally affirming a commitment or upholding a promise in a covenant previously initiated, so that the other partner experiences in history the fulfilling of this promise (cf. Gen. 17:7, 18, 21; Ex. 6:4; Lev. 26:9; Deut. 8:18; 2 Kings. 23:3; Jer. 34:18). It is legitimate, then, to conclude that the phrase "establish my covenant" in Genesis 6:18 (and in Gen. 9:9, 11, 17) refers to the maintenance of a preexisting *covenant* relationship which can only be found in Adam and rooted in creation. Later Scripture confirms this point (e.g., Hos. 6:7).

Second, contextually, not only are covenantal elements present in Genesis, such as the Lord/vassal relationship and the obedience-disobedience motif (Gen. 2:16–17), but also God identifies himself by his covenant name: Yahweh (Gen. 2:4, 5, 7, 8, et al.). Also, Adam is created as God's image-bearer and functions as a son (Luke 3:38)—relationships that are nothing less than covenantal. Third, canonically and theologically, the entire storyline of Scripture is centered on two foundational individuals: Adam and Christ (Rom. 5:12–21; 1 Cor. 15:20–21). In fact, Scripture clearly teaches that all humans fall under the representative headship of either Adam or Christ. Adam represents all that is tied to the "old creation" and "this present age," characterized by sin, death, and judgment. Christ represents all that is associated with the "new creation" and the "new covenant," which from the perspective of the Old Testament prophets is identified with the "age to come," characterized by salvation, life, and restoration of what was lost in the Fall. Given this fact, it seems difficult to think of Christ as the head of the new covenant without Adam being the head of some kind of covenant in the original situation. As God's image-bearer (and son), Adam is given the mandate to rule over God's creation, to put all things under his feet (cf. Psalm 8) and to establish the pattern of God's kingdom in this world. But, sadly, Adam disobeys, and unless God acts in grace and power, all people stand under divine judgment and wrath. Thankfully, however, God does not leave us to ourselves but instead chooses to save us by promising a Redeemer, i.e., the seed of the woman (Gen. 3:15), which drives the entire storyline of the Bible.

The significance of starting with the "covenant with creation" for grasping the Bible's storyline and *how* the covenants relate to each other cannot be overstated, for at least two reasons. First, *all* of the biblical covenants unpack Adam's representative role in the world. Whether we think of Noah, Abraham, Israel, or David, *all* of these later covenant mediators function as a subset of Adam, ultimately leading us to Christ, the last Adam. In Christ and the new covenant, all the previous covenants find their *telos* and terminus, which underscores why the new covenant age is greater than what preceded it. Even though the amount of space devoted to Adam is not large in Scripture, his role as the representative head of creation defines what comes after him. We have sought to capture this emphasis in fig. 11.3, where the first covenant's scope is as universal as creation, even though in subsequent covenants it is narrowed. Yet, as the storyline of Scripture progresses, the narrowing focus of later covenants is restored in Christ, who comes as the new covenant head and who through his obedience brings about the inauguration of a new creation (see fig. 11.4).[9]

---

[9] Figures 11.3 and 11.4 were designed by Jason T. Parry; used by permission.

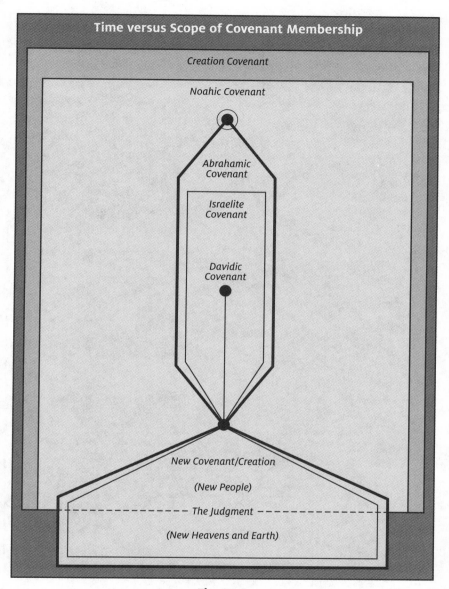

Fig. 11.3

Notes: The line corresponding to the Abrahamic covenant is bold to show that both the Israelite and new covenants are the means of fulfilling the Abrahamic covenant. The Davidic covenant is a single line because, formally, the Davidic covenant is between God and David. The Abrahamic covenant promises blessing to the nations, the Israelite covenant locates Israel in the land bridge between Mesopotamia and Egypt, and the Davidic covenant is a charter for humanity, so they all have worldwide implications in principle, but the diagram is specifically about the scope of covenant membership. The New Creation eventually replaces the Old Creation completely. In the Old Testament God makes the people first (Israel) and then the land (Palestine), and in the New Testament God makes the people first (Christians) and then the land (new heavens and earth).

Time versus Covenant Partners/Roles

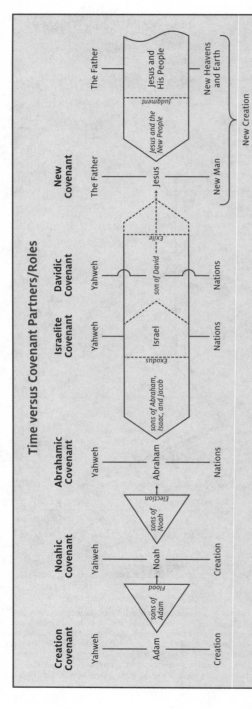

The middle section (horizontally) identifies the servant king(s)/"son(s) of God" who is/are set up over creation/nations by the corresponding covenant. The New Creation section is provisional and attempts to account for:

- 1 Cor. 15:23–24: "But each in his own order: Christ the first fruits, after that those who are Christ's at His coming, [24] then comes the end, when He hands over the kingdom to the God and Father, when He has abolished all rule and all authority and power" (NASB). The final scene is difficult to portray, since on the one hand, Christ "hands over the kingdom" to the Father, but on the other hand, God and the Lamb share a throne in the New Heavens and Earth (Rev. 22:1, 3), just as they do after Jesus' resurrection (Acts 2:33). We take "handing over the kingdom" to the Father therefore to mean that Jesus has fulfilled both his first-advent role of creating a New People and his second-advent role of purging the nations of the non-elect, so that the "hands over" a regenerate kingdom to the Father, having completed his assigned roles as priest and judge. Then the Father and the Lamb co-rule this New Heavens and Earth; Christ's "handing over the kingdom" to the Father apparently does not mean laying aside his role as a king over the New Creation.

- Rev. 20:4: Christ and those "made alive" in Christ reign during the millennium (= inter-advent period).
- Rev. 21:1: The New Heaven and Earth.
- Rev. 21:3: "And I heard a loud voice from the throne, saying, "Behold, the tabernacle of God is among men, and He will dwell among them, and they shall be His people, and God Himself will be among them" (NASB).
- Rev. 21:7: "He who overcomes will inherit these things, and I will be his God and he will be My son" (NASB).
- Rev. 22:5: The servants of God will reign forever in the New Heaven and Earth.

Fig. 11.4

Second, given the foundational role of the creation covenant for all subsequent covenants, it should not surprise us that foundational typological patterns are established in creation that eventually reach their terminus and *telos* in Christ and the new covenant (e.g., the *rest* of the seventh day in Sabbath [Gen. 2:1–3; Ex. 20:8–11], which leads to ultimate salvation rest in Christ [Heb. 3:7–4:13]; Eden as a temple sanctuary tied to creation, which finds its end in Christ as the new temple and the new creation; and marriage, which points to a greater reality, viz., Christ's relationship to his people [Gen. 2:24–25; Eph. 5:32]). In these ways, and many more, the creation covenant establishes patterns that eventually terminate in Christ and the new covenant age.

One last important point: we cannot think of the "covenant with creation" without mentioning the twofold emphasis on the entrance of sin into the world and God's initial promise of redemption—a promise that takes on greater clarity, definition, and expansion in subsequent covenants. First, Genesis 3 is crucial in describing how, in history, sin and evil came into the human race—and thus the desperate nature of human depravity, which God alone can remedy. Scripture, from beginning to end, takes the reality of sin and evil seriously. In moving from Genesis 1–2, we see how quickly humans move from a "very good" world (Gen. 1:31) to an abnormal and cursed one (Gen. 3:14–24), one now under God's judgment and under the sentence of death. Adam, after having received every blessing imaginable from God as well as the direct command not to eat of the tree of the knowledge of good and evil, and with the warning still ringing in his ears—"for in the day that you eat of it you shall surely die" (Gen. 2:17)—acts in willful, autonomous rebellion against God and thus, tragically, turns the created order upside down. In the words of Paul, humans chose to worship and serve "the creature rather than the Creator, who is blessed forever!" (Rom. 1:25). The punishment, sadly, fits the crime: death. The human race is now under a death sentence, described in a variety of ways in Scripture—bondage to sin, dead in our trespasses, under the power of sin, death, the Evil One, and so on (Jer. 17:9; Rom. 6:23; Eph. 2:1–3). But worse than all of these terrible results is that humans, who were made to know, love, and serve God, are now enemies of God, living under his judgment and wrath, and no longer in a living relationship with him— spiritually dead unto God (Rom. 8:7; Eph. 2:1–3; 4:17–19). This in the end is death—physically and spiritually—for to live in relationship and fellowship with God is life, but to live apart from him is death.

As the text unfolds, the punishment of our sin is swift, leading to God's expulsion of Adam and Eve from the garden, and his blocking entrance to the tree of life, signifying that we are no longer in life-giving fellowship with the Lord, living in his presence in terms of blessing, privilege, and relationship. In order to forbid access to the tree of life, God places the cherubim at the entrance to the garden (cf. Ezek. 1:5ff.; 10:15; Rev. 4:6ff.) and adds "a flaming sword that turned every way to guard the way to the tree of life" (Gen. 3:24). The flaming sword represents the justice and holiness of God at work in his judgments (cf. Jer. 47:6; Ezekiel 21). By this description, Scripture makes it clear that as we move across redemptive-history, the only way back to the presence of God is through God's way and God's provision, which eventually is seen through the biblical covenants and through the provision of the tabernacle, temple, and ultimately the coming of the one who is the replacement of the temple, our Lord Jesus Christ (see John 2:19–21; cf. Revelation 21–22).

In addition, there is no doubt that Adam's sin is passed on to subsequent generations, as evidenced in Cain's murderous action (Genesis 4); the common refrain in the genealogical list in Genesis 5, "and he died . . ." (5:5, 8, 11, 14, 17, 20, 27, 31); the flood (Genesis 6–9), and so on. Paul's statement in Romans 3:23—"for all have sinned and fall short of the glory of God"—is not only given by divine revelation; it is also true to the Bible's entire story. From Genesis 3 on, Scripture underscores the fact that *all* of us are under the condemnation of sin, and that the only hope for our desperate condition is found in God's provision alone. The only hope for Adam's helpless race is found in another Adam, the last Adam, who, unlike the first man (and the entire human race), does not fail, and who wins our redemption. However, before we come to Christ, the covenants progressively reveal and anticipate, in instruction and type, the coming of our Lord.

Second, Genesis 3 is also crucial in establishing God's initial promise of redemption—a promise that drives the entire storyline of Scripture, including the biblical covenants, leading us to Christ. Genesis 3 is situated in the Canon not only to establish the nature of the human problem but also to prepare for God's gracious redemption. The effects of sin are comprehensive and disastrous, but thankfully the narrative unfolds God's word of promise (Gen. 3:15). Scripture is clear: our greatest problem as humans is our sin before God. Given who God is and who we are as fallen creatures, there is a *tension* in covenantal relations between God and humans. Covenants allow for intimacy with God. God, as our covenant Lord, is present with his people, and his people enjoy rest and relationship with him as we carry out our responsibilities before him. However, given our sin, how can the holy, just, and righteous God dwell with us; or better, how can we dwell in his presence? How can God declare us right before him? Since God is holy and personal, he requires the punishment of our sin; we cannot dwell in his presence apart from our sin being vanquished. Sin cannot approach God, and God cannot tolerate it, but how can God forgive our sins without denying himself? Or, in the words of Paul, "How can God be *just and justifier* of the ungodly?" (Rom. 3:25–26).

Scripture's answer is that *God himself* must save us—he must take the initiative to act in perfect justice *and* manifest his amazing grace. And he must do so by providing a "seed"[10] of the woman, yet a greater Adam and Son, who as God the Son incarnate will perfectly obey even unto death and thus pay for our sin, reverse the alienating effects of sin in all of its death and dimensions, and usher in a better covenant (see, e.g., Phil. 2:5–11; Heb. 2:5–18). Truly, Genesis 3:15 is the *protoeuangelion*—the first gospel proclamation—which the Bible's entire storyline unfolds through the covenants, reaching their *telos* in Christ (see Rom. 16:25–27; Gal. 3:16).

THE NOAHIC COVENANT

The word "covenant" first appears in Scripture in relation to Noah (Gen. 6:18; cf. 9:9–11), but it should be viewed as a continuation of the prior creation covenant. The Noahic covenant is the reinstatement and upholding of God's commitment to creation, now in light of human sin. Given human rebellion, it would seem that humans and creation are threatened, but given God's promise in Genesis 3:15 and the description of the Noahic covenant—lasting as long as "the earth remains" (8:22)—this covenant reinforces God's intention that humans will continue to fulfill their role as image-bearers in creation. The "seed of the woman" will now come through Noah the covenant mediator and his family, and it is this seed who will reverse the effects of sin and usher in a "new creation." In this way, Noah functions as "another Adam" (Gen. 9:1–7; cf. 1:26–30)—as the new head of the human race—and is called to be an obedient son.

Yet Noah also demonstrates by his disobedience (Gen. 9:18–28) that

---

[10] "Seed" (*zeraʾ*) is a key word in Genesis. It occurs 59 times compared to 170 times in the rest of the Old Testament (see T. D. Alexander, "Seed," in *NDBT*, 769–773).

the problem of the human heart remains (see Gen. 6:5–7 with 8:21–22). Ultimately what is needed, which the biblical covenants will develop, is a greater heart transformation tied to the forgiveness of sin—literally brought about by God's Spirit—so that humans will fulfill the purpose of their creation. In addition, in its universal scope, the Noahic covenant also reminds us that God's purposes ultimately encompass not just one people or nation but the entire creation.

THE ABRAHAMIC COVENANT

Given its location in Scripture, the Abrahamic covenant stands in contrast to the judgments of God on human sin and presents anew the plan of creation. This can be seen in the way that important elements in the creation of humans are repeated in the blessing to Abraham: God's promise of a great name and seed, the multiplication of human beings, the provision of the land, a peaceful relationship between God and humanity, the restoration of the nations (Gen. 12:1–3; cf. 15:4–5; 17:1–8; 18:18–19; 22:16–18). However, unlike the situation with Noah, God does not destroy the human race. Instead, God allows the nations to exist and then calls Abraham out of the nations to become a great nation (*gôy*), i.e., a world community, a political entity, a *kingdom* in the proper sense of the word.

Here we discover the grounding to Scripture's contrast between two kingdoms, especially since the Fall. On the one hand, we have the kingdom associated with Babel and all that stands in opposition to God (Genesis 11). On the other hand, we have another kingdom, associated with God's saving initiative, which will fulfill the role of Adam and bring salvation to the nations. Throughout Scripture these two kingdoms are contrasted, but it is only through Abraham and his seed that God's salvation will come. In this light, it is best to view the Abrahamic covenant as the means by which God will fulfill his promises for humanity, especially in light of Genesis 3:15 (cf. Gal. 3:16). In this way, Abraham and his family constitute "another Adam," a calling into existence of something new parallel to creation of old, but in this case a "new creation" (Rom. 4:17). The Abrahamic covenant functions as a subset of the "covenant with creation," yet narrowed now through one family/nation, that ultimately has a universal *telos* (see fig. 11.3, which emphasizes the narrowing of the Abrahamic covenant and its ultimate universal end). In Abraham and his seed, specifically through Isaac (and then through the nation of Israel, epitomized by the Davidic king), all of God's promises for the human race will be realized—promises that God unilaterally takes upon himself to accomplish, as beautifully portrayed in the covenant inauguration ceremony in Genesis 15.

Two other elements of the Abrahamic covenant are important to stress. First, the covenant is multifaceted. It not only encompasses spiritual elements that link us ultimately to the new covenant; it also consists of national/ physical and typological elements that must be carefully unpacked as the biblical covenants unfold. Second, it also consists of unilateral and bilateral elements and it is not reducible to either one. God's action in Genesis 15 speaks of his unilateral action to fulfill his covenant promises, yet God also demands covenant obedience from Abraham in order for the covenant to continue (Gen. 17:1; 18:19; 22:16–18) even though Abraham is not always obedient. This growing tension between God unilaterally keeping his covenant promises *and* also demanding an obedient covenant keeper is only met, finally and fully, in the true seed of Abraham, our Lord Jesus Christ (Gal. 3:16).

THE OLD COVENANT [11]

In the Old Testament, the amount of space devoted to the "old covenant" is vast, yet Scripture teaches that it functions as a means to a larger end that culminates in a better covenant. This is why Scripture views the "old covenant" as *temporary* in God's plan; or better, it is a crucial part in God's redemptive purposes, yet when that to which it points arrives, the covenant with Israel *as a whole covenant package* comes to its end and Christians are no longer under it *as a covenant* (Gal. 3:15–4:7). What, then, is the purpose of the law-covenant? The answer is diverse, and truly to answer this question we must think through how the old covenant is *organically* related to what preceded it, how it advances the promise of Genesis 3:15, and how it points forward to and anticipates, in diverse ways, the coming of Christ and the inauguration of the new covenant. When this is done we find that, at its core, the old covenant's purpose was to reveal and intensify sin, and to prepare us for the coming of Christ (Rom. 5:20–21; 7:13; Gal. 4:4). Additionally, three points are important in summarizing the nature of the old covenant and its place in God's redemptive plan.

---

[11] The covenant with Israel is called a number of things. Sometimes it is referred to as the Mosaic covenant, since Moses, in many ways, served as its mediator. Moses functioned in the role of prophet, priest, and king before those offices were separated in the life of Israel. It is also called the Sinai covenant, given its location. Predominantly in Scripture, it is identified as the "old covenant" set over against the "new covenant."

First, placing the old covenant in its textual and epochal horizon, it is evident that God's establishing his covenant with Israel cannot be understood apart from his promises to Abraham. Due to God's patriarchal promises, he calls Moses to deliver his people from Egypt (Ex. 3:6; cf. 2:24–25; Deut. 4:36–38). God did not set his love on Israel because they were better or more numerous than the nations (Deut. 7:7). The basis for God's calling of Israel was not to be found in them, but instead in God's sovereign choice and his covenant loyalty to Abraham (Ex. 19:4; Deut. 7:8). Moreover, in placing the old covenant in relation to the previous covenants, we now see with greater clarity how the "seed" of Abraham is narrowed to the nation of Israel (see fig. 11.3, which presents the old covenant's scope as broad as the Abrahamic covenant, since it is now through the nation of Israel that God will bring blessings to the nations).

In this way Israel, as a nation (*gôy*) (Ex. 19:5–6), serves as "another Adam" and fulfills that role to the nations. Given its placement in Scripture, this means that it is through Israel that God will fulfill his Genesis 3:15 promise, namely to bring about a resolution of the sin and death first caused by Adam. Further evidence for this assertion is seen in how Israel as a nation is described as God's "son" (Ex. 4:22–23). This "Father-son" relationship not only hearkens back to Adam; it is also picked up later in the Davidic covenant, where the Davidic kings are viewed in this same relationship with Yahweh, thus linking all of the covenants together in one overall plan. Israel, then, as a nation, was called to serve as God's son/representative, to live before the nations and demonstrate what it looked like to be God's image-bearers, and ultimately through them to usher in God's kingdom and new creation.

Second, the old covenant is best viewed as an entire package. Scripture does not partition the law-covenant into moral, civil, and ceremonial laws; instead it is an entire unit, which governed the life of Israel and which now, in Christ, has been brought to fulfillment. Also, as an entire package, the old covenant develops in greater detail many typological patterns that ultimately find their antitypical fulfillment in Christ and the new covenant. For example, it is in the law-covenant that we see the establishment of the priesthood, which, in truth, is foundational to the entire covenantal relationship (see Heb. 7:11). Related to the institution of the priesthood is the entire tabernacle-temple-sacrificial system. All of these institutions not only serve as a means by which Israel may dwell in the land and know God's covenantal presence among a sinful people; they also point beyond themselves to God's greater provision of atonement in the servant of the Lord (see Isaiah 52–53), who will fulfill and eclipse the role of the Levitical priest (Heb. 5:1–10; chs. 7–10), bring the tabernacle-temple to its terminus in himself (see, e.g., John 2:19–22), and by his new covenant work achieve full atonement for sin (see Jer. 31:34; Heb. 10:1–18). What is said about priest is also true of prophet and king, two other offices that take on typological significance and that reach their fulfillment in Christ (e.g., Prophet: Deut. 18:15–18; 34:10–12; Acts 3:22–26; Heb. 1:1–3; King: Gen. 17:6, 16; 49:8–12; Num. 24:17–19; cf. 24:7; Deut. 17:14–20; 2 Sam. 7:8–16; Matt. 1:1–17; Rom. 1:3–4; Heb. 1:5, 13; 5:4–6). Or, think of the foundational event which first establishes Israel in covenant relationship with God, namely, the Passover and the exodus. As we work through redemptive-history, the Passover and the exodus become a pattern of a greater, new exodus/redemption to come, all of which is associated with the new covenant era (see Ex. 15:14–17; cf. Isa. 11:15–16; 40:3–5; 41:17–20; 42:14–16; 43:1–3, 14–21; 48:20–21; 49:8–12; 51:9–11; 52:3–6, 11–12; 55:12–13; Jer. 16:14–15; 23:4–8; 31:32; Hos. 2:14–15; 11:1; 12:9, 13; 13:4–5).

Third, even though the old covenant is predominantly bilateral in orientation and rightly demands obedience of the people, it cannot be reduced to this category. As with the previous covenants, one cannot understand the old covenant without also grounding it in God's ultimate promise to redeem—something that God must initiate and accomplish unilaterally. In fact, it is God's unilateral action to redeem that grounds our hope and confidence. Israel was called to be an obedient son, as was Adam and the entire human race, yet they failed. Through them, the lost dominion of humanity was to be reclaimed, but they show themselves to be unfaithful sons. The law-covenant holds out the promise of life (Lev. 18:5), yet due to sin, Israel broke the law and came under its curse. The law is "holy, righteous, and good" (Rom. 7:12), yet it cannot save; nor, because of sin, did God intend for it ultimately to save (Deut. 27:26; cf. Gal. 3:10–12), even though as a whole, especially in its typological patterns, it allows for forgiveness. In this way, the law-covenant is prophetic (Matt. 11:13); in diverse ways it points forward to God's provision of redemption, but God's righteousness comes apart from it (Rom. 3:21)—from God's own provision of an obedient Son, our Lord Jesus Christ (Rom. 3:21–31; cf. Heb. 2:5–18; chs. 7–10).

THE DAVIDIC COVENANT

The Davidic covenant is the epitome of the Old Testament covenants, a point often overlooked. It has two main parts: (1) God's promises concerning the establishment of David's house forever (2 Sam. 7:12–16), and (2) the promises concerning the "Father-son" relationship between God and the Davidic king (2 Sam. 7:14; cf. Psalm 2; 89:26–27). Given its covenantal placement in Scripture, the significance of this "sonship" is twofold. First, it inextricably ties the Davidic covenant to the previous covenants, and second, it anticipates in type the greater sonship of Christ. In terms of the former, the sonship applied to Israel as a nation (Ex. 4:22–23; cf. Hos. 11:1) is now applied to David and his sons so that the Davidic king, as an individual, now takes on the representative role of Israel. He becomes the administrator/mediator of the covenant, thus representing God's rule to the people and representing the people as a whole (2 Sam. 7:22–24). Ideally, this also entails that the Davidic king fulfills the role of Adam; it is through him that God's rule is supposed to be effected in the world (2 Sam. 7:19b).

This is not surprising if we link the covenants together. At the heart of God's redemptive plan is the restoration of humanity's vice-regent role in creation through the seed of the woman; thus, by the time we get to David, we know who will restore the lost fortunes of creation. In the Old Testament, this truth is borne out in many places, especially in the Psalter, which envisions the Davidic son as ushering in this kind of universal rule (e.g., Psalms 2, 8, 45, 72; cf. Isa. 9:6–7; chs. 11; 53). It is the Davidic king, then, who is called to be God's devoted servant/son, even functioning sometimes in priestly terms, instructing the nations in the ways of the Lord and inviting them to come under Yahweh's rule (see fig. 11.3, which captures this point by first picturing the Davidic covenant as a subset of the old covenant, and second by showing that Israel's sonship role is now narrowed in the king as the corporate head of the people).

Yet, in Old Testament history, there is a major problem in this regard. As with the previous covenant mediators, the Davidic kings are not obedient. The Davidic house does not effect God's saving reign, which leads the prophets to anticipate the need for God to provide a greater King (e.g., Isa. 7:14; 9:6–7; 11:1–10; 42:1–9; 49:1–7; 52:13–53:12; 55:3; 61:1–3; Ezek. 34:1–31). In this way, the biblical covenants tell a story: not only do they teach us who God is and what he expects of us; they also demonstrate that God must act in sovereign grace to provide an obedient Son, who will fulfill the roles of the previous covenant mediators by bringing God's rule and reign to this world by inaugurating a new and better covenant.

THE NEW COVENANT

As one biblical covenant leads to the next, all of them find their *telos* (terminus) and fulfillment in Christ, the mediator of the new covenant (see Jer. 31:29–34; cf. Luke 22:20; 2 Corinthians 3; Hebrews 8; 10). When the new covenant arrives, we are no longer under the previous covenants in exactly the same way that the people of God were in the past. Probably the most famous Old Testament text regarding the new covenant is Jeremiah 31, but it is not limited to this text, as previous chapters have demonstrated. Within the Old Testament, the new covenant is viewed as both national (Jer. 31:36–40; 33:6–16; Ezek. 36:24–38; 37:11–28) and international (Jer. 33:9; Ezek. 36:36; 37:28). In fact, its scope is viewed as universal, especially in Isaiah (42:6; 49:6; 55:3–5; 56:4–8; 66:18–24). These Isaiah texts project the ultimate fulfillment of the divine promises in the new covenant onto an "ideal Israel," i.e., a community directly tied to the servant of the Lord, located in a rejuvenated new creation (Isa. 65:17; 66:22). This "ideal Israel" picks up the promises to Abraham and is presented as the climactic and ultimate fulfillment of the covenants that God established with the patriarchs, the nation of Israel, and David's son (Isa. 9:6–7; 11:1–10; Jer. 23:5–6; 33:14–26; Ezek. 34:23–24; 37:24–28).

Furthermore, in the storyline of Scripture it is not enough to say that the new covenant merely brings about the Abrahamic blessing to Israel and the nations. One cannot understand the Abrahamic covenant apart from the "covenant with creation" so, in truth, when the new covenant arrives, we have the ultimate fulfillment of all of God's promises, the reversal of the effects of sin and death brought about by Adam, and the establishment of the new creation. Ultimately, *all* prophetic hope is tied to the dawning of the new covenant age associated with the coming of Yahweh and the Davidic king, the establishment of a new creation, the pouring out of the Spirit (Ezek. 36:24–38; 37:11–28; Joel 2:28–32), and the full forgiveness of sin (Jer. 31:34). In the new covenant, *all* of God's promises are fulfilled, as fig. 11.3 pictures.

In the New Testament, it is clear that the new covenant texts are applied to Christ and the church, which includes within it both Jews and Gentiles (cf. Luke 22:20; 2 Corinthians 3; Hebrews 8; 10). Even though the new covenant is made with the "house of Israel and Judah" (Jer. 31:31), Scripture applies it to the church *through* the work of Jesus Christ, David's greater Son, the true Israel and the last Adam. Minimally, whatever complex relations exist between Israel and the church, Israel is related to the church in a typological relation *through Christ*. Probably the most distinguishing difference between the two communities is that Israel is a *mixed* community (i.e., constituted by believers and unbelievers), while the church is a *regenerate* community (i.e., constituted by believers born of the Spirit and forgiven of their sin). This difference is not only taught in the New Testament; it is also anticipated in the Old Testament, specifically in Jeremiah 31. The Old Testament anticipates that the community of the new covenant is no longer mediated through various leaders but instead is mediated directly through Christ, our great prophet, priest, and king, and that the *entire* community is now a believing, Spirit-filled and empowered people, who know God in a saving way (Jer. 31:31–34).

No doubt, Christians still await the consummation of the age, but even now we enjoy the firstfruits of the new creation and participate in the promised "age to come" realities. Individually and corporately, Christians are God's new covenant people (e.g., Rom. 8:1; 2 Cor. 5:17; Eph. 2:1–22), and it is in Messiah Jesus—as last Adam, true Israel, and David's greater Son— that *all* of God's promises are fulfilled. In Christ, Jew and Gentile are now the one new man, the church (Eph. 2:11–22). Together and equally, we inherit *all* of God's promises in Christ Jesus our Lord.

In this light, it is crucial to see that in Christ and the inauguration of the new covenant, *all* of God's promises to Israel are fulfilled (Acts 28:20). Because of Christ's work, the promised Holy Spirit is poured out at Pentecost in fulfillment of Old Testament restoration promises. As the church first takes root in Jerusalem (Acts 2), then spreads to Judea and Samaria (Acts 8), and then expands to the Gentile world (Acts 10–11), God's restoration promises begin to take place before our eyes. Because Christ is the last Adam and the true Israel, the true and literal seed of Abraham (Gal. 3:16), *all* of God's promises to Israel (which includes the nations) are fulfilled in Christ and inaugurated in the church. God has not replaced Israel by the church; instead, he has brought Israel's role to its fulfillment in Christ and to Christ's people.[12]

In this regard, even though Romans 9–11 can be interpreted in a number

---

[12] On this point, see Alan J. Thompson, *The Acts of the Risen Lord Jesus: Luke's Account of God's Unfolding Plan*, New Studies of Biblical Theology 27 (Downers Grove, IL: InterVarsity Press, 2011).

of ways, it does not teach that God's future purposes for national Israel and Gentiles are different. There are no outstanding promises for national Israel which are not first fulfilled in Messiah Jesus and then given to Christ's people, the church, comprised of believing Jews and Gentiles. In other words, in the unfolding of the covenants, *all* of God's promises are now yes and amen in Christ (2 Cor. 1:20).

As Christians today, we no longer are under the previous covenants *as covenants*, even though the entire Scripture is for our instruction (2 Tim. 3:15–17). Instead, in Christ we are beneficiaries of his all-sufficient and victorious new covenant work, and we live our lives as God's new covenant people and all that that entails. Thinking through the biblical covenants not only allows us to understand better God's glorious plan of redemption; it also leads us to worship, serve, and adore our glorious Savior and Lord. In Jesus the Messiah, God the Son incarnate, the promised age is now here, even though we still await the consummation. In Christ, the triune God has laid bare his mighty arm to save. In Jesus' obedient life and death, the desperate plight begun in Eden now finds solution and the new creation is won, as the church now cries, as she awaits the return of our Lord, "Come, Lord Jesus" (Rev. 22:20).

In a summary fashion, here is our understanding of the relationships between the biblical covenants and the basic backbone of the entire metanarrative of Scripture. "Kingdom through Covenant" nicely captures what we are seeking to communicate. The task of "putting together" the biblical covenants is at the heart of "thinking God's thoughts after him" and "bringing every thought captive to Christ" (2 Cor. 10:5). It is our prayer that this book in some small way has helped us better understand something more of the depth and riches of God's Word. When all is said and done, may this book lead not only to a greater understanding of the biblical covenants, but to a true knowledge, enjoyment, and glorification of our great and glorious triune covenant God in the face of our Lord Jesus Christ, our new covenant mediator and head.

GENERAL INDEX

1 Samuel, book of, and the people's request for a king to lead them, like the nations surrounding them, 188–189

2 Samuel, book of, 189–190; theme in that kingship in Israel must be subservient to Yahweh, the Great King, 191

'ābar bĕrît (Hebrew: to transgress a covenant), 61

Abraham, 51; comparison with Adam and Noah, 94; covenant/treaty of with Abimelech, 58–59; failure of as a covenant keeper, 115–116, 123, 127; identification of with the kind of king-priest rule that Melchizedek represents, 101; in the Genesis plot structure, 94; key points in the Abraham narratives, 98; as a new Adam, 94, 100, 107, 119, 126, 134, 264; overview of God's dealings with, 97–98; as the paradigm of faith for Jews and Gentiles, 35–36; as a priest, 99–100; as a priest (and blessing) to the nations, 122, 125; as a royal figure, 100, 104; "seed" of, 42–43. See also covenant with Abraham

Acts, book of, 216

Adam, 126; expulsion of from Eden, 262; failure of as a covenant keeper, 95, 126; as a gardener, 87; headship of, 258; as a Levite, 89; "other Adams" or "little Adams," 40, 41–42, 251; as a priest in the garden sanctuary, 90, 134, 147, 194, 216; as a type of Christ, 40–51, 51. See also covenant with creation; Fall, the

'ādām (Hebrew: son of God, servant king), 79

addîr (Hebrew: prince, mighty one), 237

Alexander, T. D., 43n37

allegory, distinction from typology, 38–39

'am (Hebrew: people), 167; as a kinship term, 103

apologetics, 24

'ārar (Hebrew: curse), 102

ark of the covenant, 89–90, 90; capture of by the Philistines, 189; Jeremiah's promise that the ark will become obsolete, 231; the return of the ark in 2 Samuel 6, 189

atheism, 21n5

ba'ăbûr (Hebrew: on account of, in order that), 199

Babel, 51, 95, 104, 134, 264

Barr, James, 82

Baudissin, W. W., on the root of "holy" in Hebrew, 148

Bavinck, Herman, 22

Beale, G. K., 27, 28

bēn (Hebrew: son), 192–193

bĕrît (Hebrew: covenant), 47, 49; first occurrence(s) of in the Bible, 57, 59; as a loanword in Egyptian texts, 49; pronominal suffix on in the Old Testament, 117–118

biblical theology, 20, 23–24, 31; definition of, 22–23; and diachronicity, 23n11; Enlightenment approach to, 21; evangelical approach to, 21–22; as a hermeneutical discipline, 23, 25; and intertextuality, 23; and intratextuality, 23; and the post-Reformation emphasis on "whole-Bible theology,"

SCRIPTURE INDEX

24:9–11	146
24:12	136
24:12–18	166
24:15–18	179
25–40	75, 90, 133, 137, 139, 147
25:8	89, 216
25:9	82
25:16	90
25:18–22	88
25:40	72, 82, 84
26:31	88
28:12, 29	159
31:12–18	162
31:16	220
32:15–20	179
33–34	183
34	179, 180
34:10	180
34:10–27	179
34:27	136
34:27–28	179
34:28	137, 138, 151
40	90, 146
40:34	216

Leviticus

3:17	63
7:12–18	166
7:26–27	63
8–9	43n38
17:11	256
18–20	153
18:5	267
19–20	149
19:2	149
19:18, 34	153
19:26	63
20:26	149
24:8	220
26:9	257
26:11–12	232
26:12	17, 88
26:40–42	220
26:42	136

Numbers

3:7–8	89
4:20	90
6	148
8:26	89
12:6	224
12:6–9	190
14	183
18:5–6	89
23:21	189
24:7	267
24:17	189
24:17–19	267
25:6–13	51

Deuteronomy

1–30	180, 181
1:1	170
1:1–4:43	169
1:1–28:68	177
1:3–5	169
4:12	71
4:13	137, 138, 151
4:13, 23	180
4:31	136, 180
4:36–38	266
4:39	154
4:44	170
4:44–28:68	169
4:45–11:32	173
5:1	169
5:1–6	181
5:2	181
5:2, 3	180
5:3	181, 182
5:6–21	151
5:7–10	151
5:8	157, 158
5:15	163
6:4–9	169
6:5	169, 173, 175, 176, 181
7:2	180
7:6–11	142
7:7	266
7:7–9	128, 185, 186
7:8	266
7:12	180
8:18	180, 257
9:5	185
9:9, 11, 15	180